Alex Ferguson

A Year in the Life
THE MANAGER'S DIARY

edited by Peter Ball

First published in Great Britain in 1995 by
Manchester United Football Club plc
Old Trafford
Manchester
M16 0RA

in association with
Virgin Publishing Ltd
332 Ladbroke Grove
London
W10 5AH

A catalogue record for this book is available from the British Library.

ISBN 1 85227 521 9

Produced by **Zone Ltd**

Designed by **offspring**

Photography: **Action Images, John Peters and Paul Massey/FSP**

Printed by **Butler & Tanner Ltd**, Somerset, England

Contents

Acknowledgements

Thanks to Brian Kidd for his continual assistance, and to people who gave specific help on this book. In particular, Jane and Cecily for their work on the tapes, Louise Newman and Andrew Syer for their diligent sub-editing, Rachel Jervis at Old Trafford for compiling the match statistics, Maurice Watkins, Justyn Barnes and James Freedman.

to **Cathy and my family**

1
Pre-Season

Monday 18 July

Yesterday was the World Cup Final in Los Angeles. Today we began our pre-season training. Brian Kidd and I always meet with the coaches and plan exactly what we are going to do from the day the players return.

Not everyone was back. Bryan Robson, one of the greatest names in the club's history, has gone to be player-manager at Middlesbrough. Clayton Blackmore has joined him and Mike Phelan has also left. There were a couple of absentees, too. I let Roy Keane and Denis Irwin, our two Irish internationals, return later because they had been involved in the World Cup and needed a break. David May, our signing from Blackburn Rovers, was the only new face, although I have added several of the 1993 youth team to the first-team squad. The rest are the team who won the double two months ago – the first United team ever to do it.

However, that is history. Now we have to prepare for a new season and face fresh challenges. The players are capable of winning a lot more; they are still a young team and can get better. The only question is their desire. If they still have that, nothing is beyond them.

The European Cup was the only blot on our great record last season. This year we go straight into the Champions League section. Even though it is still a month away, it is exciting. The European Cup is the great challenge, but there is also the challenge of winning the Premiership for a third time. Blackburn and Arsenal will be our strongest opponents, but the team I think will pose the greatest threat are Newcastle. Still, we'll see.

Tuesday 26 July

Bryan Robson rang me at 8am this morning. He is beginning to find out what being a manager involves. It seems ridiculous that there is just no real preparation for managers – you are a player one day and then responsible for a club the next.

We have a new physio, David Fevre, who has joined us from Wigan Rugby League. He suggested buying some new equipment, and we needed some new stuff for the gym, anyway, so I put it to the chairman Martin Edwards.

"It's essential," I said.

"I can pass all the small stuff," he said, "but the £40,000 for the Cybex… I'll need to discuss that with the board."

There are three areas where money has to be spent: the team; the ground; and the future. There has never been any problem with money when it is needed for improvements to the team or the club. The supporters can see the development at Old Trafford, which is beautiful now, and they are proud of it. But as far as the future's concerned, we have some work to do. United needs a new training ground because The Cliff, our main training area, is too small. The FA blueprint for the game's future means that we will be operating Sunday football for 14-, 15- and 16-year-olds, and coaching on Sundays for our nine-to thirteen-year-olds, so facilities are going to be important.

Apart from The Cliff, we have Littleton Road, but it doesn't have the facilities to house everything, so we are carrying out a survey to see where to put things. At the moment we're considering keeping The Cliff as the first team's headquarters and for a clinic where injuries can be treated, and building a new place at Littleton Road to accommodate everything else. We would keep two dressing rooms at The Cliff for the youth team to use on Saturdays.

One of the major problems with Littleton Road is that it's very exposed and the wind howls through the place. It could be a good training ground, but it would cost a lot of money. The next problem is deciding what is more important: to build an extension to the stand, to sign a player to help keep you at the top, or to build a new training ground.

Nowadays I am happy with our squad. In 1989 we went for broke and bought five players. In order to encourage the directors to take that step, we made some sales. I'd sold McGrath and Whiteside along the line, we got rid of Gordon Strachan before the end of that season, we got rid of Jesper Olsen during the season, and players such as Graeme Hogg and Chris Turner leaving also helped the package.

With United you are never sure how much you have to pay for players. Clubs put on an extra nought as soon as United's name comes into it – in fact, I think they put on an extra two or even three noughts in the hope they'll get one.

But we went for freedom-of-contract players, so it wasn't too bad. You knew you weren't going to get murdered, although we went to the top end of the tribunal, paying £1.5 million for Nottingham Forest's Neil Webb.

I always got the impression that the tribunal was going to be more impressed with Brian Clough than me. I remember him saying to them:

"Don't think for a moment that we can buy a player for £1.5 million. All that stuff you read in the paper about John Sheridan joining Forest, it's absolute nonsense."

They sat listening to him, then said: "Yes, fine. Thank you Mr. Clough."

Four days later he bought Sheridan! But that was the top end. The price for Mike Phelan was sensible. Norwich wanted £800,000 but we were only prepared to pay £700,000, so we agreed to split the difference.

Friday 29 July

Arrived in Dublin for a short tour. We were mobbed when we arrived at our hotel, with Ryan Giggs as the main target.

Saturday 30 July

Dundalk 2 United 4

We began badly, which was not all that surprising at this stage of our preparation, but we won comfortably enough in the end. It gave the press a few good stories.

Monday 1 August

Shelbourne 0 United 3

A much more convincing performance than the last. We strolled it.

Wednesday 3 August

Wolverhampton Wanderers 1 United 2

A really stunning occasion. A good game and the ground was packed – Wolves took record numbers of receipts. Molineux is magnificent now. They feel like a really big club and one which will be a major power in the near future.

It was strange to see my son Darren on the opposite side. I negotiated the move for him.

Graham Taylor, the Wolves manager, asked about taking Keith Gillespie on loan, but I told him I couldn't do anything until the Champions League section of the European Cup is over. Then it would be good for the boy, because he needs to play at a decent level to gain some experience.

Thursday 4 August

Arrived in Glasgow for the Ibrox International Challenge Trophy. It has involved more travelling than we wanted to do. We got back late from Molineux and it seemed that no sooner had we got off the bus than we were getting back on it.

Friday 5 August

United 1 Newcastle 1 *(lost 6-5 on penalties)*

A good game. It confirmed my suspicions that Newcastle will be a real threat to us – perhaps the biggest this season. But they are further on in their preparation than we are.

Saturday 6 August

Rangers 1 United 0

A nightmare, not so much because we lost, but because Cantona was sent off. We are already without him for four European matches; now we will probably lose him for some Premiership matches too. It was the same old story. He was kicked, didn't receive justice from the referee, and took matters into his own hands. I'm not sure whether he actually touched the boy, anyway, but it was a silly tackle.

Ibrox is a fabulous stadium – the second magnificent stadium we have visited this week – and it is a really great club. I was disappointed in the fans, though; they were much more hostile than I had expected. I made a point about that in the press conference, partly because I wanted to give them something to talk about other than Eric.

I don't think playing in this tournament at this time of year was right for us – certainly not so soon after the Wolves game. I'm not sure about the format, anyway. Playing two matches on the Friday evening made it a very long night for spectators: they were there for nearly five hours. I mentioned to Walter Smith, the Rangers manager, that perhaps they should make the games an hour long, rather than the full 90 minutes.

Sunday 7 August

Eric spent last night in Glasgow. It seemed a good idea to keep him away from the hassle he would get from the press if he came back to Manchester. I got a call from a friend who I'd asked to keep an eye on him.

"You're OK," he assured me. "He's in a club with Ally McCoist."

"WHAT?"

Ally is noted for enjoying himself. But it's OK in Glasgow. They are real football people and although there would be a bit of banter, they would be pleased to see him and he wouldn't get the hostile treatment that supporters in London or Liverpool would dish out.

Tuesday 9 August

I came to Prague to watch Sparta play Gothenburg in the European

Cup. The winners will be in our group in the League.

Wednesday 10 August

Sparta Prague 1 Gothenburg 0

An interesting game. Gothenburg are a strong side and I expect them to win the tie. They might have got a draw last night if they had been a bit more positive. Sparta are a typical East European side – good technically, playing it around and then making sudden bursts.

Friday 12 August

The FA Charity Shield marks the start of the season. We want to put on a show, but I have some problems. I didn't really want to use Roy Keane or Denis Irwin because they were late back for training. Roy is struggling a bit with the groin strain he suffered in the World Cup and Paul Parker has been having problems with his ankle.

Sunday 14 August

United 2 Blackburn Rovers 0

You can't read too much into the score because Blackburn were really below par. I'm sure they will become contenders, but I don't think they will be our greatest challengers this time. Blackburn are a hard working side; they compete all the time. But Newcastle are a better footballing side and with the hunger for success up there, this might just be their year.

One of the main talking points of the match was the number of bookings – seven in all. Lee Sharpe, Steve Bruce and Ryan Giggs all got booked. Sharpey and Bruce were fair enough, but I thought Giggs was a bit unlucky. It is a bit ironic that he should be booked for a tackle because the idea of the new mandate is that it will protect players like him. I think Philip Don thought that because he had booked three Blackburn players, he had to come down on us.

The fans were incredible – we virtually took over Wembley. We had great support in Ireland and Glasgow, but this game was amazing.

Tuesday 16 August

Middlesbrough 0 United 3

Cwmbran 1 United 3

A double header with a difference. We had the Middlesbrough game for Clayton Blackmore's testimonial and the Cwmbran match as a memorial game for the referee Frank Martin, so we divided the forces. Giggs and Hughes went with the Cwmbran team and I took the rest to Middlesbrough. We had Kevin Pilkington in goal because Peter Schmeichel was on international duty and Gary Walsh is off sick. Kevin was the goalkeeper in the youth team and was pretty good, so if I have to use him I won't have too many worries.

Afterwards, Robbo asked me about taking Keith Gillespie on loan. I told him I couldn't do anything until after the Champions League was over, which was exactly what I had already said to Graham Taylor. Robbo said I should let Keith go to him because of his United connections. I replied:

"Yes, but Darren's at Wolverhampton and blood's thicker..."

Robbo wasn't pleased.

Wednesday 17 August

The Premiership managers had a meeting with Ken Ridden, the FA's man in charge of refereeing, to talk about the way the laws will be applied under the new FIFA directives about tackles from behind. The FA is determined to implement it thoroughly.

I'm all in favour. It will help protect skilful players, but I don't think it will work. There are bound to be inconsistencies; some referees will stick to it and some won't. I said what I thought, but Ken insisted that they are going ahead with it.

Friday 19 August

Tomorrow the season begins. I am always excited at the start of a new season and very eager to get going.

2
The Season Begins

The Season Begins

Saturday 20 August

United 2 QPR 0

A dramatic start to the season: QPR had Clive Wilson sent off in the first ten minutes. Paul Parker didn't even last ten minutes, but he went on as sub and we had virtually won the game by that time. We made hard work of it until half-time. QPR are a well coached, positive team and they caused us real problems in the first half. But once Mark Hughes had put us a goal ahead, almost immediately after the interval, things began to open up for us. They had one or two chances, but when Brian McClair got our second, that was it. The only blot on the game for us was Paul being sent off. Within minutes of coming on to the field, he brought down Les Ferdinand as he was breaking through. Obviously, with them losing Clive Wilson and us losing Paul, the sendings off dominated the game and the inquest at the press conference later.

I felt sorry for the referee, because there wasn't a nasty tackle in the game; the feeling between the two sets of players was good. Even Gerry Francis and I didn't fight, and we've exchanged views once or twice over the years!

But in a "nice" game, the referee had two situations he had to deal with. On each occasion a forward was going by the last defender and was in a "through" position – that is, he would have been through. Andy was going by Wilson, and although they had a covering defender, he was on the other side of the pitch, so essentially Andy was through. It was the same with Les Ferdinand. I actually thought he stumbled a bit, but he was also clear once he was past Paul.

So the referee had no alternative under the new rules. But what worries me is that we have a new edict every year, which gets forgotten six weeks into the season. Even more worrying is that we will have inconsistencies. We've had two sendings off in our game, which didn't have a bad tackle. There are no reports of anyone else going off in the Premier League – are we to believe that everybody else was beyond reproach? If not, then we have got problems.

I'm delighted that there is a clean-up process. We shouldn't have any situations like the one last year when Garry Mabbutt was elbowed in the face and had his cheekbone fractured. If tackles from behind are stopped, then great – all managers should be positive about that. But it's something different every year. Last year it was professional fouls; another year it was encroaching on free kicks; once it was tackles from behind. But they do it every year and then get fed up with it because inconsistencies arise. That's what I'm worried about. What if there were other players who should have been sent off today and weren't?

I know Ken Ridden said at the meeting that referees will be dealt with if they don't comply within a month but, in the meantime, the clubs which get the strict referees will suffer. Now I will definitely lose Paul Parker for our game at Leeds; Gerry will lose Clive Wilson for an important game – possibly even three. If there are obvious inconsistencies will the FA wipe out those suspensions? The FA made the rule, and it should make sure it is applied fairly.

Apart from that, it was a satisfactory first day. We didn't play that well, in fact during the first half we didn't get going at all, but we stepped up a gear in the second half and won well enough. One or two members of the team aren't quite ready yet. I didn't want to play Denis Irwin, but had to because Paul is only just back in training, so all in all it was OK. I will have to think about Roy on Monday, because he is desperate to play at Forest for the first time since we bought him.

Venue: Old Trafford *Att:* 43,214

	Manchester United	*goals*		**Queens Park Rangers**	*goals*
1	Peter Schmeichel		1	Tony Roberts	
12	David May		2	David Bardsley	
4	Steve Bruce		4	Steve Yates	
6	Gary Pallister		6	Alan McDonald	
3	Denis Irwin		3	Clive Wilson	
14	Andrei Kanchelskis		7	Andy Impey	
8	Paul Ince		14	Simon Barker	
9	Brian McClair	68	8	Ian Holloway	
5	Lee Sharpe		11	Trevor Sinclair	
10	Mark Hughes	47	9	Les Ferdinand	
11	Ryan Giggs		20	Kevin Gallen	
Substitutes					
2	Paul Parker (70 mins for 12)		12	Gary Penrice (82 mins No.9)	
25	Kevin Pilkington		13	Sieb Dykstra	
16	Roy Keane (70 mins for 5)		16	Danny Maddix (88 mins No.20)	

Sunday 21 August

I went to watch my son Darren play for Wolves at Notts County. They drew 1-1.

Before I went, I watched *Goals on Sunday*, which confirmed all my fears. We had two players sent off in our game – rightly so under the new guidelines. But then in West Ham's game, Alvin Martin rugby tackled someone who was breaking clear and didn't get a red card. They should wipe out the red cards for Clive Wilson and Paul Parker.

Monday 22 August

Nottingham Forest 1 United 1

In terms of possession, I thought that we controlled the game and we got a great goal from Andy, but there's always a threat with Forest. They keep so many players behind the ball, but then you make a mistake on the edge of their box and they pounce. In the first half there was a poor shot which was blocked. It rebounded out to Bryan Roy and immediately Forest counter-attacked. That threat was there all evening.

Their goal was a typical example – a breakaway when we had been attacking. Collymore did well running at us and he hit a great shot. But Pallister hesitated because he was worried about tackling. The referee was really firm – he'd booked three players in the first 20 minutes and Pally didn't want to risk a mistimed tackle. Paul Ince hesitated because he thought Pally was going to reach it, but Collymore hit a great shot. Afterwards, some people criticised Peter Schmeichel, but when we saw it replayed on the monitor, it was a hell of a shot. He hit it with unbelievable power, it was only inches inside the post and at the height goalkeepers hate. It was going like a rocket six inches from the ground. He proved a dangerous customer for us. He's got pace and power and two very good feet.

Roy Keane got booked for his first challenge – I think that was to appease the home fans. It's amazing the way supporters react to a player coming back. Here's a player they got for nothing, so they made £3.75 million out of him, which virtually funded their team. While he was there he worked his tripe off for them. The year they got relegated, I thought it was Keane versus the rest – he was the only one who realised the urgency and the desperate situation they were in. I certainly don't think he deserved all the nonsense he got from the Forest fans.

That sort of thing never seems to happen at Old Trafford. Paul McGrath got a bit of a raspberry from our fans the first time he got back, but it's very rare. They are great to former players: Kevin Moran always got a great reception; Ray Wilkins got a standing ovation when he was taken off before the end in one match with QPR. Not just former players, either. Gary Lineker scored his final goal here, it was the last game of the season, there were 46,000 in the crowd and he got a bigger ovation than we did.

Before the game I phoned Ken.

"It's not going to work," I said. "We had two sent off and then you see things like Alvin Martin's rugby tackle. There's no consistency, there's going to be anarchy."

But he said they would take a look at it on film and, if the referee hadn't obeyed the instructions, they would act. We'll see.

Venue: City Ground *Att:* 22,702

	Nottingham Forest	*goals*		Manchester United	*goals*
1	Mark Crossley		1	Peter Schmeichel	
2	Des Lyttle		12	David May	
3	Stuart Pearce		4	Steve Bruce	
4	Colin Cooper		6	Gary Pallister	
5	Steve Chettle		3	Denis Irwin	
7	David Phillips		14	Andrei Kanchelskis	22
8	Scott Gemmill		8	Paul Ince	
10	Stan Collymore	26	9	Brian McClair	
11	Steve Stone		5	Lee Sharpe	
14	Ian Woan		10	Mark Hughes	
22	Bryan Roy		11	Ryan Giggs	
Substitutes					
12	Jason Lee		2	Paul Parker	
23	Malcolm Rigby		25	Kevin Pilkington	
9	Lars Bohinen (80 mins for 22)		16	Roy Keane (55 mins for 11	

Tuesday 23 August

Flew to Gothenburg to watch the second leg of Gothenburg v Sparta Prague tomorrow. We are playing Spurs on Saturday, and I would have gone to watch their match with Everton, but it is more important for me to see Gothenburg (or Sparta), because they are our first opponents in the Champions League. Les Kershaw, our chief scout, has gone to watch Spurs.

Wednesday 24 August

Because of flights I had to come out yesterday. That gave me a day off today in Gothenburg, which was really good. Before the game I went to sort out our hotel for our game there, then had lunch with Nestor Lauren.

The hotel is the one we used when I was at Aberdeen and we won the European Cup Winners' Cup. Thanks to Nestor, we got this hotel out in the country sorted out before Real Madrid, our opponents in the final, had even begun to think about where they would stay. It was absolutely superb and no one knew we were there. I haven't been back since, even though I've been to Gothenburg quite a few times, but we will definitely use it for our game there. Funnily enough, Johann Cruyff's assistant was there, and Barcelona are going to stay there when they play.

I had expected Gothenburg to win. I thought that they would be far too strong and too good tactically for Sparta. What amazed me was how patient they were; never in any hurry to win the match, they just took their time. They played in a certain way and were disciplined throughout.

Sparta played 5-3-2 at the back. They had a one-goal lead from the first game in Prague, and I don't like the mentality of Eastern European football. They say: "We'll not lose a goal here and we're through." But because they keep everyone back, they lose possession elsewhere. They were surrendering the ball in other areas of the pitch. As the game was going on, I kept thinking: "Surely they are going to do something about this." They had one or two wee forays, but you couldn't see them attempting a single shot at a goal!

Gothenburg just ate away at them. They kept at it and kept at it and kept at it. They had no great imagination for the game, they aren't a Milan or a Barcelona, but they are solid and resourceful.

They started off playing long balls, but then, after about 20 minutes, began passing it, as they kept turning Sparta back towards their own goal. Sparta started to defend on the edge of the box, but once Gothenburg got their first goal, it was a foregone conclusion. They won easily. Sparta made an effort in the last ten minutes because they knew that an away goal would enable them to go through. They ended up playing the goalkeeper at centre-half for the last five minutes, which was unbelievable. I'd better not tell Schmeichel in case he gets any ideas!

It was an interesting game to watch. Gothenburg will be tough opponents for us. They are organised, disciplined, have a lot of experience, a number of Swedish internationals, and, as a team, have played in Europe constantly so they know what it's about.

Thursday 25 August

I took the 7am flight from Gothenburg to Amsterdam via Copenhagen. The connections were perfect and I got into Manchester at 8.45am and went straight to training.

Friday 26 August

We travelled down to London to play Spurs.

Saturday 27 August

Spurs 0 United 1

When I got home I watched the game on Match of the Day and I said: "Christ, we're the luckiest team in world." But we won quite comfortably, really. It just goes to show how deceptive television can be. They had put just about every Tottenham attack of the game into the TV version, so it looked as if we were under pressure the whole time. The truth is that Steve Bruce put us ahead quite early on in the second half and we actually dominated the match. I said to the lads after the game: "That was more like Manchester United, apart from the last ten to fifteen minutes."

At the end, Schmeichel made three great saves and Spurs missed a penalty. That was strange because it usually will deflate a team, but the penalty was their first chance and it set them off and running. It was amazing. It was after the penalty miss that they all got their chances. Whether we'd breathed a sigh of relief and relaxed, I don't know, but until then, from the third minute when Sheringham shot across the face of the goal to the last fifteen minutes, we totally dominated the match. We should have been four or five up. We were positive, we were confident, we kept possesion and created chances, we were more like ourselves. It was a good result because there had been a great surge in confidence at the Tottenham camp. They really thought they were on their way.

My team talk was made for me by all the hype surrounding Spurs this week. They signed Jürgen Klinsmann and Ilie Dumitrescu, the Romanian who did so well in the World Cup, and there is a buzz around the place. Ossie is putting his faith in all-out attack – they won 4-3 at Hillsborough on the opening day of the season and beat Everton on Wednesday. Spurs had six points deducted by the FA because of financial irregularities but all the talk in this morning's papers was that they would win the Premiership despite the deducted six points.

I said to the team: "Well, we really have been written off. We've won two championships, we did the double last year, and you can probably go and get 5-1 against us here this year. Spurs are 3-1 and they're not even playing that well. Klinsmann's the new messiah and we're the bit-part players. So all you can do is hope that you don't get done by six."

That was the theme. But the team knew themselves. They had been reading the papers all week and were ready for it. I didn't think Tottenham had any chance of doing to us what they had been doing to other teams.

Venue: White Hart Lane *Att:* 24,502

	Tottenham Hotspur	*goals*		**Manchester United**	*goals*
13	Ian Walker		1	Peter Schmeichel	
22	David Kerslake		12	David May	
23	Sol Campbell		4	Steve Bruce	
14	Stuart Nethercott		6	Gary Pallister	
3	Justin Edinburgh		3	Denis Irwin	
9	Darren Anderton		14	Andrei Kanchelskis	22
5	Colin Calderwood		8	Paul Ince	
8	Ilie Dumitrescu		9	Brian McClair	
7	Nick Barmby		5	Lee Sharpe	
18	Jurgen Klinsmann		10	Mark Hughes	
10	Teddy Sheringham		11	Ryan Giggs	
Substitutes					
16	Micky Hazard (57 mins for 5)		19	Nicky Butt	
30	Chris Day		25	Kevin Pilkington	
6	Gary Mabbutt		20	Dion Dublin	

Wednesday 31 August

United 3 Wimbledon 0

The return of 'Ooh Aah' Eric was fantastic. He gave an unbelievable performance and scored a goal, but his all-round play was just exceptional. It was a good team performance, we were really positive. Wimbledon had a few injuries – Holdsworth was out, and of course John Fashanu has gone to Villa – but 3-0 will always be a good score against them.

Joe Kinnear, the Wimbledon manager, stayed behind after the game for a chat. He is quite a character. He let me know that Liverpool were about to sign John Scales and wanted to know if we wished to get involved. I had made enquiries about Scales once or twice, but Wimbledon hadn't been prepared to let him go.

"If I'd known that you were going to sell I might have been interested," I said, "but I've got David May now and he is more than adequate. I think he was the best I could get at the price." Joe said he was looking for £3 million for Scales and I replied:

"There's one thing for you Joe, you are a great seller!"

Joe told me he needed a centre half, so I suggested he signed Alan Reeves from Rochdale. I said:

"He'll not let you down. He is a good steady performer, has a good attitude, is a determined so-and-so and his pace is all right. He isn't the tallest centre half, but he'll put his head in."

Venue: Old Trafford *Att:* 43,440

	Wimbledon	*goals*		**Manchester United**	*goals*
1	Hans Segers		1	Peter Schmeichel	
2	Warren Barton		12	David May	
12	Gary Elkins		4	Steve Bruce	
4	Vinnie Jones		6	Gary Pallister	
18	Steve Talboys		3	Denis Irwin	
6	Scott Fitzgerald		14	Andrei Kanchelskis	
26	Neal Ardley		7	Eric Canton	40
19	Stewart Castledine		9	Brian McClair	81
25	Mick Harford		5	Lee Sharpe	
16	Alan Kimble		10	Mark Hughes	
20	Marcus Gayle		11	Ryan Giggs	84
Substitutes					
7	Andy Clarke		20	Dion Dublin	
21	Chris Perry		25	Kevin Pilkington	
23	Neil Sullivan (64 mins for 19)		19	Nicky Butt	

Thursday 1 September

The Cliff is virtually deserted. It is very early in the season to have an international week, particularly one with a free Saturday. For the first time in my career I'm going to take a few days off during the season.

My mother-in-law has not been too well, so my wife Cathy is going up to Scotland for a few days to stay with her. I said:

"All this is a bit of a strain for you, so why don't we go away for a few days first?"

I suggested Marbella, where Mr Midani, one of United's directors has a country club. But Cathy said:

"I'd rather go to a city. How about Brussels?"

"How about Rome?" I said. "I've never been to Rome."

She agreed, so we are off to Rome on Saturday.

Friday 2 September

This morning the chairman, Martin Edwards, told me he'd had an inquiry from Coventry about Dion Dublin, our big striker. He asked me what I thought and I replied:

"We can't really let him go, we might need him for Europe. We are struggling for English players for the European games as it is."

So Martin said: "Is there any price you would let him go at?"

"There is always a price," I said. "If someone offered £2 million for Dion, we'd have to think about it. We've got Paul Scholes coming through and Brian McClair can play up front. It's just the European games I worry about."

We left it at that.

The European rules are a problem, and with Mark Hughes over 30, and Welsh, we have been thinking about a replacement. We talked about strikers at a staff meeting and I asked Tottenham about Teddy Sheringham, who is a good, intelligent player, but not young. First they said £5 million, then they came back and wanted £4 million plus Mark Hughes. No wonder Alan Sugar makes millions at the rate he does.

The player I would really like is Andy Cole, but when I asked Kevin Keegan he just laughed.

Saturday 3 September

Cathy and I flew out to Rome at lunchtime. We are staying at the Sheraton, which is on the way into the city from the airport. The Roma training grounds are about 200 yards away, so I may drop in to see them train.

Sunday 4 September

We went to watch Roma v Foggia this afternoon. It was an interesting game and Foggia were really impressive. They are a very good, progressive young side.

Watching the game made me wonder whether Britain is the only country implementing the new FIFA guidelines because nothing appears to have changed here, there were plenty of strong tackles. Referees are strong in Italy and they send off quite a few players, but there was no doubt that they let a lot of players get away with things that would be punishable offences in England now.

Italian football has changed. Until about six or seven years ago, it used to be "Oh, you've got the ball so we'll retire to the edge of our penalty box and wait." But they don't play like that any more. They press the ball all over the field – every good Italian team does that now, so the game is far more competitive than it's ever been in Italy.

We'd just settled down to watch the game and I said to Cath:

"This is great. Nobody knows me, we can sit and enjoy a game in peace for once." But I spoke too soon, because all of a sudden, the president of Foggia came up to us, accompanied by an Italian agent who had recognised me.

The president was saying what a good team Foggia are. And there do seem to be some more progressive young coaches coming in. At Parma, the coach had apparently gone off to run a restaurant for a while before returning to football. There are others at Sampdoria and Cremonese who seem to be coming in with a fresh approach.

Monday 5 September

We spent the day in the city. Rome is beautiful. I like all the little piazzas and fine restaurants.

Tuesday 6 September

I watched Roma train today: the youth team at lunchtime and the first team at 4pm this afternoon; which I suppose was sensible considering the climate – the weather was beautiful. I couldn't say I learnt a lot, but it was interesting. I was particularly interested in the amount of time they spend on warm-ups. Again, perhaps the weather has a lot to do with it, but they took a long time on them.

Wednesday 7 September

We had an early start, a 7am flight back to London. I had a Managers' Association meeting today and there's the launch of the ITV European coverage tomorrow.

Our four days away were great, but I felt guilty about being away during the season and, when I got on the plane, I couldn't wait to get back.

As soon as we got into the terminal at Heathrow I switched on my mobile and checked my messages. One of them said to "phone Mr Edwards urgently."

I phoned Martin from the airport and he said:

"I've had this bid for Dion from Coventry and I don't know what to do. I spoke to Brian Kidd this morning because I knew you were travelling. But they've offered £2 million."

"£2 million," I said. "Jesus!"

"What do you think?"

"Well, we need him for Europe, you know that," I said.

"If we have any injuries, we would really be struggling. But on the other hand, he isn't going to get into the team and Scholes is coming through."

I have a lot of confidence in Scholes. But, nevertheless, I still had slight doubts about it and finally said:

"I don't know what you do."

"I've already talked to Dion," he said.

I thought that was fair enough because Dion might have wanted to turn them down anyway, so maybe there was no point in getting excited about it. But I had this uneasy feeling about it.

Then I went the League Managers' meeting. As an organisation it is not given as much weight as it should be. The players get a huge amount of money for the Professional Footballers' Association out of the TV contract and we are trying to get a share, too, to help fund it. As I said, "Who do the TV people get the most cooperation from? The managers!"

We also discussed the benevolent side of the business. We have a fund set up to help managers who are struggling – and to ensure that those who are sacked get their pay-offs within a reasonable period of time.

It is a good organisation and has Steve Coppell as its full-time chief executive. We've got a lot of plans for the future if we can get the financing right – managers' courses, influencing coaching in the country, and so on.

I checked in to my hotel, then went out to Wembley to watch England play the USA. Dearie me. They had offered the USA £25,000 to beat England. They should have made it £250,000 then they might have had a go. It was an absolutely pathetic performance by the USA. If England had wanted to score six, they probably could have. Shearer's second goal was the highlight of the entire match.

Thursday 8 September

ITV has the rights to the Champions League games and has also bought the rights to the Arsenal games in the Cup Winners' Cup, so George Graham and I went along to the press show at which this was announced. I've always got on well with the ITV football people because I believe they are really concerned about the game.

But my mind was elsewhere. Dion had gone to talk to Coventry. I rang the club and spoke to Kiddo, who told me that Paul Scholes had been injured in the reserve match yesterday and was having a scan to see if the damage was serious. I then spoke to Martin Edwards and said: "Can't you put a brake on any negotiating with Coventry until after the European matches – or at least until we know what's happening with Scholes, because if he is injured badly, we will be very short of players?"

But Martin said:

"It's difficult, because they need him now. And what if he signs while he's there?"

If Dion has signed, I have to accept it.

Cathy had flown on straight to Glasgow from Heathrow to see her mother. So I took a plane back to Manchester and went to The Cliff.

Dion arrived and he hadn't signed for Coventry. I imagine he is hoping for better terms.

"What do you want to do?" I asked him.

"Well, I'm not really getting a game here," he said. "I don't have any complaints, you've been great. I've really loved it here, but I really do need first-team football."

"But you may get a European medal this year," I said.

"Yes, but you are talking about six or seven games in a season, which is not enough for me. You've got Cantona and Hughes and Scholes coming through. I don't think you are ever going to make me a first-team player and, at this stage in my career, I really do need first-team football."

I couldn't argue with that; you have to be fair to the player. Dion showed a keenness to go and I can understand his position. We have been offered good money for him – £2 million is a lot of money for a player and although I am sure he will get goals anywhere – so I accepted that he should go.

"If that's the way you feel, I understand," I said to Dion. But everyone here will miss him. He is a smashing lad with a really great personality. I have a lot of respect for him, he is a good pro, a good trainer and a really good finisher. He was just unlucky because he was injured shortly after being signed by United, then we bought Cantona and there wasn't really a place for him. On top of that, we couldn't really match him with anyone.

His best partner was Scholes – they were brilliant together in the reserves, absolutely brilliant. They scored goals all over the place.

We heard that Scholes's injury wasn't too bad, thank goodness. You only get a player like him perhaps once in a decade. He's small and stocky, not what you'd call a Ryan Giggs in terms of running power, but he's sharp and quick about the ground in short distances. He's got a brilliant football brain and he's tough– mentally, tough too. So you know he is easily a "United" player. He needs experience. We must put him in situations where he has to perform in order to find out how good he really is. He has enormous potential and in some ways reminds me of the young Kenny Dalglish.

So it was a funny week to be away.

Now it is just a case of waiting for everyone to come back from their trips. I always worry when players are away on international weeks. Not only because they might get injured, but because the journeys and change in routine sometimes take it out of them.

Friday 9 September

Dion signed to Coventry today. I hope we have not made a mistake.

The international players returned to Manchester. The Irish lads had been to Latvia and Andrei had been to Russia. I still don't think we've got the international system right. Perhaps they should revert to playing on Saturdays and cancel the club programmes. As it is at the moment, the players sometimes return totally jaded. It is a big deal for them emotionally. Take Kanchelskis. He has a five-and-a-half hour journey to Russia, three or four days there, then he plays a match, has the same journey back to England on the Thursday and is expected to be ready to play for us at the weekend.

There's always a lot of banter when the international players come back, discussing who won and who lost. Keith Gillespie, our young winger, played for Northern Ireland for the first time this week, against Portugal in Belfast. Ireland lost and, although the reports suggested he played quite well, he was disappointed with his performance.

Joe Kinnear has bought Alan Reeves. I'll have to phone Rochdale and get a commission!

Saturday 10 September

As our match is on television, we trained today. Although this gives us an extra day to prepare after the internationals, it telescopes things next week, which is not ideal with our first European Champions League match with Gothenburg on Wednesday.

Sunday 11 September

Leeds United 2 Manchester United 1

Today was our first defeat by Leeds since they came back up – and since Howard Wilkinson joined them. In a way I was quite pleased for him, we don't ever want to experience that sort of reaction from their fans again.

When I saw their team I said: "They're going gung-ho, they are going all out to win this one, and they are either going to beat us or we'll slaughter them." They had put all their attacking players in whereas, in the past, they have been very cautious.

If we had got the first goal we might have won well. But we didn't. It was a really disappointing performance and an unusual one, because playing at Leeds usually gives us an edge. You can feel the hatred, the animosity, and that usually makes us sit up and defend really well. But this time, our defending for the two goals was poor. We just didn't cope at all. They out-fought us, they ran faster and harder and their supporters carried them over the hill. We might have snatched a draw at the last – I put Nicky Butt on, who did well, and after we got one back they had to hang on. We had a charge at the end, but we didn't deserve anything. It was a bad result and a disappointing performance from us.

I put Nicky on with half an hour to go. At 2-0 down, I thought: "Well, let's see what he can do, because he has to be an option for Wednesday due to the three-foreigner rule." The fact that he played well was just about the only positive thing to come out of that game.

I said to the players after the match: "Now you know what it is like losing here." I hope it never happens again. The Leeds supporters were awful. Even if I was pleased for Howard, I almost want his team to be relegated because of their fans. I don't think they deserve to be in the Premier League. Such hatred really is incredible. Apparently, a TV camera caught some woman screaming abuse at me. When it gets to women behaving in that way you wonder what chance have we got? I just cannot understand why people like that go to football. You get the same at Chelsea and West Ham. And I just cannot understaand the mentality of supporters like that.

You could understand the animosity better between Liverpool and United, because they are just down the road from one another. Liverpool's supporters have been known to put incredible pressure on referees, but every club in the country would like to have supporters like them.

You can't say the same for Leeds. I went with Archie Knox to see them play Crystal Palace some years ago, and the venom and threatening attitudes were just the same - you're expecting a pitch invasion at any moment. Palace scored twice in quick succession. One of them was controversial – I think Ian Wright scored it – and it was questionable whether it was offside, but we left 20 minutes before the end because we thought it might get out of hand, the whole thing was so nasty.

The person I feel for is Howard Wilkinson. He has done an unbelievable job at Leeds. He has brought in race-relations people, he has brought in Cec Podd, the former Bradford fullback to do the PR bit, but I think it's an impossible task – even their own players know it. The Leeds supporters chanted "Don Revie" during the minute's silence for Sir Matt Busby at Blackburn and the players were really upset by it. If fans ever lost a game, that was it. The players just weren't up for it after that, they were so sick.

Apart from the supporters, Leeds is a good club. We get on very well with them and there's never any bother on the pitch. Of course, games are competitive and tackles can fly in at times, but there's never any trouble. In the first semi-final of the League Cup a few years ago we had a bit of a battle with them and two or three got booked, but that was the most there's ever been. They compete with each other, there's aggression, players will foul one another, but they get up and get on with the job. Once or twice I've thought things were going to turn nasty, but it's never happened.

It was one of these careless performances which sometimes surface with us–if there is a criticism of us it is that we never finish teams off. We get in front and then play around. In the past two years we've only had a couple of 5-0 victories – over Coventry and Sheffield Wednesday – which is unusual for a team which has won the championship twice in that time. You can usually point to quite a few four- or five-goal victories for championship sides, but we're not that kind of a team. Usually, when it surfaces, it is in games we are well in control of. In the big games you can't afford it.

I think there was no doubt that Andrei and Ryan, who had run his socks off for Wales midweek, had a drop in performance today. It was definitely down to the internationals. But Leeds had one or two players who had also been involved, so we had no excuse.

I also wondered if a few of our players were thinking ahead to Gothenburg. If you look at some of our other performances this season, they've been alright, they've not been been bad, but we've never really hit a high as a team so far, and you wonder if anticipation of the Champions League has a bearing on that. It is understandable in a way, because our present players recognise that last year's performance against Galatasaray comes up in any appraisal of them as a team. I've even said it myself. We did the double and we've been in the final of the League Cup, and there is only that one blot, which is hard to ignore. And with that sort of blemish on their personal achievements, it can sometimes deflect their attention away from the bread and butter stuff which is most important.

And the other thing is that we've won the championship twice now, with points to spare. In this country, you can never say that you've won with comfort, because it is too competitive. But we have had a bit of leeway at the end of the last two seasons, so perhaps the players are feeling that they should concentrate on the Champions League, because we will be all right in the Premiership.

Venue: Elland Road *Att:* 39,524

Leeds United	*goals*	**Manchester United**	*goals*
1 John Lukic		1 Peter Schmeichel	
2 Gary Kelly		12 David May	
6 David Wetherall	13	4 Steve Bruce	
4 Carlton Palmer		6 Gary Pallister	
15 Nigel Worthington		3 Denis Irwin	
10 Gary McAllister		14 Andrei Kanchelskis	
11 Gary Speed		7 Eric Cantona	74
14 David White		8 Paul Ince	
19 Noel Whelan		9 Brian McClair	
26 Phil Masinga		10 Mark Hughes	
8 Rod Wallace		11 Ryan Giggs	
Substitutes			
9 Brian Deane (30 mins for 14)	49	5 Lee Sharpe (63 mins for 9)	
13 Mark Beeney		25 Kevin Pilkington	
5 Chris Fairclough (87 mins for 26)		19 Nicky Butt (63 mins for 11	

3
Into Europe

Monday 12 September

As a result of playing on Sunday, we have had to compress our preparations for the game with Gothenburg, but we just had a loosener and ran through one or two things.

Deep down, I am apprehensive about the game. People don't realise how good Swedish football is. There is a lot said about them being part-timers, but this club have been in Europe – and done well – every year for the past ten years.

I keep thinking back to my days at Aberdeen and as a player, asking myself how we handled these games. I try to jog my memory and think 'Europe' again. I look back at the year we won the Cup Winners' Cup and the game with Barcelona. In the end I always return to the same things: patience and possession of the ball.

Tuesday 13 September

At the start of the season I said to Brian Kidd "We are really going to have to concentrate on the team we pick for Europe." It's got to be spot on. We can't afford another game like that at Galatasaray, where I left out Sparky. Tactically, I felt it was the right thing to do that day, but perhaps they knew they'd got the advantage. Of course we haven't got Eric, who is banned for the first four matches following last season's match against Galatasaray, and Roy Keane is still out with his groin, which is becoming worrying. But we still have selection problems because of the three-foreigner rule.

At least I can be reasonably confident about Nicky Butt now. He virtually picked himself after his display on Sunday. But although that is a help, there are still problems. Do I gamble and leave out Denis Irwin, play Lee Sharpe at left back and play Ince, McClair and Butt in the middle? Or do I play McClair with Sparky? The biggest risk would be to play Irwin, leave McClair out and play Butt in midfield with Giggs through the middle and Sharpe wide left.

What I finally decided to do was to play Irwin, leave out McClair, but play Sparky on his own through the middle, with Giggs left and Sharpey tucked into midfield with Nicky and Paul Ince.

Because of Eric's ban, the Galatasaray game still hangs over us. The atmosphere reached fever pitch over there. I think one or two of our players were walking around saying: "What have we come into here?" The atmosphere, the place, the whole thing was perhaps a little too much for us. You don't get European games of that nature very often nowadays.

When I was at Rangers there were one or two games which were like that. We played in Zaragossa and Bilbao, which was terrible. They had a lot of problems with their crowds. I played in Bilbao three times, and every time it was just as intense. But nowadays UEFA are so strict on crowd control and threats about throwing teams out of the competition that you rarely have to encounter a Galatasaray-style situation. I hope the atmosphere has improved when we go there this time.

Newcastle won 5-1 in Antwerp, which is exceptional.

Wednesday 14 September

United 4 Gothenburg 2

In my team talk I said: "This game is never going to change. When you are playing in Europe you think you are doing well and then the roof falls in. You cannot rest for a minute. If you are not vigilant, if you are not alive to situations and if you don't defend properly, then you've got one hell of a night ahead."

We started off really well. We hit the bar and our free kicks and corner kicks were causing Gothenburg all sorts of problems. We were well composed and disciplined in the middle of the park. Then came the sucker punch.

Just when you think you are about to crack that team, they go and hit you. We won the tactical battle to start with, because they thought we would play Sharpe wide left with Giggs through the middle, so they played 5-2-3, which was positive but meant that we had more in midfield – and won there.

But they felt it was a game they could score in. Having seen us at Leeds they had every reason to feel that way. But it was a bad goal for us to lose. One lad got down the right, hit in this low curving cross and Peter was stranded. The defenders didn't cut it out and Stefan Petterrsson nipped in front of Peter and scored. You say to yourself: "You can't defend like that in Europe." You hope that if you lose a goal, it has got to be a worked goal, one that they've earned. But we handed it to them on a plate.

But credit to the team, they buckled down and showed character and perseverance, and we equalised before half time. In fact, we should have gone in ahead, because Ryan got through with only the goalkeeper to beat. He tried to lob him, but Ravelli saved.

It was a long ball from Peter. The defender let it go behind him, Ryan nipped in and it bounced high. Part of the problem when the ball is coming over your head and you are looking up there is that you lose your bearings about where the goal is and where the keeper is and how far out you are. When it finally came down, the keeper had hesitated, so Ryan had the chance to hit it, but instead he decided to wait and lob. The goalie came again and Ryan went for it, but the keeper reached up and blocked it. I said to Ryan: "You should have hit it right away." So many things have happened to the kid in such a short space of time and he is struggling a bit.

I always say to goal-scorers when they are not having a great time: "Don't be clever in front of the goal, always blast it. Make sure you hit the target and hit it hard." If the goalie has to save, the crowd shout: "What a save," but if you try to sidefoot it or lob, or try to go round the goalkeeper and lose it, they are disgruntled. If you blast it and the keeper saves, they always clap. It's something Ryan will learn in time.

So it was level at half time. That ten minutes is vital because you have got to get your message over quickly. You've got to get them all sat down, get their cup of tea or water or whatever they are drinking and ensure that they're concentrating on what I'm saying. There were only two or three points to make today. To Schmeichel I said: "It's important that you calm them down at the back, because we are all over the place at times, we're diving at people."

I told Giggsy to sit a bit deeper and said to Sharpey that he should make runs through the middle. Giggs had come in a bit during the first half and had blocked a lot of Lee's space. In the first half Lee was a spare player for us.

That was about all I said. People find the idea of Peter calming anyone down a little funny because he can get quite excitable himself, but he is important at organising us.

We got a great start after the interval with Andy's goal. If there's a ball that inspires hate, it is the one that drops just outside the penalty box. It's a matter of keeping the ball down and getting it on target. Andy was lucky, it went through someone's legs and we were ahead.

We all leapt up on the bench and I said to Kiddo: "Right, that's good.

Let's get control now and we can enjoy it." But when you are manager of Manchester United, you can't expect that – it's impossible. There's a suicidal streak in the team which means we're always going to make matches entertaining.

Gothenburg got an equaliser from a free kick which deflected off the wall when Peter went the wrong way. At the time I thought it deflected off Nicky Butt, but it turned out that Stefan Rehn, who was on the end of the wall, had stuck out a foot and changed direction, which was quite sharp of him. Schmeichel didn't stand a chance. Rehn had come on as sub when they put on another midfield player to try to counter us in the middle of the park. At that point you say to yourself: "This is not going to be our night." But then Paul Ince hit a great shot, which hit the woodwork and Giggsy got in to turn it in.

I didn't realise it at the time, but the goalkeeper got a touch on it and it fell nicely for us. Normally if you get a touch on a shot like that it will go over the bar, but this time it hit the underside of the bar. Even if we hadn't scored from that, it was such a great shot that I think it would have lifted us, anyway.

I said to the players before the game that one of the reasons Gothenburg lost to Sparta in Prague was that they backed off and allowed their opponents shooting opportunities from a distance. I told them that the same could happen in our game. In the first half we had two or three chances as a result. Nicky Butt had a shot, Denis Irwin had a shot from outside the box, so did Andrei. And this time too they backed off and Incey hit this hell of a shot.

Ryan followed it in well, but the pleasing thing about it was that Nicky was beside him to make sure. I always say you can get an extra six goals a season by following things in. I always refer to Denis Law. I used to do it myself. The way they play offside these days makes it very difficult when you are actually running from the edge of the box. I look at pictures, and every time you see a ball going towards the net and the goalkeeper flopping on it on the goal line, there is Denis standing over him. I keep telling them about that. "Look at Denis! He's right on top of the goalkeeper!" So it was good to see Ryan and Nicky following things in.

That goal put us in front and Sharpey's goal was the icing on the cake. A typical United performance – we made it difficult for ourselves, but we played with style, too.

Venue: Old Trafford	*Att:* 33,625		
IFK Gothenburg	*goals*	**Manchester United**	*goals*
1 Tomas Ravelli		1 Peter Schmeichel	
2 Pontus Kamark		2 David May	
3 Magnus Johansson		3 Denis Irwin	
4 Joachim Björklund		4 Steve Bruce	70
5 Mikael Nilsson		5 Lee Sharpe	
6 Mikael Martinsson		6 Gary Pallister	
7 Magnus Erlingmark		7 Andrei Kanchelskis	48
8 Stefan Lindqvist		8 Paul Ince	
9 Jesper Blomqvist		9 Nicky Butt	
10 Jonas Olsson		10 Mark Hughes	
11 Stefan Pettersson	27	11 Ryan Giggs	33
Substitutes			
12 Dick Last		12 Gary Neville	
13 Johan Anegrund		13 Kevin Pilkington	
14 Stefan Rehn (44 mins for 10)	50	14 Paul Scholes	
15 Patrik Bengtsson		15 David Beckham	
16 Magnus Gustavsson		16 Simon Davies	

Thursday 15 September

My main feeling about last night is one of relief. Starting with a win was vital. Nine points will get you through for certain. Eight points should do. Now we've got two points, so we need another six from five games, which hopefully we will manage.

That win gives us a cushion. We can go to Galatasaray now knowing that we don't need to win. We 'll be disciplined and make sure it's a bloody hard night for them. Barcelona beat Galatasaray last night, which was the perfect result for us.

Nicky did well again. You can only give young players a chance and then it's up to them to take it. The best thing you can do is to encourage them. But the next question, if he gets a few games now, is to decide when to take him out so he can progress again. With players like Keane and Ince being so young, Nicky's progress can be monitored easily. There will come a point when he will say: '"Right, I'm good enough to stay in," or not, as the case may be.

I feel he has all the qualities to be a top player. He's got a desire to win, a bit of hunger about him and his determination is good. He's got great running power, he's good in the air, and he's a good finisher. He has qualities similar to those of Roy Keane. Some say he's a Bryan Robson – there's great eagerness to look for a new Bryan Robson at our club! Keane is as close as you can possibly get, and Butt is not far behind.

Sometimes Butt gets carried away and holds the ball and tries things out, but he is much better when he plays it early. He runs well and sees spaces up ahead of him – he's pretty good for a young lad. He is quite competitive going into the box, too. He really is the type who will get goals. He was a bonus in terms of finding a player to give the team a bit of balance and the extra ingredients necessary to play in Europe.

The performance made me think that perhaps their minds were on the

Gothenburg game last weekend against Leeds. But if players are taking anything for granted, Newcastle's performance in Antwerp will wake them up and make them realise that they can't take the league for granted.

The fixture list is such that we can't relax for a moment. We are playing Liverpool on Saturday – that's in two days time! So we have played Leeds, our first European game and Liverpool within a week. And that week didn't run from Saturday to Saturday, either. Because Leeds was a TV game, it was literally a week, seven days; Sunday to Saturday. I really do wonder who drew up the fixtures list, because I can't believe a computer came out with Leeds one week, Liverpool the next and a European game wedged in between.

If it really was the computer then it didn't have the right parameters fed into it. It is ridiculous. We're supposed to represent England, and if we do well it helps the other clubs by improving the seedings in European competition. And to make the Leeds match a Sunday match into the bargain! This week, because Arsenal are playing tonight in the Cup Winners' Cup, they are playing Newcastle on Sunday. I don't know whether Liverpool would have agreed to us switching.

Friday 16 September

Les Kershaw, our chief scout, went out to Barcelona to watch the game with Galatasaray. He said Galatasaray had expected to get a result. Before the game he was talking to one of their directors. Apparently, they really fancied their chances, think that the team is pretty good and that it's only a matter of time before a Turkish side wins the European Cup. Les said they were really sick afterwards.

I worry a bit about having to play Liverpool after coming off a European match with all its emotion. Last year we had to play them midweek, immediately after losing to Aston Villa in the Coca-Cola Cup Final at Wembley. It was difficult, because playing at Wembley takes it out of you, and it took us a while to get into the game. But this time at least we can bring Eric back and Brian McClair to freshen things up. And this time we are going into it having got a win.

The real decision, which I need to think over, is whether to play Choccy or Sharpey in midfield. If Choccy plays it will make us tighter against them in midfield; but Sharpey did well on Wednesday. He is an important option for us in Europe and I don't want to be knocking him down after a good performance.

The other worry is Sparky. He hasn't been training, and players of his build need to train the whole time. The lighter players can get away with it, but big men need consistency.

Like every other club, we have had one or two problems with young players caught drinking. You tell young players before they come: "There are two ways you get into my office. One is because you are doing well; the other is because you've behaved badly."

This week I caught one of our young players in a hotel bar with a glass of beer in front of him. I brought him in today and said:

"There are two fines. One is a week's wages, the other is two week's wages. One week is for telling the truth, two weeks is for telling a lie. You saw me in the hotel."

He told me it wasn't his beer, but his cousin's.

"I wasn't drinking," he pleaded.

"Okay, it's two weeks' wages."

"I wasn't drinking."

"I saw exactly what you were up to," I said, "I sat down and spent ten minutes watching you drinking."

His face went white. "I'm sorry, Boss," he said, his voice cracking.

Afterwards you laugh about it, but you can't condone it. You can't allow that with young players. You try to educate them, you explain how vital it is.

Drink is a problem in our game. More so in England than in Scotland. It seems to be the mentality, this macho English thing. When I came down here, it was a particular problem at this club, so I gathered everyone together in the gym and said:

"I'm not going to change, I just don't agree with it. If anyone can come along and explain to me how drink makes you a better player, and prove it, I'll go along with it. But until then, you are all going to have to change."

This team do have a night out, but the one thing that does please me is that they all go together now. The last two years when they won the Championship they went to Chester Races together. This year there was a problem – some Scousers created a scene. But I spoke to the manager at the course, and to the people who invited them, who all said that my team's behaviour was impeccable. A lot of people said they were being provoked all day, and even had to endure people throwing champagne over them in the box. But, as I said, I've got quite a moderate situation here. I know what they are doing during the week. If they go out during the week they get punished, they know that. Mostly I know what they are up to because Manchester is a small place. I get phone calls every morning and the players know that. If anything happens, it only takes a few days to filter through to me. We've got one or two exuberant lads, but as they grow up in the club the exuberance evaporates. They get a sense of purpose easily here in terms of how important winning is. The defeat at Leeds will have helped that sense of purpose because it gets home the message: that everybody wants to cut our throats.

I do hear stories about other clubs and players' drinking episodes which are hair-raising. I don't think there is anything wrong if players go out for a drink on a Saturday night, particularly if they go out together. The Chester thing was a special case – they'd won the double and the season was over.

I don't understand it, personally. For me, the night you win the trophy you celebrate and that's it. I'd have a few glasses of champagne and stay up chatting into the small hours, not wanting to go to bed – although this year after the Cup Final I was tired, I think I had too much champagne in the dressing-room. But the Chester trip and the Christmas bash when they have in the wives is understandable. More regular drinking is a problem in the English game. But how do you stop it?

Saturday 17 September

United 2 Liverpool 0

It was a very similar game to last year's. In the first half last year Liverpool dominated midfield by putting an extra man there, and it was the same on Saturday. Peter Schmeichel had to make three great saves – so did their keeper, but ours were from breakaways which we might have scored from. We never really dominated the game.

But then, after half time, things turned round. Tactically, I was right when I thought I should play Choccy. He would have gone up against Barnes, who was the key man for them, and left Molby. But because Paul Ince played towards the centre it meant that Barnes was free all the time in the first half. Andrei isn't the best at coming into the middle of the park to pick people up.

I should have played Choccy, except that it was always likely that he would come on in the second half to go up against Molby. I just had to see how Sparky was going to react after half time. When I asked him how he was feeling he said he was all right, but there was no life in him. And when big lads like him don't train, there are always problems. So I took him off, put on McClair to make runs from midfield against Molby, and left Eric on his own up front.

Eric really came into his own. He was magnificent. And McClair began making runs, causing Liverpool all sorts of problems because Molby couldn't possibly run back with him; he hadn't the legs. Roy Evans took Molby off and brought on Phil Babb, their new £2.5 million centre half, to stop McClair. But before that could take effect Kanchelskis scored, and then we got a second goal very quickly.

We finished with a good result, and, in the last half hour, we played some of our best football so far this season. Their legs had gone a bit, and the disappointment of losing two goals so quickly put them off too.

Roy Evans said in the press conference afterwards that he had made a mistake in putting on Babb in place of Molby. I think it was the right thing to do. It certainly wasn't why they lost – they were going to lose it anyway. Sometimes taking the blame is not a bad thing to do, but in this case it really wasn't necessary.

Liverpool have done really well by Roy. He set the standard for his management when he didn't take Wright and Dicks on the pre-season tour. I can't judge the rights and wrongs of the situation, and I don't know whether he was right to do it publicly, but he saw what he thought was a problem and attacked it right away, which was dead right.

We should probably have left Sparky out, but he wanted to play. He has always risen to the challenge of Liverpool over the years: he has always been the cavalier; the buccaneer; snapping around at them. He has been an influence on our team and my thorn in their side.

Every time we play them they are moaning and groaning at him. The day I came we had him and Norman Whiteside against Hansen and Lawrenson. They must have been glad to get home, they were absolutely on pins and needles playing against Sparky and Norman. Sparky has always been that way in the big games. To see him giving such a muted performance tells you that he wasn't fit.

The only thing that spoilt the win was Eric picking up a yellow card for a lunge at Ruddock. It was the usual Eric 'Red Mist'. Ruddock had just elbowed him in the face and he didn't get any justice from the referee, so he took matters into his own hands. In fairness, the referee might not have seen it because there were two players around Eric, but it was a severe blow. Ruddock has something of a reputation and the referee should, perhaps, have been more aware. But it wasn't just the elbow, it was goading, too. Ruddock put his hands on the back of Eric's neck and pulled his collar down. He kept doing it, kept annoying Eric. Eric kept turning round, but of course that was going on while the referee was following the game. He had done it two or three minutes before the incident, and he did it afterwards, too.

I was screaming at Eric from the side.

"Leave him! Ignore him! We're winning, don't get involved," I shouted.

But the moment Ruddock started trying to take the mickey out of him by pulling down his collar he'd had enough. So I think the booking was right. I don't think it was as bad as it looked, but his feet were off the ground.

Part of the problem is Eric can't tackle. He couldn't tackle a fish supper. I keep saying to him : "Why do you try to tackle when you can't tackle?"

Fortunately that was the last of it. The game died after that and, in fairness to Ruddock, he did not try for retribution. I think he knew he was skating on thin ice anyway.

Venue: Old Trafford *Att:* 43,740

Manchester United	*goals*	**Liverpool**	*goals*
1 Peter Schmeichel		1 David James	
12 David May		2 Rob Jones	
4 Steve Bruce	20	Stig Inge Bjornebye	
6 Gary Pallister		12 John Scales	
3 Denis Irwin		25 Neil Ruddock	
14 Andrei Kanchelskis	71	14 Jan Molby	
7 Eric Cantona		15 Jamie Redknapp	
8 Paul Ince		17 Steve McManaman	
5 Lee Sharpe		9 Ian Rush	
10 Mark Hughes		10 John Barnes	
11 Ryan Giggs		23 Robbie Fowle	
Substitutes			
9 Brian McClair (59 mins for 10)	73	6 Phil Babb (71 mins for 14)	
25 Kevin Pilkington		13 Michael Stensgaard	
19 Nicky Butt		7 Nigel Clough	

Sunday 18 September

On last night's *Match of the Day* Alan Hansen made an issue about David May's positional play. It was a load of nonsense. He was in a central position in the bit of film he chose because it followed a free kick, not because he had taken up a bad position.

Centre half is David's best position, but he's been playing right back for us. He's got to get used to thinking of every game as a Cup Final, which is something he didn't do at Blackburn. So he is having to adapt to playing in a new position and in high-pressure games all the time. It is like a Cup Final every week. That is the nature of the club.

The focus on David is a bit unfair, because he did quite well on Saturday. At half time I said to him:

"Just assert yourself. Go for it. Don't be sitting in between players. You're sitting off McManaman. You're a good tackler, he's not the type who is going to murder you for pace, he's quickish, but he's not lightning; not Kanchelskis or Giggsy. So go and commit yourself. Get in a few tackles against the lad." And he did much better in the second half.

We are in mayhem at the moment: Steve Bruce got booked for a tackle; David May's been noticeably worse, but he didn't get booked. Nobody knows what is going on. I watched Blackburn and Chelsea this afternoon and there were some really aggressive tackles. By the end of the game there were four bookings, although, in truth, it should have been six or seven. There was nothing like that in our game yesterday and yet we ended up with five bookings.

Monday 19 September

A couple of weeks ago Ryan Giggs's girlfriend Dani Behr, who presents *The Word*, stated in a magazine interview that Ryan went down to London a couple of nights a week and she came up here to Manchester a couple of nights. I questioned Ryan about it and said:

"You haven't got the energy to be going down the road all the way to London every Saturday, and Wednesday, it's just not possible."

But Ryan told me that the article was nonsense. "Pre-season I was going down there quite a bit and she was coming up, but since the season started, I haven't been. I don't know why she said that – I suppose she might have done the interview a while ago and it has only just appeared."

He knows he won't do himself any favours by running back and forth to London all the time. But yesterday's *Sunday Mirror* had got hold of the story and written that I had banned him from going, which was totally untrue.

Ryan got a bit of stick from the lads about it. The great thing about a football dressing-room is all the banter. As a player I loved it and I still enjoy listening to them arguing and mickey-taking. They think I'm in there to check up on them, to see whether they are showing signs of having had a night out on the town. But I enjoy just being in there and soaking up the atmosphere.

When you stop being a player, you miss all the banter. Obviously my life's different now, but I remember when I played at Dunfermline going out for lunch with the lads and not getting home until really late in the afternoon because we'd spent hours plotting tactics, using napkins and sauce bottles.

There was a period when we were doing great at free kicks. We had a different one every week. We used to go back in the afternoon and work on them: Paton; Edwards; Hugh Robertson; and myself. I remember one week when we played Celtic, who were the top team at the time. I was at a "do" during the week prior to the game with Billy McNeill, who said to me scornfully:

"You can try all your free kicks on Saturday. You've no chance, because we know them all."

When Saturday came, the first goal was a free kick. You should have seen Billy's face. He was never the best of losers, but he looked like thunder.

"Aye, you've got them all but you've nae got that one!" I said as I ran by him.

There is a bit of banter among the staff. We do ante-post betting with teams we've picked at the start of the year who we think are going to win their leagues, picking the top four. So, on a Monday morning, anyone whose teams have had a bad weekend gets awful stick.

Norman, our kit manager, is a great one for that. He is a fantastic man. We call him the "chief executive of the kit". He puts up with all sorts of abuse from everybody. He is in before 8am every morning and everything – all the kit – is spot on.

Norman actually joined the club as minder to George Best, to look after him and make sure he got to training. George had a house built in Cheadle, where he held a housewarming party. Norman took Sir Matt along. There were all these actresses and models coming out of the door, each one with longer legs than the last. Sir Matt said: "Good Heavens," and Norman says that that was the moment when he knew he was beaten.

He's always pulling faces at people. Once he was in the old dressing room–or rather the second dressing-room, the one the players moved into temporarily while the rebuilding was going on – and I was having a go at him.

"For Chrissakes will you get these kits sorted out. You've got the short sleeves out," I barked.

He was saying: "Yes Boss, no Boss," but as I was turning away, I looked in the mirror and he was pulling faces behind my back. But he was doing it almost so that I would see him do it.

These days he's got an assistant and three or four laundry girls.

"It's an empire you're building," I said to him. "You're like all the bloody rest, all building castles at Old Trafford, and yours is the biggest!"

Gary Walsh came through his first game back in the 'A' team, against Blackpool. It was good timing, because Schmeichel came in this morning feeling his back. He injured it on Saturday, so Gary will play against Port Vale. So will Roy Keane.

Tuesday 20 September

Tomorrow we will play the young players. Because of European commitments we've got to use all our resources and, anyway, it is time players like Paul Scholes, Keith Gillespie, David Beckham and Gary Neville took the next step. We'll have a firm base. I shall play Denis Irwin, Roy Keane and David May at the back, and put Choccy up front so that there is someone with experience in there.

We've been talking about it for two years now and if they are not given a chance now it will be too late, they will go to other clubs who will get the benefit of the training they've had at United. I have no doubts about their ability or their temperament.

David May and Roy will play at centre half. Port Vale is a good football team, so we can afford to play the pair. If they'd been a team that play up-and-unders to big forwards, then I'd have had to think about playing Pally.

You need height in English football at centre back. There is no question about that. Gary Neville's natural position is centre half. He is an organiser, a good tackler, his pace is good, his distribution is good, but unless he grows another two or three inches he is going to get beaten for height. In Europe he could fit in at centre half quite happily, but when you play against teams like Crystal Palace, Wimbledon or Blackburn, you've got to be able to head the ball. It's the same with Chris Casper, Gary's partner in the youth team. He needs a few extra pounds in weight and if he gets it, he could be a top centre back.

Either way they could both have good careers playing in other positions if they don't develop enough physically to make it at centre back. Gary is playing at full back and is comfortable there. I've always believed in identifying a player's weakness and, if that weakness could deter him from being the top player in the team, working out where else he would fit in.

Gary's younger brother Philip is a fabulous player, too. He might have played in the game tomorrow, but he was injured a week last Saturday. He has been playing far too much football. It is 20 September today and he has already played 23 games this season. It's unbelievable. It's down to the number of games he plays with the England youth team. I'm bored out of my skull listening to the number of friendly games England have that he's got to play in – and the training programmes. It's crazy. The FA says schoolboys should play a maximum of 50 games per season, but I think it should be monitoring the number of games they play right up to their twenties. That's what we do here and from time to time, the apprentices get rests.

get rests.

In the last two years the FA has taken them away in pre-season, without any preparation, to play friendly games. I don't know what they are trying to do and can only think they are trying to prove that young players can break through the pain barrier.

And they are playing the long ball. My scouts have come back and said that they have just wellied it up the pitch. England national teams! I think Terry Venables has a big job ahead of him sorting it out. But we are going to give Philip a good rest because he is going to be a really good player.

Gary Walsh is back, which is good to see. He is undoubtedly the unluckiest player I've ever had. He had an appendicitis and then on the first day back he went down with chickenpox. When I came to the club it looked as though he was going to be an outstanding keeper. In fact he was tipped as a future England keeper. In those days Chris Turner was the keeper at Old Trafford. He was a good keeper, but we played a game against Tottenham, and he was chipped from about 16 yards.

I said to him: "You are always too far off your line, Chris."

I had been watching the reserves. Gary Walsh was only 19 at the time, but he was unbelievable – he almost filled the goal. I've never seen a better goalkeeper on one against ones, either. So, I put him in against Villa. It was 3-3, and he might have done a wee bit better at the front post on one of the goals, but Villa had the Birmingham Air Crew at the time, with Andy Gray and Thompson. They were really aggressive, but Gary was doing well. Then he got a head injury in Bermuda and since then he's had a catalogue of disasters.

Last season I spent ages trying to get him a club. Joe Royle had him on loan for a time and would have taken him on except he had faith in Paul Gerrard, but there wasn't much interest. Then he came on as sub at Ipswich and played against Southampton and Coventry, where he was absolutely phenomenal. I then got half a dozen managers coming to me and saying: "What are you doing about Walshy?" I replied: "I'm not doing anything with Walshy, you've had your chance. I need him for Europe and that's that." I'd let Les Sealey go by that time, so I really needed Gary. I really feel for Gary, and hope he can go on. He is only 26, so he could still have a great career.

Wednesday 21 September

Port Vale 1 United 2

It was a really good performance. Paul Scholes scored two goals. The first was a defensive mistake, but the second was a really good header. Everybody worked really hard. They got the goals at the right time too, because they did tire in the last fifteen minutes.

The youngsters' inexperience helped them in a way. They really didn't have a care, they just attacked. Their performance was totally lacking in fear. It was difficult for Port Vale because there were men streaming forward wanting to join in the game. Having the two centre backs, Denis Irwin and the goalkeeper gave the young players a good base and, with Choccy up front, we had experience in the right place.

I hadn't announced the team yesterday, but one reporter snooping around The Cliff found out and there were a lot of complaints from outsiders. There were suggestions that we would be reported for fielding a weak team, and the local Stoke MP had a moan about Port Vale supporters buying tickets under false pretences because they had expected to see Cantona and Giggs.

But I think our supporters wanted us to do what we did. They've never seen some of the young players, even though there has been so much talk about them. It was important for the fans to see them, particularly in a situation that wasn't too easy. I felt that it was important to play them all together, because there may come a time when I have to play two or three in a Premiership game.

Gary Neville came in this morning suffering from food poisoning, so we sent him home and told him to drink plenty of liquids and see how he felt in the afternoon. He was OK, but while we were waiting for the coach at the Four Seasons, I was standing with Choccy, Denis Irwin and Gary Walsh. I said to Walshy:

"What about young Neville? He's got food poisoning.

"Oh," said Gary, "I've never had that."

"Knowing your luck, you almost certainly will!"

Venue: Vale Park	*Att:* 18,605		
Port Vale	*goals*	**Manchester United**	*goals*
1 Paul Musselwhite		13 Gary Walsh	
2 Bradley Sandeman		27 Gary Neville	
3 Allen Tankard		12 David May	
4 Andy Porter		16 Roy Keane	
5 Gareth Griffiths		3 Denis Irwin	
6 Dean Glover		31 Keith Gillespie	
7 Kevin Kent		2 David Beckham	
8 Robin Van Der Laan		19 Nicky Butt	
9 Martin Foyle		9 Brian McClair	
10 Lee Glover	7	24 Paul Scholes	36 & 53
11 Tony Naylor		18 Simon Davies	
Substitutes			
12 Ray Walker		5 Lee Sharpe	
13 Mark Van Heusden		25 Kevin Pilkington	
14 Mark Burke (70 mins for 11)		30 John O'Kane (75 mins for 2)	

Thursday 22 September

Schmeichel came in this morning and said: "I've got a problem. I don't think I can play on Saturday."

"You be ready for next Wednesday, that's all I'm worried about," I said.

We will want Peter out there. He had a great game over there last year when we drew 0-0. But it is fortuitous that Gary is back.

I'm a bit worried about Nicky Butt. He had a collision late on in the game last night and we had to take him off because he had double vision. The trouble is he keeps on getting it. We've sent him to see all sorts of people, but no-one can find anything wrong with him. I will take Paul Scholes with me to Ipswich, just in case, and I think I will play Keith Gillespie. I've got to think about Wednesday, it is so important. If I can have Andy and Giggsy really flying on Wednesday, really nice and fresh, it will be a big help, and so I will probably play Keith and play Sharpey on the other side.

There will be one or two others knocking on the door fairly soon: David Beckham had a good game last night. He's a big, gangly lad, and, it seems, a late developer; he's only just beginning to get his strength. We used to bring him to games in London – he was our mascot at West Ham when he was 12. His mother used to say to me:

"I don't think David will grow."

I disagreed and said: "I do, look at his father. And you're not small yourself."

We don't get many players from London because usually they don't want to leave, but David's family are daft about United. He is going to be a good player. He watches the senior players, he practices all the time, his quality in the use of the ball is fabulous, and he works all the time on his technique.

Friday 23 September

We flew to Ipswich. David May had picked up an injury on Wednesday, which meant that I had to play Sharpey at left back. I decided that I wanted to involve Paul Scholes and Nicky Butt as much as possible, bearing in mind next Wednesday, so I decided to leave Gillespie out. Also, it was a chance for Roy Keane to play his first game in midfield but, with his groin strain, having Nicky as a sub made sense. To help Roy, I will play three in midfield with him in front of the back four, which is the role

I want him to play in Turkey. That means Eric will be on his own up front with the two wingers. We need to win this game, so I don't want to use too many of the young players.

Mark Hughes has been in the gym all week, on the machine building up his groin. He has worked really hard, so we hope we ran get him in trim by Monday before we fly out to Istanbul.

Saturday 24 September

Ipswich 3 United 2

It was one of those inexplicable games. We actually played some of our most penetrating football of the season. We had 25 strikes on goal and 22 corners to Ipswich's four. We should have won by I don't know how many goals. Their keeper had an outstanding game!

For the first goal, Ince hit the bar. He was on the ground and he put his head in his hands and groaned with dismay, and took his time in getting up. Now, whether that would have prevented the goal, I can't say, but they passed it out wide and, because Incey wasn't back, nobody went to the boy in the wide position and he crossed it in. Sharpey, who hadn't been well before the game, got caught running inside two players and they scored. And Walshy did really well to get a hand to it.

We then went 2-0 down completely against the run of play. As a team we worked really hard. And, like all the best United teams, they fought like hell to try and get back into the game. All the best United teams have had that fighting spirit, and it is a trademark of the current side.

We got it back to 2-2. Anyone listening to the radio who knows United well would have thought "they'll win now." That was what we thought on the bench. Ipswich had had a hard week, having lost on both Monday and Wednesday, while most of our team didn't play midweek, and we were running over the top of them.

For the winning goal, it looked as if the ball was going out of play for a throw in. Usually the pitch is slightly cambered at the sides, and everyone stopped. But it seemed to catch a curve on the pitch and come back in again. When that happens, you know you're out of luck because on most pitches the camber means that every time the ball goes towards the touchline it goes out. But at Ipswich it slopes in, so Yallop kept on running and crossed. Then Sedgley's shot hit Keane and flew into the net.

Sharpey went to the dentist yesterday to have an abscess removed, so he was feeling pretty rough. We got the Ipswich doctor to look at him before the game, but he said he could only give him a light painkiller because anything stronger would show up if he was picked for a random drug test. The other thing was that it might have made him drowsy. So, there was nothing we could do for him. Lee just had to suffer. We took him off after half time, but considering the state he was in, he played well.

We had an aborted take-off on the way home. It was the first time I've experienced one. At the time I didn't think too much about it – I suppose I was a bit numb because we'd lost. But when I came in I told Cathy: "Oh, no! What happened?" And you could see the panic in her face. And then you start thinking about it. And it is a funny feeling, particularly at this club.

Sir Matt always used to say we should take two jets; that teams shouldn't all travel together. I know Arsenal used to split the party up all the time, but in the modern world engineering has improved, so it's not really something we think about. Also how do you divide the party? And if you do opt for two flights, in one way you are doubling the risk.

Venue: Postman Road	*Att:* 22,559		
Ipswich Town	*goals*	**Manchester United**	*goals*
1 Craig Forest		13 Gary Walsh	
19 Frank Gallop		3 Denis Irwin	
6 David		4 Steve Bruce	
5 John Wark		6 Gary Pallister	
8 Gavin Johnson		9 Roy Keane	
4 Paul Mason	15 & 43	7 Andrei Kanchelskis	
7 Gerraint Williams		8 Paul Ince	
18 Steve Palmer		5 Lee Sharpe	
14 Steve Sedgley	80	9 Brian McClair	
12 Claus Thompsen		7 Eric Cantona	71
24 Adrian Paz		11 Ryan Giggs	
Substitutes			
9 Bontcho Guentchev (77 mins for 24)		24 Paul Scholes (62 mins for 73)	
13 Clive Baker		25 Kevin Pilkington	
17 Simon Milton (89 mins for 5)		19 Nicky Butt (85 mins for 9)	

Sunday 25 September

We had the players in for a loosener this morning because Wednesday's match is so important. It was important to to get the stiffness out of their legs today because we have a four-hour flight tomorrow.

Giggs and Sharpe have changed their hairstyles in the past couple of weeks. Lee did it first, then Ryan followed suit. There was a story in one of the tabloids this morning claiming that Reebok, Giggsy's boot sponsors, were unhappy about it. According to the story it was "an insider" who told the journalist, so I said to Ryan:

"Have Reebok said anything to you about being unhappy with your hair?"

"No, they think it's terrific," he said.

I was always going on at them about their hair, but they have to have the latest fashion. You see players changing their hairstyles all the time, but because it's United, it becomes a big story. Black players have suddenly started having really short hair – to the point where they are almost bald. I think Dion might have been the first to do it.

In my day the style was the DA. My ma said: "Don't you dare come in here with a DA!" When I was an apprentice I wondered whether I should get one, but I wasn't sure if I was brave enough.

I was always telling Sharpey to get his hair cut. "Every time you take a corner you're flapping it up out of your eyes first."

I like the players to be smart. I don't like long hair, but that's purely on practical grounds. I don't see how you can play with hair flopping into your eyes. You have to give yourself the best chance you can of operating in a game and, if you can't see properly, you are giving the opposition an advantage.

Players must make sure they have done everything possible to aid their performance. That means eating sensibly, training properly during the week and getting enough sleep. If a player does all those things and then we still lose, at least they can say they were properly prepared.

The next part is: how did we lose a game or why did I play badly? Perhaps it was just an off day, which all human beings have – mind, as a manager you can't afford too many off-days. But self-examination is vital if you are going to succeed. As the manager I have to assess myself and my preparation. Did I pick the right team? Were the tactics right? You need to do that even before watching the video of the game.

The other vital thing is responding to adversity rather than lapsing into depression. I remember a manager who had never touched a drop of alcohol in his life until he became manager of St Mirren. He ended up drinking a bottle a day. A bottle a day!

You mustn't let things get you down. Perhaps that is why people with a temper are better suited to management than more placid types. They can spark a reaction because losing means something to them.

Everybody can handle success in the sense that they like it. But not everybody can handle losing. That is part of the make-up of top management – or of any successful person – they have to be able to thrive in any situation, especially a bad one, and know how to handle it well and then get over it.

The longer the players are with us, the more care they take in preparing themselves. It is good to watch that develop in people, it's part of the job satisfaction.

Obviously you get job satisfaction from winning trophies, but also from knowing that players respond to you. It's great to watch young players coming through the system, doing well and not undergoing a change in personality. Take Giggsy. He's not really changed, he's the same good lad. Sometimes players get carried away, so I say to them: "I want you to go home to your mother just the same as when you came to us."

Monday 26 September

We trained at The Cliff in the morning. We had hoped to have Sparky with us, but he needed another session in the gym. I'm sure he will be OK, though.

Roy Keane and Denis Irwin had injuries, so I'm having a rethink about the game. Paul Parker is due for a medical in London on Wednesday, but I could see from the way he trained that he was on the mend and might be able to help out.

"You were great, you looked as if there's nothing wrong with you," I said to him.

"I feel all right," he said. "It's just now and again I feel the weak spot aching a bit."

"Well, I'm going to take you with me."

I told him that he may have to play in the game if Keane isn't fit.

Tuesday 27 September

We trained at the stadium today. Roy Keane declared himself fit but he and Denis were still lingering doubts. During training, Giggsy came over and told me his calf was feeling tight. I said: "Just ease yourself through it without doing anything."

Afterwards, Brian mentioned that he'd thought Ryan hadn't looked too bright. I said I'd told Ryan to take it easy because his calf was troubling him. Brian thought he should have opted out, but I said:

"No, all the press were there, which was why I told him just to do a little."

I want to play Peter Schmeichel, Andrei, Ryan and Sparky, so it will come down to a choice between Denis and Roy. For weeks I have wanted someone who can sit in front of the back four and look after Kubilay, who is the Turks' most dangerous player. Roy can do that very well.

Kubilay can play wide – he did some of the time against us last year – but whenever we've watched Galatasaray this season he has played off the front pair.

Wednesday 28 September

A few Galatasaray fans came along the Bosphorus in boats last night and made a bit of noise outside our hotel which overlooks the river, but it wasn't anything serious.

Some of the lads had money stolen from their hotel rooms, but that can happen anywhere, I suppose.

We found a ground near the hotel and gave Denis and Ryan try-outs. They were both OK, but it is one of those things – you can take a risk with a forward because it is not going to cost you the game if they let the side down. But never take a risk with a defender. And with Paul Parker on the bench I didn't want two risks on defenders, particularly with Denis having a hamstring injury. I was worried that if Denis's hamstring went it would put us under pressure straight away.

Wednesday evening

Galatasaray 0 United 0

The game turned out to have a good result and we put on a good professional performance. Looking back I thought we could have won had we gone for it a bit more, but we kept our discipline and did what we wanted to.

The result was the same as last year's match; the game itself had some similarities. Everything else was totally different. The stadium had improved dramatically since our last visit: they have obviously done a lot of work on it. The security was different, too. They couldn't do enough for us. After the episode in the preliminary round in Luxembourg when the fans misbehaved, I think they know they are on their last chance. Before the game they kept making announcements to their fans, reminding them that if there was any trouble they'd be out of Europe. This year there was no police presence in the tunnel, which was what caused the problem last time.

I don't usually go on to the pitch during the warm-ups, but this time I thought I would. I stood out there for about an hour while the team got ready. The atmosphere was great; very loud, but all good-natured. When the team came out for their warm-up, they started singing their songs against United and one or two of the lads started dancing. They loved it.

Tactics in Europe are different. You are up against people who work on tactics all the time. Having watched them and planned for Kubilay to play behind the front two, they went and played three up with Kubilay playing wide left. They had obviously watched us and, for some reason, decided that Kubilay should play against David May.

I'd said in my team talk that if Kubilay did play as a winger, just to leave him as winger and for Roy to play centre midfield as usual. That was the way it turned out, so none of the players were confused about what they should have been doing.

That meant that Roy Keane had no-one to play against. In some ways that was good for us because he picked up a lot of scraps outside the box and so we were able to keep possession quite easily at times. But because their central midfield was deeper, it meant Mapeza was on the ball all the time. When teams come to you, you are better to keep things tight rather than having players all over the field. Our objective was to use Andrei and Ryan to try to stretch Galatasaray and turn them back towards their own goal. Then Nicky Butt and Sharpey could go and support as much as they could, but making sure that the three defenders – Pally, Bruce and May – were always there, with Keane sitting and Ince doing as much as he could.

Apart from a couple of lapses, the team did well. Nicky Butt gave the ball away in the first five minutes and they could have scored, but Pally recovered well to get a good tackle in. We kept it quite quiet. We were a wee bit unlucky with one or two things ourselves – Sparky had a great effort blocked when it looked as if it was flying in.

At half time, the only point I made was about possession.

"Make sure we don't end up going nowhere and then passing back to the goalkeeper," I said. I hate that type of possession.

In the first twenty minutes of the second half we were all over the place. Kubilay kept floating about and they increased the tempo. That was expected, though. A team who are not doing well at home are likely to get a rocket from the manager at half time. For the first twenty minutes I felt we needed two or three players to hold the ball and keep passing it. It didn't matter who they gave it to, they needed to keep passing it, to make early passes to keep possession and kill Galatasaray off. Once we were over the first twenty minutes, I was quite confident. What I was looking for but didn't get was the final penetration to bring us a goal.

We were a bit unlucky. Nicky Butt and Roy Keane started to tire in the last 15 minutes, which was understandable – it was only Nicky's second real outing and Roy hasn't played many games. Giggsy eventually came off with calf trouble, too.

We almost got lucky with one shot from Andrei. The goalkeeper lost it, Brucey put it back in and Andrei lobbed it, but the defender did absolutely brilliantly. He had Sparky going in on him, but he didn't take his eye off the ball for one minute, he just guided it away for a corner.

Venue: Ali Sami Yen *Att:* 30,000

Galatasaray	*goals*	**Manchester United**	*goals*
1 Ghintaras Stauce		1 Peter Schmeichel	
2 Gotz Mapeza		2 David May	
3 Korkmaz Bulent		3 Lee Sharpe	
4 Kaya Sedat		4 Steve Bruce	

5	Korkmaz Mert	5	Nicky Butt
6	KerinoghuTugay	6	Gary Pallister
7	Altintas Yusuf	7	Andrei Kanchelskis
8	Sancakli Saffet	8	Paul Ince
9	Sukur Hagn	9	Roy Keane
10	Hamzaoglu Hamza	10	Mark Hughes
11	Turkiylmaz Kubilay	11	Ryan Giggs
Substitutes			
12	Erdem Arif (45 mins for 6)	12	Paul Parker (65 mins for 11)
13	Cakir Osman (76 mins for 8)	13	Gary Walsh
14	Bolglu Nezihi	14	Paul Scholes
15	Arsla Cihat	15	David Beckham
16	Uruk Okan	16	Gary Neville

Thursday 29 September

We got home finally about 5am. A four hour flight back. Then I couldn't sleep–one of those nights where you go to bed, you can't sleep or you doze and keep waking up. Cathy is in Glasgow at her mother's, so I went home and put the teletext on. I got up at 8am, read the paper, went back to sleep. I got up again at 9.45. It is horrible, your whole day is gone. You are totally knackered, yet you know that you have a game on Saturday, and the chances are it is going to start badly and finish badly. I always say after European matches "Make sure you start right. You can understand if it goes towards the end of the game, but if you start badly it never comes."

Money wasn't the only thing to disappear from our hotel rooms. I didn't notice at the time, but my personal organiser has disappeared, with all my engagements and lots of telephone numbers. I rang the hotel, but it wasn't in the room.

I watched Aston Villa beat Inter Milan 1-0 and win their UEFA Cup tie on penalties. It was an exciting performance, the best by an English team in Europe for some years and a real contrast to Blackburn's defeat by Trelleborgs. But Blackburn rely on forcing errors, a bit like the old Wimbledon, and I don't think you can do that in Europe. You've got to probe and create, be patient, work the ball around, but Blackburn were just knocking it forward.

Friday 30 September

Paul Parker had a great last 20 minutes when he came on as sub on Wednesday. Nevertheless, he is still worried about his ankle so we have rearranged his appointment to see the specialist for next Wednesday. Hopefully he'll get a quick diagnosis, because I really want him to play against Barcelona. He is the player who could do a job on Romario for me.

Very few players have the discipline, the mental toughness that Paul has. If I ask him to go and play against John Barnes, he'll do it and Barnes won't get a kick.

Barcelona lost in Gothenburg, so Barcelona can only get ten points now. If they do, the maximum Gothenburg can get is eight points, and Galatasaray seven. So now we are looking for eight points. I wonder if it might have been better for us if Barcelona had won because it would have got rid of Gothenburg. The good thing is that it tells you that Barcelona are not unbeatable. Sometimes teams seem larger than life and have incredible reputations, but often, when you come up against them, they aren't so frightening. Some years ago, when Maradona was at his peak, Barcelona came to Old Trafford and Graeme Hogg was up against him. I wouldn't put Hoggy down as one of the best centre halves to play for Manchester United, but that night he didn't give Maradona a kick. And you see from the performance of Aston Villa last night how the British spirit can lift a side. The really passionate support helps players. If we get a night like that at Old Trafford, the players can really be inspired by the crowd. We shouldn't go into it thinking what happens if Romario gets the ball, or Koeman, or Stoichkov or Hagi, who had great World Cups. We have the stage and the players too–Roy Keane had a great World Cup. You just make sure you don't build the opposition up into monsters, so that the players are afraid of them.

The Gothenburg game was strange because Barcelona went 1-0 up and our report said they could have been five up. They were in control but then lost it by two late goals. This illustrates the point I repeatedly make to the players about Europe: you can do well in terms of performance; but sometimes you don't win. But you can be outplayed possession-wise in European games and still win at home.

That is always the worry when you are away - you can play well and still get beaten 1–0. I keep stressing that message to the players, that they need to be really vigilant. You think you are doing well and then the roof falls in right on top of you. They can have easy possession, they build up very slowly, and then all of a sudden in the last third they increase the pace and it catches you at times.

And when you make a mistake, they capitalise on it right away. Nicky Butt hit a pass and Tugay, who was their best player on Wednesday, intercepted it. And the moment he cut it off, he was lifting his head, looking to see what he could do with it. And he threaded a pass right through us to the big centre forward, Saffet. Fortunately Pally saved the day.

The variation in Europe, the way danger can suddenly hit you out of nowhere, and the huge differences between home ties and away ties has always intrigued me. As a player I went to Cologne with Rangers. They had two World Cup players in Overath and Weber – who scored the second goal in the final against England in 1966. We murdered them at Ibrox and came away with a 3-0 lead.

Then they murdered us. We lost 3-0; they got the third goal about two minutes from the end, and it went into extra time. But, if anything, the pace they had to play at to get back into the game meant that by the time it went into extra time they were knackered and we won on an own goal.

In one game at Aberdeen we annihilated Hamburg. We were 3-1 up, with two minutes to go. Then we missed a penalty and they scored with the last kick of the game. We'd had a player taken off, and we were waiting for the ball to go off to put a sub on. Instead of the final score being 4-1, it was 3-2 and they went through.

Another game in Aberdeen was against Gothenburg. We drew 2-2 and lost on away goals. We were 2-1 up. Then, in the last minute, Willie Miller got caught in possession, the ball was played through and they scored an excellent goal. Again, it was the last kick of the game. Had they not got that final goal we would have been in the semi-final of the European Cup. And that is the nature of european competition. And the more experience the players get of that, like last year against Galatasaray, the better prepared they will be. One of the important lessons of management is learning in adversity. And it is the same for players until you get to the point where they learn the final lesson and say "I've had enough of this, I'm not going to make that mistake again, because it costs so much."

When I first came to United, losing a game could cost you sixth or seventh place. Now losing games can cost you first place. You lose a semi-final and it costs you the final, so everything is at a higher level now.

Gothenburg know exactly how to play in Europe. No matter what teams they have had over the years, they always do well. They seem to have a formula and they get by.

After the game on Wednesday I did the usual press conference. Then, on the plane back from Turkey I did the usual follow-up conference for the daily papers, then went to the back of the plane to do one for the Sunday papers.

One journalist asked about "the spitting incident". I was baffled. Apparently, Roy Keane was supposed to have spat at Kubilay.

The next day it was all over the papers, even though none of the journalists from the dailies had said a word about it to me on the plane.

Mark trained today. We never do much on a Friday anyway, but when you've had a game like Wednesday's, and the travelling, you can't. He needs to play to keep his fitness up, so I may play him against Port Vale on Wednesday, too. Apart from Ryan, who will be out for ten days or so, everyone's fit.

While we were in Turkey, Eric had been having treatment for a groin injury. He will come back in, but then we lose him again next weekend because France have a game. Russia want Andrei to join them on the Friday, but they are only playing San Marino, and our staff team would beat them. Hopefully we will be able to keep him until after the Saturday game.

The international system still isn't right. There has been talk of Scotland, Northern Ireland and Wales invoking the five-day rule so that they can have players on the Friday before matches, but I don't think it's feasible. Nobody is going to cooperate for friendly matches if they do that.

We play Everton tomorrow. They have had a disastrous start to the season, and their manager, Mike Walker, is already under pressure. But you always worry about the game after a European tie, particularly after the amount of travelling to Turkey, it is important for us. Newcastle are six points clear and we don't want to let them get out of sight. Everything is buzzing, they are all flying off as soon as the ball is passed. They all have good control and they all want to play. It is very different from Blackburn. David May believes the main work at Blackburn is on setting up play – centre back to full back, back to centre back and into the channel, or full back to winger, back to full back and into the channel. When they got that early goal against us last season, all you heard from their bench was "put the ball into the corners."

Ipswich play Southampton tomorrow. Ipswich must have used up all their luck for the season against us last week. But teams often have very bad runs after beating us. When Chelsea beat us at Stamford Bridge last year they didn't win another game for months. Whether they get so wound up against us and put so much into the game that they are flat afterwards, or whether it is because they are still doing laps of honour for weeks afterwards I don't know.

Saturday 1 October

United 2 Everton 0

During the early part we did quite well, but the second half was really flat, because the body is tired after the travelling–and sometimes the brain is tired too. The way Everton defended high up the pitch, on another day they would have been caught by Eric, who can thread passes through, and we would have done well, particularly with such quick, wide players. But it wasn't to be, simply because there was a tiredness there. We got the result, and there was never any real question of us losing, although Schmeichel had to make one or two saves, and we didn't sparkle.

And although Eric wasn't tired from the trip, he had missed training all week and it showed. When he came in I said to him "Are you sure you are alright?" and he said "Yes, I'll be all right," but you could see he had missed the training. People like Eric and Hughes must train; the players with powerful builds; the Roy Keanes and Pallisters; must train. They have too big a frame to miss it. Lee Sharpe is the same. If you chart Sharpey's progress as a footballer, all his highs have been when he is fit.

Big lads need to be fit, they need to do plenty of training, to have regular habits of work, in order to keep themselves in shape. And Eric and Sparky need to make sure they get some really hard training to get the momentum going again. And if Eric is away with France next week, hopefully he will do that.

There were six bookings during the first 27 minutes, some of them just ridiculous. Sharpey was booked for kicking the ball away when he didn't hear the whistle. The refereeing was erratic and there wasn't a single booking after the interval. You wonder if an independent observer had had a word at half time.

Had a chat with Mike Walker afterwards. He is under pressure because there is constant speculation in the papers about his future. I told him to stop reading the papers; after all, where's the sense in torturing yourself?

I was right in my prediction about Ipswich. They got thrashed at Southampton.

Venue: Old Trafford *Att:* 43,803

Everton	*goals*	Manchester United	*goals*
1 Neville Southall		1 Peter Schmeichel	
4 Ian Snodin		3 Denis Irwin	
5 Dave Watson		4 Steve Bruce	
26 David Unsworth		6 Gary Pallister	
16 David Burrows		12 David May	
19 Gary Rowett		14 Andrei Kanchelskis	41
8 Garaham Stuart		8 Paul Ince	
17 Joe Parkinson		16 Roy Keane	
7 Vinny Samways		7 Eric Cantona	
3 Andy Hinchcliffe		10 Mark Hughes	
11 Daniel Amokachi		5 Lee Sharpe	88
Substitutes			
18 Stuart Barlow (86 mins for 8)		24 Paul Scholes	
2 Matt Jackson		13 Gary Walsh	
12 Jason Kearton		9 Brian McClair (75 mins for 10)	

Sunday 2 October

Everton are signing Trevor Steven and taking Ian Durrant and Duncan Ferguson on loan from Rangers. Mike Walker didn't mention that in our chat yesterday.

Newcastle won again. I keep saying to myself, and to the players "just keep in there until December and we're in with a great chance." We'll get going again in December, there's no question about that. But it has been sporadic so far. There have been wee moments–Wimbledon was excellent; parts of the Liverpool game–we finished brilliantly against Liverpool; there were little bits yesterday; little bits against QPR; a good performance at Nottingham Forest. But we have been patchy in other games. We had good penetration at Ipswich, but threw three goals away. We have to strike a balance, where you say 'there's a few who got eight out of ten today'. That's what wins you games. If you get all your players getting eight or nine out of ten, you win your games. But at the moment we are making a rollercoaster of it. And changing teams all the time has meant we haven't had consistent form.

Monday 3 October

We have a few injuries. Roy Keane has gone to have his groin scanned to see if there is any real damage. Paul Parker is having his check up this Wednesday. Eric's away with France, and it looks as if we are going to lose Andrei for Saturday. Today Mark Hughes had his first full training session since the start of the season. We're in October and it's only his first full session.

Trevor Steven didn't sign for Everton, but they are taking Duncan Ferguson, reportedly for £35,000 a week for a three-month period – a lot of money.

Tuesday 4 October

We have the second leg against Fort Vale tomorrow, where we will play the young players again. It will be harder for them this time.

We have a Spanish journalist with us for four days. Part of the UEFA requirements for the Champions League is that journalists must be given access. We have quite a controlled situation at Old Trafford, with a new press room up in the main stand, some distance from the dressing-rooms. I encourage the boys to go up there for press conferences after the games, and I always go up myself. But television operates from a base in the tunnel and the new UEFA regulations give journalists the right to go down there too, which creates chaos.

We get quite a lot of journalists visiting. We've just had a request from a Finnish journalist who wants to come over and do a big feature on United. I think every country in the world has done it and it gets to be a real pain, because they want to come, cameras and all, to talk to me and to meet every player.

Until about a year ago, we used to give journalists a lot of access. But it has got to the stage now that we just can't cope because there are so many high profile players in the team that we are swamped with requests. We don't mind the odd coach – we had a man from Japan last week. Bobby Charlton looked after him and he was fine; he didn't get in the way. But some of them you just can't get rid of. They get into the staff room, the medical room, they want to have lunch with you and they seem to forget that we have a job to get on with – and that we need a bit of privacy. The other difficulty is that you have to make sure journalists are being looked after because you don't want them writing detrimental things about the club.

The demands at this club are enormous. We have a group of handicapped supporters here today to meet the players. Of course you are glad to do it, but we have tried to organise it so that they do come in groups at a time. Otherwise it would be never ending.

All the interest that players like Ryan and Lee, Paul Ince and Eric arouse means there is always someone waiting to meet them, to get their autographs or to be photographed with them. Sometimes you can hardly get in and out of The Cliff for people hanging around the gate.

We do like to participate in charity work as much as possible; hospital visits, or, as I mentioned before, having handicapped people to visit. It is no exaggeration to say that there are people who have had years put on their lives by just meeting the players.

Wednesday 5 October

The injuries continue: Steve Bruce's knee is beginning to grumble – it always plays up once the season's really got going. We are a bit concerned about Denis' hamstring. He keeps having twinges, so we will have to give him some special exercises in the gym to build up strength. Roy is going to have to have an operation on his groin. It's a hernia, which he got training with Ireland during the World Cup. If we can get him through the two Barcelona games before the op it will be a great help. The specialist said to give him a game a week to get through until then. I shall play him at Sheffield, but he is definitely out of Ireland's match against Barcelona next Wednesday and the question then is should he play in the match against West Ham or not.

Sparky is getting in a full week, which is good. He is not effective when he isn't in full training. If you look at his scoring record this season compared to last, that is down to not training. He's going with Wales next week, which should boost his fitness. It might also help my popularity in Wales. *Wales on Sunday* ran this coupon for people to fill in if they thought United were being unfair to Wales by pulling Ryan out of one or two matches. They sent me the coupons with a letter of protest reading: "United let Wales down." So I phoned and asked whether they were doing it to get publicity. I said: "Do you think I could tell Mark Hughes not to play for Wales? Is that what you think? Because if so, you don't know Mark."

It was the same with the game at Port Vale. Everybody wanted to see Ryan Giggs. But it is ridiculous to think that Ryan will be able to play in every game this season. We have always rested him for a period during a season. He is still only 20 and I think he is still growing.

There are so many demands on Ryan. People criticise me for not giving them access to him, but if you let one in the others get the huff and he'd be seeing people every day. When he's 23 or 24 he'll know what's going on, and who he wants to talk to. I don't want to spend my life telling him who he should and shouldn't be talking to, but every week some magazine wants to do a profile on him. It never stops. People forget that our business is football.

Paul Ince has finally signed his new contract. We did well last year, with a lot of the players signing long contracts: Pallister; Bruce; Giggs; Sharpe. Schmeichel finally signed after a lot of debating. This year Paul's has been protracted, partly because he started talking about tax in the papers, which created a problem. It was all down to his testimonial, but the chairman has now sorted things out. I don't think there is any doubt that his emergence as a top player has been due to his coming to Manchester United. he had all the basic raw material there - two great feet; a terrific header of the ball, a great spring; great pace; a terrific tackler; and he could dribble and could pass. But as with a lot of young players you've then got to take all the raw material, sort all the bits out and make a player, and I think that was the case with Paul.

I think the talk about Italy might have got to him, with agents dangling incentives under his nose, but I think he knew that Italy wouldn't have suited his lifestyle. Not many people go there and settle in that environment and enjoy it.

So now he has signed we can take a deep breath of relief and look at

CARLING
CARLING
CARLING

Strain man: Fielding questions at the pre-match press conference in Barcelona

Contemplating the tasks ahead in the solitude of the bootroom

In the presence of the man who made Manchester United

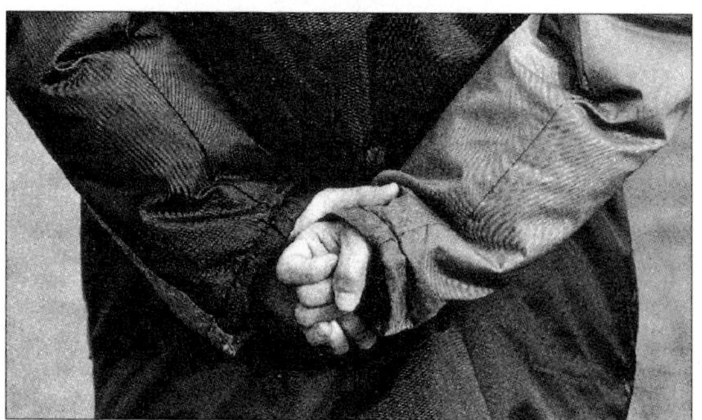

The manager's the guy with the white knuckles

Under pressure

Life in a goldfish bowl: surrounded by the world's press at the Nou Camp

My close partnership with Kiddo has reaped rich rewards

Grey skies, but there's sunshine in our hearts

Not fast enough lads - do another lap!

Keeping a close eye on developments at the Cliff

Incey makes a false start while my attention is elsewhere

Club rappport: Giggsy and me share a chuckle

Football: serious business or a funny old game?

I love the spirit and camaraderie at United

For once, alone in the Theatre of Dreams

the team. Hopefully we'll have this gang for the next few years. But each year there is always one coming to the end of their contract. It is vital to stagger all the contracts so if it came to the point where someone did leave, it would be one rather than two or three.

At the moment we are negotiating with Sparky. He wants a three- or four-year deal, which at his age is asking too much. It is not easy, because you are not just dealing with a player but you are dealing with agents and lawyers and accountants nowadays, and that can go on and on and on.

Wednesday evening

United 2 Port Vale 0

Port Vale started off really well. They could have been two up in the first ten minutes, but Gary made a terrific save from a header. We had the nucleus of the senior side, at least at the back. You have to make sure that you are going to be hard to beat, so we had Walshy in goal and David May and Gary Pallister in the centre of the defence. I put Casper and O'Kane at full back, and O'Kane did really well, playing a big part in one of the goals.

We had an experienced forward in McClair and, in midfield, Nicky Butt – who has now got real experience in first team football from playing in the team in European games. Nicky was named man of the match despite missing a penalty. That is a great asset–a player who can take a penalty without it affecting his game.

Simon Davies played well, too. He's a big, powerful lad and came to United as a colt. I remember seeing him as a lad of 14. He was this big, gangly boy, who I never thought would have enough strength because he was so thin. In those days his legs were like matchsticks, but he has come a long way since then. He's got good control, good pace and confidence and he has got a trick, he has this shrug of his hips and his shoulders, so he can beat a man.

I went in afterwards and told them:

"I've just heard the draw and we've got Liverpool."

I was only winding them up - the draw is not till tomorrow morning. But they were all really excited about the prospect of playing Liverpool, they had no fear at all.

Venue: Old Trafford *Att:* 31,615

Manchester United	*goals*	**Port Vale**	*goals*
1 Gary Walsh		1 Paul Musselwhite	
2 Chris Casper		2 Bradley Sandeman	
3 John O'Kane		3 Allen Tankard	
4 Nicky Butt		4 Andy Porter	
5 David May	61	5 Neil Aspin	
6 Gary Pallister		6 Dean Glover	

7	Keith Gillespie		7	Tony Kelly
8	David Beckham		8	Kevin Kent
9	Brian McClair	34	9	Martin Foyle
10	Paul Scholes		10	Lee Glover
11	Simon Davies		11	Mark Burke
Substitutes				
12	Graeme Tomlinson (64 mins for 7)		12	Robin van der Laan (73 mins for 8)
13	Kevin Pilkington		13	Arjan van Heusden
14	Gary Neville (76 mins for 11)		14	Joe Allon (73 mins for 11)

Thursday 6 October

Well, we didn't get Liverpool. We got Newcastle! It will be the same again: the youngsters will play. In the team I pick I will make allowances for their strengths. We will need some experienced players and I won't play all the young ones, but Butt, Gillespie and Scholes will all play.

Overall, the two games the youngsters played served to confirm what I already knew: that they all have real strength. Their technical ability and temperament is good, but what we don't know yet is whether they have the real capacity to go right to the top: to play on the big stages; against the best players; in games against teams who are going to man-mark them and be rough with them.

You never know about a young player until they've got through the first year and into the second; when they are playing against teams which know them and are planning tactics against them. Then you see how they handle it – and how they handle success, which is the biggest problem in football for a manager. Some players get completely carried away with it. In most cases you rely on the boy's father to be down to earth and sensible - as Ryan's mother is. A stable family background helps.

I like my players to be married. I was married at 24. You can't tell a player to get married, but if they are, it's a bonus. Paul Ince got married within about a year of arriving here and it really settled him down.

Then there are the players who most girls in the country would love to go out with, players like Ryan and Sharpey. They think it's a great life, having all these girls running after them, so it is difficult to imagine them settling down, but you hope they will eventually. It helps their game, there's no question about it.

Friday 7 October

We are without Andy and Eric tomorrow because of internationals, so Keith Gillespie will play. In the end I did not play Sparky against Port Vale because he needed training, but he will be in tomorrow. Ryan is still injured, though.

We have had some great games at Hillsborough over the years, and it has always been in a good atmosphere - passionate enough, but good tempered.

Saturday 8 October

Sheffield Wednesday 1 United 0

I said to the lads after the game: "Enough is enough." We've seen it three times this season already, throwing games away. I told them I wouldn't put up with any more.

"We've got to get it sorted out and that obviously means making one or two changes. But there's something wrong. The players we've got in this dressing-room are good enough to win every game."

Somehow we looked a bit sluggish from the start - it was strange because usually these games are really gung-ho, but we were slow to start. Trevor Francis said to me afterwards:

"We were expecting a barrage straight away, but it was really slow."

I agreed with him but couldn't explain it because there was a big crowd and a good atmosphere – all the things we usually respond to.

Even though we didn't really play, we should have been four or five up at half time. Keith Gillespie had a good start and should have scored, but he ran offside - inexperience. He knows he didn't need to run it. But if we had scored then, we would probably have won easily.

Keith had a really good game for us. Towards the end he stopped dropping back and started wandering a bit, which is a problem with young players. I took him off and put on Paul Scholes towards the end, because if you are down you should always have the maximum number of potential goal-scorers on the pitch as possible. But Keith is going to be a good player. He has good composure, good temperament, is a good crosser of the ball and is a really nice boy - no big ideas and no pretensions.

I think the bits of injuries we've had, and the inconsistencies of team selection, haven't helped us, but that's not all. There's carelessness, too, which we will have to eradicate. The whole thing is unacceptable because we cannot afford to let Newcastle get too far away.

I'm not sure how much the European competition is responsible for it. I'm sure it has an effect. Thinking back to my experiences with Aberdeen, we lost on the Saturdays before the quarter-finals and semi-finals of the Cup Winners' Cup the year we won it. The same thing is happening here, so I hope that's a good sign.

Before the semi-final, it snowed in Aberdeen and we lost 1-0. We could have won the treble that year, but we missed four penalty kicks. Wee Strachan missed four penalties during the run-in that year. Every time it cost us the game and we lost the league by one point. We just threw our chance away. Even in the last game we needed to win 5-0 as long as Dundee United only drew. We won 5-0, but Dundee scored five minutes before time.

Venue: Hillsborough	*Att:* 33,441		
Manchester United	*goals*	**Sheffield Wednesday**	*goals*
1 Peter Schmeichel		13 Kevin Pressman	
2 Paul Parker		2 Peter Atherton	
3 Denis Irwin		12 Andy Pearce	
4 Steve Bruce		17 Des Walker	
6 Gary Pallister		3 Ian Nolan	
8 Paul Ince		29 Lee Briscoe	
5 Lee Sharpe		16 Graham Hyde	
31 Keith Gillespie		11 John Sheridan	
16 Roy Keane		14 Chris Bart-Williams	
10 Mark Hughes		9 David Hirst	44
9 Brian McClair		10 Mark Bright	
Substitutes			
12 David May (60 mins for 2)		4 Ian Taylor (65 mins for 14)	
13 Gary Walsh		23 Lance Key	
24 Paul Scholes (76 mins for 31)		20 Gordon Watson (88 mins for 10)	

Sunday 9 October

The refereeing in our game was poor. He booked Sharpe for absolutely nothing, then he booked Steve Bruce for a tackle from the back when he clearly took the ball. I've checked it twice on the video. Then, because he had booked two of our players, be booked Pearce when he actually played the ball. Later on, Pearce twice brought down Ince on the edge of the box, and the ref didn't do anything, because if he had, it would have necessitated sending Pearce off for two bookable offences. So he didn't want to know.

I watched Southampton v Everton on *Match of the Day*, and even though there were all sorts of things going on, there wasn't a yellow card in sight. As far as I'm concerned, there wasn't a single tackle in our game but there were four bookings. It was the same last week when we played against Everton. I think the trouble is that our games are all like cup-ties and the referees just can't cope.

We've got players like Steve Bruce on four yellow cards already, and he hasn't produced a tackle to make a hair move on anyone's leg yet.

Monday 10 October

It's international week, so most people are away. Only Steve Bruce, Brian McClair, Lee Sharpe, the injured and the youngsters in at The Cliff.

Spoke at a charity dinner at Old Trafford in aid of adolescents with cancer.

Tuesday 11 October

I flew to Belfast to watch a young goalkeeper I had been tipped off about. It was a cup-tie and a local derby. Some of the tackling! Finally this boy was taken off with a badly broken leg. That quietened things down. I felt sorry for the ref.

Without doubt Ireland has got the best word-of-mouth communications of any country in the world. I was supposed to be here anonymously, wearing a cloth cap. When I arrived, though, it turned out that everybody in the town knew I was coming. Probably the worst thing you can say in Ireland is "keep this to yourself".

Wednesday 12 October.

I enjoyed my trip to Ireland – it sort of revitalises your faith in people. They are so hospitable and easygoing that you come away feeling totally refreshed. The only thing I can't handle is the drinking – I don't know how they do it. It's just Guinness, Guinness, Guinness. Incredible. In the bar they didn't even seem to order pints, they just continually topped the glasses up.

And they always say: "Would you like a drink, Mr Ferguson?"

And I say: "No, thank you."

"A cup of tea then?"

"Aye, I'll have a cup of tea."

But then they bring biscuits and sandwiches, too. The Scots are the same. I remember when Brian McClair's contract at Celtic had expired and we went up to talk to him. On the drive up, the chairman Martin Edwards said:

"Do you know, the one player from the great teams that I've never met is Jimmy Delaney."

So I phoned Jim Rodger, a very good Scottish journalist who I've known since I was about fifteen and said:

"Jim, here's a request, Martin Edwards is with me, and he's never met Jimmy Delaney."

"Where are you?"

"I'm driving to Glasgow."

"Where are you going?"

"Jim, I can't tell you that."

But you can tell Jim anything and he'll never tell a soul, so I let on that we were going to see Brian.

We dropped in to see Jimmy Delaney on the way back. When we drove up to the house, they'd laid on a real spread. They'd got out the tablecloth and there were sandwiches and scones, cakes, meat pies – the lot.

The chairman said to me afterwards: "Why do Scottish people do that?" I told him it was part of the culture. If someone comes to your house for a cup of tea, particularly in the afternoon, you put the lot out.

Keith Gillespie scored this marvellous goal for Northern Ireland in Vienna. This morning I was looking at the paper over breakfast in the hotel, and I saw BBC 2 were showing Austria v Northern Ireland. I thought I'd watch it so I sat down and turned on the TV. There was nothing on. I thought maybe it was an 8pm kick off, but still nothing doing. Then I turned on teletext. I had been looking at an Irish paper, of course! Still, I managed to catch Keith's goal later on *Sportsnight*.

Thursday 13 October

There was talk last week of Pat McGibbon, our reserve centre half, going to Bradford on loan, but it turns out that both their central defenders are OK after all, so I had to go and tell the boy to forget it. It's a pity because I think it would have been good for Pat and I think he was looking forward to it. But there's a chance that he might be in the next Northern Ireland squad.

Alan McDonald got a yellow card in Vienna – his second – so he will miss the next game against Ireland in Belfast. I would be happier if Pat had an experienced player to play alongside if he does get called up, but I think he could handle Niall Quinn. He didn't give Chris Sutton so much as a kick in the 'B' international at Hillsborough last spring. In two or three years Pat will probably be a very good player, but at the moment he lacks confidence. But he has been much better this season.

Mark Hughes was brilliant in training today. His finishing was good and he is looking fitter. He has trained all week, because he didn't go with Wales, so hopefully he will be a bit more like the real Mark. It has been a worry, because an injury when you are 31 can be serious. Mark's knee is bad because he had cortisone injections when he was younger and now there is crystallisation on the bone. Hopefully the training will help.

Another dinner engagement – this time a Jewish organisation attended by Mike Edelson, one of the United directors.

Friday 14 October

You always think that international week will be an easy week, but they never are. I've had something on every evening this week and we have friends down from Aberdeen tonight.

There are a few priests who come to Old Trafford all the time. One phoned the house last night about a lad who is dying. He went to the World Cup, but since he came home he has been unable to eat and is just fading away. Apparently his mother's a doctor and just can't understand it. I wrote a letter which I hope will give him some enthusiasm back. We are always getting requests for tapes for people in comas. Usually a member of the family arrives and records a message in the hope they respond to it.

It was Cath's birthday yesterday. She never reminds me. My niece was staying with us this week, so before I went away on Tuesday she said:

"Don't forget Auntie Cathy's birthday. Do you want me to get a card?"

I said yes. I asked her to leave it in the bottom drawer of the desk in my study. I found it last night. Before I went in to dinner, I left it on the stairs. I wrote: "PS. You thought I'd forgotten!" She said:

"I told everyone not to tell you – Darren, Jason and Mark."

They all reminded me, of course.

I've been watching a video of Barcelona. Romario's back. He didn't play against Gothenburg but he's back in. It's going to be a really tough game for us. We'll have to draw up some tactics against Romario. I've just got to make sure I do my homework on that one.

I really need Paul Parker. He is a major part of my thoughts, because picking the back four will be crucial. I need Keane, Hughes, Giggs and Sharpey as well. I also need Schmeichel. I may have to rest Andrei, even though I don't want to.

It will be a great night, but I am apprehensive about it. Perhaps the World Cup did it. Romario was the player of the tournament, but Stoichkov was good too, and they are coming on the back of that. Romario hasn't played much since then, but when he returned on Sunday they won 4-3.

I haven't had a chance to watch them playing live because most of their games have been on Saturdays, and when they did have a Sunday match, so did we. We've got the videos, though. Les Kershaw has seen them, so has Eric Harrison, so we should have a good appraisal of them.

The important thing is that we don't build Barcelona up into monsters, and that we make sure that we've got our own pattern of play. We will have to be very aware tactically, but if we can score two goals at home, I don't think anyone can beat us.

Saturday 15 October
United 1 West Ham 0

Well, we won and that was about all you could say. We played quite well during the first half, but Ryan went off at half time, and the second half was very much a performance which said "we've a big European game on Wednesday". West Ham had five in midfield and played with only one up. And, although it stopped us, it meant they never even looked like scoring.

Venue: Old Trafford	*Att:* 43,795		
Manchester United	*goals*	**West Ham United**	*goals*
1 Peter Schmeichel		1 Ludek Miklosko	
12 David May		2 Tim Breacker	
3 Denis Irwin		4 Steve Potts	
4 Steve Bruce		5 Alvin Martin	
6 Gary Pallister		12 Keith Rowland	
8 Paul Ince		14 Matthew Rush	
5 Lee Sharpe		6 Martin Allen	
14 Andrei Kanchelskis		10 John Moncur	
7 Eric Cantona	44	26 Don Hutchison	
10 Mark Hughes		19 Mike Marsh	
11 Ryan Giggs		7 Tony Cotte	
Substitutes			
19 Nicky Butt (45 mins for 12)		7 Ian Bishop	
13 Gary Walsh		21 Tony Feuer	
9 Brian McClair		22 Adrian Whitbread	

Sunday 16 October

We have a reserve match tomorrow, but it is difficult because I'm not sure which of the young players I'll need for the European match. I brought everyone in today because we had to be absolutely sure that everyone fit. I said to Choccy:

"Do you fancy playing in the reserves tomorrow?"

He said: "Aye, no problem, I could do with a game."

So that was settled. Then I told Keith he could play tomorrow because Andrei's fit and I don't need to keep him back.

I will keep back Beckham, Scholes, Butt, Davies and Gary Neville, though. The rest can play and it will give some of the youth team a chance to play in the reserves.

You could feel the buzz of anticipation about the place. We didn't do much – Brian gave them a good stretch for 20 minutes, and they all had a wee 'box' - six or seven against two playing one-touch possession games in a confined space (the box). We do it all the time. It's good for touch and passing and the players enjoy it.

Sunday is a good day to come in. You only get a few supporters so it's nice and tranquil and Brian and I can sit and have a chat about things without constant interruptions. I probably get more out of Sundays than a lot of people do.

When I got home I had three tapes of Barcelona to watch – and I watched football on television, too. I watched the first half of the Bolton-

Oldham game and taped the second; then I watched a few bits of the Italian followed by the Ipswich v Sheffield Wednesday match on Sky. Then it was back to Barcelona. Cath was really fed up because I went up to the bedroom and took notes while I was watching.

Monday 17 October

I had to break the news to Steve Bruce that I am leaving him out of the game. We need someone to go one-on-one on Romario and I've chosen Paul Parker. He has the pace and he is the best man-marker in English football. But telling the captain I was leaving him out is one of the less pleasant aspects of my job. He didn't agree, but he took it well.

I phoned Paul Doherty, the head of sport at Granada TV and asked him for a tape of the European cup final. It arrived a few hours later so I watched it tonight.

I was a guest at the Marks & Spencer centenary celebration.

Tuesday 18 October

The reserves did well last night. Because I kept back a few of the regulars, some of the youth team got a chance to play in the reserves. We had a rehearsal today with the reserves playing the part of Barcelona. Paul Scholes took the role of Romario, but he twice spotted Peter Schmeichel off his line and chipped him. Peter went mad.

I watched the European cup final again, and I'm even more convinced that I have got the tactics right. We won't copy what Milan did, because we have different players, but it is vital to make sure we defend deep. My thinking has been about stopping four players - Koeman, Guardiola, Romario and Stoichkov. It is vital to make sure we defend deep. We must withdraw to 25 yards from goal, so we defend on to the situation, rather than defending at the halfway line, because Koeman's passing means he can put deadly balls in behind you.

I very seldom let the players watch videos. I know a lot of managers do, but I think it is important that the information comes from you, not from the video. It's the manager's job to instruct the players. You are supposed to spot things and put them right. I use videos for my own information, not to convince myself about something, or to confirm what I thought about a game. I would never use a video to say: "Well boys, I've watched the video and we should have scored another goal and we shouldn't have conceded that one." If I did that, the video might as well be running the club, not the manager.

I went out to dinner with Sir Richard Greenbury, the chairman of Marks & Spencer; I got back at about midnight and watched Newcastle's UEFA Cup match with Bilbao. Newcastle were 3-0 up then let Bilbao back into it. It ended 3-2.

Wednesday 19 October

I went to bed about 1.30 last night, and woke up again at 3.55. I couldn't sleep, so I ended up watching the video of Barcelona v Gothenburg. Nervous anticipation. I haven't done that for a long time, but it is such a big game, and I want the preparation to be absolutely perfect for this one. Of course you can't be perfect, but you do your best to be as near perfect as possible in all aspects. You could probably list 3,000 points in a game of football, but I try to concentrate on the essentials. Who are the influential players? Where's their strengths? How do they organise themselves defensively, what are their set pieces? And then thinking about organising our own defence.

I watched the European Cup Final again. I'm sure I've got it right.

Wednesday evening

United 2 Barcelona 2

There's a fantastic buzz about Old Trafford. Today's match was one of the most exciting I've ever been involved in. When we were 2-1 down with about 12 minutes to go, and looking as if we might lose, I still said to myself "I'm really enjoying this!" But then it all changed. We got an increase in the tempo and we were brilliant again for the last 12 minutes, as we had been at the start.

It was an inspirational performance again. We played so well, we were ripping them apart down the flanks and we went ahead. Then the team relaxed for a moment. Will we ever learn?

Bakero, who was perhaps the smallest player on the pitch, got a free header because Paul Parker missed a cross. For a time they really controlled the game. We defended well by dropping back, but Koeman still hit some fantastic cross-field passes in the game: the ones which drop an inch over your defender's head, which was magnificent. We kept him quiet for the first half-hour, but when we went ahead, they moved him into midfield which gave him extra freedom because Sparky wasn't anywhere near him. Next, Bakero started to go towards their front, which took Ince back but opened up the midfield for Barcelona.

But then we upped the tempo, Lee Sharpe got the equaliser with a back heel or drag back, and we took over again. We might have won it – Paul Scholes did brilliantly, but came in from the left and tried to chip. The ball floated just fractionally over. A great bit of skill, but I said to him afterwards: "You should have blasted it!"

Gary Pallister was raving about Romario and the moves he made. He said he'd never played against a better footballer. "I've never known a player look over his shoulder so much, every time he went to get involved in the play he was looking to see where I was," Pally said.

It seemed like half of Scotland had come down for the match. There were 50 people in my office. I needed elastic walls to fit everyone in. We had a big family party at the match–Darren, Jason and Mark all came along. Darren came back to stay the night, my brother-in-law was down from Scotland, one of Darren's pals was there and my grandson was staying with his mother Tanya. Jason had to drive back to London after the game because he starts work early tomorrow. Sky is covering the Chelsea match.

Venue: Old Trafford *Att:* 40,064

	Manchester United	*goals*		**Barcelona**	*goals*
1	Peter Schmeichel		1	Carlos Busquets	
2	Paul Parker		2	Fernandez Abelardo	
3	Denis Irwin		3	José Guardiola	
4	David May		4	Ronald Koeman	
5	Nicky Butt		5	Sergi Barjuan	
6	Gary Pallister		6	José Maria Bakero	49
7	Andrei Kanchelskis		7	Luis Cembranos Martinez	
8	Paul Ince		8	Hristo Stoichkov	
9	Roy Keane		9	Miguel Angel Nadal	
10	Mark Hughes	18	10	Romario de Souza Faria	34
11	Lee Sharpe	80	11	Aitor Beguiristain	
Substitutes					
12	Steve Bruce (69 mins for May)		12	Sanchez Jara (67 mins for Beguiristain)	
13	Gary Walsh		13	Julian Lopetegui	
14	Paul Scholes (67 mins for Butt)		14	Jordi Cruyff (46 mins for Luis)	
15	Gary Neville		15	Sacristán Eusebio	
16	Simon Davies		16	Guillermo Amor	

Thursday 20 October

We left Old Trafford at midnight and got home about half past. Cath had taped the game so we sat down to watch it. The great thing about European football is that it seems to extend your life. I always seem to go to bed later after European matches because of the adrenalin rush they give me.

When I got in, two old friends, Hugh Keevens and Roger Baillie, who are journalists from Scotland came to see me. Hugh's father worked with mine in the shipyards and I've known Roger since he was a young lad. His great claim to fame is that he was given a free transfer by both Rangers and Celtic. Roger went out with Jock Stein's daughter and then with Scott Symon's daughter, but they both turfed him out.

When the players came in for their massages, there was a real buzz about the place.

Last night was an uplifting occasion for them. You could feel the atmosphere, the game had really given them a lift. They came in and they were ranting and raving. Listening to them was a really good experience for me.

I know now that we can get to the European Cup final. Barcelona came pretty close to winning yesterday's game and hopefully we will meet them in the final.

I was severely criticised for leaving out Steve Bruce and I'm disappointed that people didn't understand why I had done it. One or two people pointed to the fact that Paul Parker missed the cross for Bakero's goal, but you don't pick a team expecting one player to miss a cross. You expect the press–or at least some of them–to get it wrong, but I was a bit surprised that Jack Charlton didn't realise the significance of the team selection. I had tea with Brian Moore and Bob Wilson yesterday and I gave them my team selection then. Bob's immediate response was: "I was wondering what you were going to do about Romario and I think that's a first-class decision."

I was talking to Kiddo about the game. "I hope we don't pay for that dropped point," I said. I don't think we will.

One of the papers wrote that Barcelona had 59 per cent of the game, while we had 41 per cent, which is interesting. I believe we had the greater penetration, probably the better chances, and produced the more exciting football. But their patience and the acceleration of their game in the last third was phenomenal.

4
English Interlude

Friday 21 October

We're playing Blackburn on Sunday, which gives us an extra day to prepare. We did some work on crossing today, which we don't usually do on a Friday. After playing Barcelona, though, having an extra day to prepare for Blackburn is a godsend.

It is some programme we've got: Barcelona; Blackburn away; Newcastle twice; then Barcelona again; all in 15 days. After that there's Manchester City and Aston Villa. People expect United to drop some points there because they don't believe we could possibly win all those games. If you group them all together it looks formidable, but that's why we say take it one game at a time. And that fits in with the way it works, because you are so wrapped up in the big game coming up that you don't get a chance to look beyond it.

It is half-term week in Scotland and we have had three Scottish boys with us all week. It was a great time for them to come because it meant they got to see the Barcelona game. Trust the Scots to pick the right week!

We find it hard to get Scottish schoolboys to join the club because they can sign for Scottish clubs on schoolboy forms at 12 or 13 whereas we can't sign a Scottish boy until he is 16 and has left school. But these three are very promising kids, we think we've got a chance with them, and we are working very hard to make sure they come up. They come here on their school holidays – that's all we can do until they are 16 and we can sit down with their parents and mark out a career for them.

Saturday 22 October

It was a normal Friday – at least in the morning. We just did a light session. If we'd been playing today it would have been extra difficult for us. As it is I've had to think about the team. I'm not prepared to risk Paul Parker again, although we have put off his operation until after the return in Barcelona. David May is injured, so I thought carefully about playing Gary Neville at right back. But I think Blackburn are going to create real physical challenges, so Roy Keane's strength and experience will be vital.

And after Wednesday, playing full back will give him an easier role.

Blackburn have a lot of physical presence. Reports of their game against Liverpool said that Shearer and Sutton gave Ruddock a really hard time . And Ruddock is one of those types who, against somebody weaker, will exploit that weakness. No matter how well Liverpool played, Blackburn just ground them down.

When picking teams you have to be aware of that. They have an effective and powerful way of playing. Everyone tackles like hell and you have to contend with that. I don't want us to defend too high up the pitch. They play mainly with balls through the channels, much the same as Wimbledon used to play. All their set-up play and playing around from the back four to the wide players is to create space around the channels. To make it work, their two wide players do a phenomenal job. They are up and down all the time – they support, they defend.

In the afternoon I went to watch Manchester City play Tottenham. I was sitting there at Maine Road laughing at the comical situation. Every time somebody attacked it looked as if it was going to be a goal. In all honesty, Spurs' football was magnificent – and they lost 5-2! They absolutely slaughtered City in terms of possession of the ball. But every time City attacked, it looked as if they were going to score because their crossing was so good. The way Spurs played, there was no way they could protect the back four. From the days of the Brazilians, when you have the ball you all play, and when you lose it you all defend. But when Spurs lost it they had five left stranded up-field. And so the full backs got pulled inside into cover positions because the midfield was absolutely bare. So they were all tight and the wingers had plenty of time and space to cross the ball.

The weather helped too. The rain does something to the game. It just gives a wee edge to the passing and, because of that, the defenders are put out of the game more easily. I love the early part of the season when the pitches are good and there is a bit of rain and the ball is flying off the surface. If you are an accurate passer, that's what you want. That match was a great advert for the game.

Felt a bit below par today, I seem to have picked up a virus.

Sunday 23 October

Blackburn Rovers 2 United 4

A great result, a very good performance, but a controversial and slightly bitter afternoon. Blackburn did not lose with any grace, it has to be said. We got a soft penalty for which Henning Berg was sent off when we were losing 1-0, which made them absolutely furious.

The atmosphere was really bad – their players were angry, the fans were badly behaved and our directors got some stick in the boardroom afterwards.

But it wasn't the penalty that decided the game. They were ahead again at 2-1 and it was us getting back into the game then that decided it. They had ten men, but you can still play with ten men. We were drawing with Charlton in the Cup last season when we were reduced to ten men, and we still managed to win 3-1. We played really well to win today, because they had the lead and then pulled Sutton back in front of the back four – presumably to take Cantona – and just left one up, so it was difficult for us. But after going through what they did against Barcelona on Wednesday, the players showed incredible depths of stamina, and the real will to win.

The penalty came minutes before half time. Lee Sharpe did well breaking into Blackburn's box ahead of Berg. You tell players that when they are in that position they must cut across the defender and put the onus on him. Sharpey did that, and went down as Berg challenged from behind. Those on our bench all went up for a penalty. I went up, Kiddo went up – all the players went up. And the referee gave it, then sent Berg off. I don't believe a player should be sent off for that, a penalty is enough. But that's the mandate the referees have, and there is nothing you can do about it. But the Blackburn team were going bananas. After we'd scored, when the ball was put on the centre-spot, Sutton just kicked it away. He had already been booked, and he was dicing with death – he could have been sent off too – but the referee had clearly decided to calm things down.

Then the whistle went for half-time. Blackburn were still ranting when they came off. Kenny was waiting for the referee. I said to him: "Leave it, Kenny, you can't win that one." But he was fuming, and the poor old ref got a real bit of stick. And as we went past the TV monitor I saw a replay from another angle, and I thought it was a soft one. I asked Kiddo whether he'd seen it on the monitor and he said: "Yes, it was definitely a soft one!" That was what I told the press after the match, although I told them I thought it was an honest decision because the referee was looking at it from behind and, from that angle, there was no question about it, it looked like a penalty. And I think in big games like that the referees tend to give the advantage to the home side on the whole, so I don't think you could question his sincerity.

That brought us level, because we had got behind early, which is the last thing you want against Blackburn. It was a bad goal from our point of view, although a brilliant strike by Warhurst. We started slowly, as we tend to do after a midweek game, and they looked fresher and stronger than us to start with. They are a very determined team, who pull people back and then hit you on the counter attack. We had most of the possession and were in their half a lot more than they were in ours, but they kept catching us on the break. Ripley spent the entire time sitting in front of Berg, but Wilcox had a couple of breaks. He made great runs down the left and, although they didn't have any direct chances, they still had us on edge.

Bruce and Pallister were magnificent. On that wet surface it is very dangerous for defenders. I'd said beforehand that Shearer and Sutton are the fulcrum of their side – everything is played to them and most of the goals come from them. If you can stop that, you've got a great chance against them. And Bruce and Pallister were absolutely brilliant against them, and then, sod's law, Warhurst goes and hits this lob from forty yards. Peter made a mistake, came and punched it straight to him, but it was a brilliant strike, inches under the bar. Bruce was on the line, but he daren't touch it with his hand because he would have been off, and Schmeichel was stranded miles away. A fabulous strike – if you tried it a hundred times you probably would never do it again.

Then, after the penalty, we went behind to another untidy goal – Hendry getting his first of the season. I thought at that stage: "Is it going to be one of those days?" But the players kept at it, they showed great resolve. There is no question they are powerful men, with fabulous depths of stamina.

The deciding factor was United getting back into the game after falling behind. We passed the ball around well, and that exploited our numerical adavntage. Andrei Kanchelskis is having a great season and scored twice today. Roy Keane was fabulous in spite of getting a nasty kick from Le Saux in the opening minutes. And, for the second game running, Paul Ince was magnificent. Mind you, Incey needed to be magnificent to take the heat off him. A newspaper quoted him as saying: "I'm better than Bryan Robson," and he took some terrible stick from the lads on the bus.

"I never said that, I wouldn't say that," he insisted, but they said:

"Well, you'd better get yourself out of that one."

He said: "I'll have to play well won't I?" and I replied:

"You can't rest on Barcelona, because Robbo had many nights like that."

Peter Schmeichel knew he had made a mistake and said:

"I was absolute rubbish today."

"As long as you are aware of that, it's not a problem," I said. "You've had great games this season, you've saved us, so there comes a time when the players owe you one."

That's what teams are about. To win a big game you probably need eight good performances. You always have one or two players who are indifferent. I've probably only had half a dozen games in my life when everyone was absolutely magnificent. But if you get eight playing well, that should win you the game.

The atmosphere was a bit hostile. The crowds at Elland Road, Chelsea and West Ham are awful and it wasn't as bad as that, but there was a hostility in the air that I couldn't understand. We seem to get it a lot in these Lancashire towns – I've been to Bolton with the reserves, and there are lads of 18 and 19 singing that appalling song about Munich.

The one place we don't get it is Burnley. When we go there, all we get is people coming up to us and saying "You're not going to let Blackburn win it are you?" I'd love to see a cup tie between Blackburn and Burnley. It'd be some match, particularly if it went to a replay. Bodies everywhere!

After the match I went to the Northern Football Writers Awards Dinner. I'd still got the virus hanging around, and I would happily have gone straight home, but I thought I ought to show my face.

Venue: Ewood Park		*Att:* 30,260			
Manchester United		*goals*	**Blackburn Rovers**		*goals*
1	Peter Schmeichel		1	Tim Flowers	
16	Roy Keane		20	Henning Berg	
3	Denis Irwin		2	Tony Gale	
4	Steve Bruce		5	Colin Hendry	51
6	Gary Pallister		6	Graeme Le Saux	
8	Paul Ince		7	Stuart Ripley	
5	Lee Sharpe		24	Paul Warhurst	13
14	Andrei Kanchelskis	52 & 82	22	Mark Atkins	
7	Eric Cantona	45	11	Jason Wilcox	
10	Mark Hughes	67	9	Alan Shearer	
19	Nicky Butt		16	Chris Sutton	
Substitutes					
9	Brian McClair (82 mins for 19)		25	Ian Pearce (84 mins for 2)	
13	Gary Walsh		13	Bobby Mimms	
31	Keith Gillespie		17	Robbie Slater (84 mins for 22)	

Monday 24 October

I still felt ill, so I stayed in bed until lunchtime. We have a busy week ahead with the two games against Newcastle, and half-term, which means the car park at The Cliff is packed with fans, and a lot of boys for us to work with; potential signings from up and down the country.

The press was full of the penalty incident, with almost everyone saying that it was a bad decision. But I've now watched it 50 or 60 times, freeze frame, slow motion, all the different angles and I think it was a penalty. Watching it, it was certain that Sharpey did well, Berg was pulling at him as he went into the box, and because of the position he was in, Berg had no chance of making the tackle. They said he played the ball, but the ball hit him, he didn't play it.

A lot of the response has been way over the top, and I think it is because it is United.

Tuesday 25 October

Peter Schmeichel came in this morning raving: "That effing car park, you can't move," he said in that big, booming voice of his. He got a predictable response – he is always picked on because he is always moaning. The lads keep telling him he's a German, which he doesn't like. He gets slaughtered, because although he is massive, no one in the dressing room is frightened of him, because behind the bluff he is completely normal. He just loves to be domineering.

The central figures in the dressing room are the leaders and the ones who are picked on for a bit of fun. Brucey is a central figure because he is this bouncy character who is always saying outrageous things. Pally gets the mickey taken for being lazy – it's "You have a lie down now, Pally" because he's always lying on the table.

Then there are the quiet ones: Eric sits there and takes it all in and just laughs at them. Sparky never says a word; Ryan tends to be quiet; as does Denis Irwin. Choccy will have a word of wisdom. He is such a clever, witty person, with a dry sense of humour and an oddball mentality. He's got a really weird sense of humour and you'll think: "How on earth could you come out with that?"

The great thing has been watching them as they grow up together. The longer they are together, the better. They know each others' weaknesses and they are quick to pounce. And, if anyone gets carried away, they don't half sort it out, as they did Incey on Sunday.

As I said before, I love going in and hearing the banter and they all wonder what I'm doing there. They think I'm checking up on how they dress in the morning, or if I can smell drink, but I love the banter.

You can put a timetable on the arrivals; who is going to walk in first, second, and so on. There is a pattern to the time they each arrive. Giggs is two minutes up the road and he's always the second last to arrive, beaten only by Mark Hughes. Sparky is incredible – I think he leaves his bed at 10am and he's in at twenty past. He flies through Wilmslow. There must be something in the water in Wales!

Walshy used to be in the reserve dressing-room, but with all the young players coming in, we moved him into the first-team dressing-room. But since he moved we've had injuries and all the players tell him to get back to the reserve dressing room, because he's brought a jinx in. I said to him:

"Well, Walshy, it's worth considering. Think about it from the team point of view. You've got to think about going back in there."

He's not happy about that at all!

Tomorrow we have the first of our two matches with Newcastle: the Coca-Cola Cup-tie at St James's Park. The big one for us is the Premiership match at Old Trafford on Saturday – we have to win that to close the gap. Tomorrow I shall play some of the youngsters, but I want Newcastle to play their full team. I shall play some of the senior players, I don't want the young ones up there like lambs to the slaughter because it could be damaging for Saturday.

So I'm not certain what to do. I've decided to leave Kanchelskis behind and play Gillespie instead. Keith is a very good player. I think I will play most of the youngsters because there are one or two of the older players who still have strains hanging around that I'm not happy with and I don't think I can take the chance with the Barcelona game looming. But, without actually saying so, I implied to the press that I would play most of the senior players so that Newcastle will play their strongest side.

It is a difficult one, this. I've never been into a game in my life wanting to lose. But I've got two chambers in my mind working. One is telling me, "Alex, don't go for the League Cup, forget about it," and the other is saying "getting beaten is not on the agenda of Manchester United." So I have got to wrestle with my conscience about this, about what is right for the club and how much I put into it. But I think what I will be saying to the players is 'go and enjoy it. Enjoy the atmosphere and entertain, give the crowd an insight into what we are.'

Kevin Keegan set that up in this morning's papers. He came out with some stuff about how we have got the best youngsters – I'm sure it wasn't a coincidence, what with us going up there tomorrow with a young team. It's Shankly stuff, psychology, "the biggest and the best in the world, the American dream".

I used to do that as a young manager. When I was the manager of St

Mirren I'd say: "My job is to make sure we can climb Mount Everest with our slippers on." Kevin is trying that . It is amazing the heights people can reach through confidence and belief, but when that fails, what do you fall back on? There has to be a different psychology then, the realistic part of management. Kevin will learn that. I'm sure Shankly had a few red faces over the years.

Ben Thornley came on as a sub in the reserves the other night. He's made better progress than we had expected, but unfortunately he has had problems with one of his knees and the time might come where he has to have quite a major operation on it.

But hopefully we'll get him back to a very good degree of playing because he was without doubt an absolutely tremendous young player. When he made his debut, he came on as a sub against West Ham and you could see he was edging towards first-team football. His reserve performances were excellent and he's a good finisher, too.

We actually thought of him at the Wembley game with Oldham. I think Sharpey was injured at the time and Ryan had just had a wee spell when maybe he'd gone a bit quiet. Then, lo and behold, Ben gets a really bad injury. We had to work hard not just with Ben, but his family too, because they're so close. We had to really work hard at that. But he's doing all right.

One or two of our young players have suffered bad injuries. When I came to the club, young Nicky Wood looked as if he'd make a superb player. We played him in a cup-tie with the first team, but he was always complaining about his back. It turned out to be serious and he had to finish with the game. Fortunately, Nicky was an intelligent lad, he has a degree, can get a career and can have another life, no problem. It's not as if he's hit the brick wall and has nowhere to go.

"What's going to happen to me?" That's the question any young player is going to ask when he gets an injury "If I'm out of the game, what am I going to do?"

Maiorana had a bad injury, as Ben Thornley did, and it is disturbing to see players with great potential stopped in their tracks. Maiorana never got it back, and he could have been a really top player. But it got to him badly, he got depressed. I kept trying to smooth him along and told him to keep working at it, but words of comfort are really of no use to the player. It's like when something goes wrong in your life and people tell you to keep your chin up, but no one's got an answer to your problems; no one tells you how to keep your chin up.

Wednesday 26 October

Newcastle United 2 United 0

The boys did well. In the end I went with the young players, but didn't place any at the back. I started with the idea of Irwin, Sharpe, Bruce and Pallister, which gave me an experienced back four. I was going to talk Incey into being sub and then play the rest of the young ones – except McClair – up front, interchanging with Scholes.

But then Incey said: "Boss, I don't want to be sub because I'd want to go on after ten minutes."

I wasn't sure about Eric. Yesterday I asked him if he wanted to play, but he said:

"I think Scholes deserves to play, they won the game at Port Vale, you should stay by them."

I'd never had any doubts about their ability, but what you find out about at times like this is their temperament, their ability to cope on the big stage. It was a pleasure to see them with the confidence to play one-twos just outside the penalty box to get themselves out of trouble. That said a lot about them. We came under huge pressure at times, we had moments of fortune, we got bodies in the way of shots, all that sort of thing. But we had some excellent attacks as well and we might even have gone in one up at half-time, because Steve Bruce had a header cleared off the line. It was a good game, we were never overrun, we gave as good as we got for more than an hour and I couldn't see Newcastle scoring. They were beginning to sweat a bit and I thought I was going to have to carry out my threat to play six up for the last ten minutes, because I said to them beforehand: "No draws!"

In the end we just got a bit tired and, once they got one, they could have punished us more in the closing minutes, but we held on.

We ended up with a few knocks. Sharpey got injured and won't be fit for Saturday, and Nicky Butt is also looking doubtful.

After the match I said that I hoped Newcastle would do well, and I do. They have been a breath of fresh air, they try to win matches, and they play in the right way. Newcastle have scored more goals than anyone in the Premiership. They had a few easy games to start with and that has built up their confidence. Now they are trying things, they are inventive.

Venue: St. James Park *Att:* 34,718

Manchester United	*goals*	Newcastle United	*goals*
13 Gary Walsh		1 Pavel Srnicek	
27 Gary Neville		12 Marc Hottiger	
3 Denis Irwin		6 Steve Howey	
4 Steve Bruce		15 Darren Peacock	

19	Nicky Butt	3	John Beresford	
6	Gary Pallister	27	Philippe Albert	82
31	Keith Gillespie	19	Steve Watson	
28	David Beckham	8	Peter Beardsley	
9	Brian McClair	11	Scott Sellars	
24	Paul Scholes	9	Andy Cole	
18	Simon Davies	28	Paul Kitson	87
Substitutes				
15	Graeme Tomlinson (72 mins for Sharpe)	10	Lee Clark	
25	Kevin Pilkington	30	Mike Hooper	
5	Lee Sharpe (52 mins for 3)	18	Steve Guppy (63 mins for 9)	

Thursday 27 October

It takes a fair amount of work to organise the young boys we've got with us this week, to keep getting them to come here for visits until the time comes when they leave school and can take up residence in our School of Excellence. When I first came here, I worked really hard to change our youth system, altering the scouting and our commitment to it. But other clubs have followed our lead and are trying to catch up with us.

No two managers are alike. The problem is that over the years the demand on managers who have come to this club has increasingly been to win the Holy Grail. We've all suffered for that, we've all felt the pressure, whether it be me or Ron Atkinson or Dave Sexton or whoever. And when you are trying to chase the end of that rainbow, it can sometimes mean that all the other things are peripheral. If you take the attitude that you've got to get the Championship, then other branches fall off. Then, all you've got to fall back on is what the first team are doing. My belief has always been to build on youth from the word go.

When I joined East Stirling, with two or three weeks to go to the start of the season, I said to the chairman: "Could I see your player file – the list of players?" He coughed and spluttered, then a couple of days later produced the list. This was the day before the pre-season training started. They started when their holidays were finished, because they were part time. It was then that I discovered he only had eight players!

I said: "Mr Chairman, you know you need eleven players to start a bloody game of football – you do know that don't you?"

He said: "Yes, I am aware, I'm well aware of that. We'll have a meeting."

So I went to the meeting and he said: "We'll give you £2,000 to get five players."

I replied: "You need two subs, by the way."

Even in those days I was working away getting youth, holding trials locally and bringing teams youth teams through from Glasgow to play the local youths.

At St Mirren I did really well. I had a great desire at that time to get young players. I held trials every night, Sunday mornings and Sunday afternoons too. They'd started St Mirren Boys' Club and we used that as the basis of our youth. Not everyone wanted to play for St Mirren Boys' Club, but at least it was a base you could get local boys into.

I went scouting at Saturday-morning games. That's how I learned to scout for players. There was all the old school at these games–Bobby Calder, Jimmy Dickie was with Manchester United at the time–and he's still here. And there was John Barr of Leeds United, who brought all these Scottish players into Leeds. We used to stand together and chat and that's how I'd get to know them.

Then I twigged. They knew all the players already and they'd get me talking so I wasn't concentrating on watching the game. So I started to stay away from their line. I'd go and watch on the other side of the ground and not go near them. I used to regularly end up eating sweets, talking and not watching the game at all. They were clever so-and-sos. They knew the players, they knew all their addresses. But sometimes you could get to meet the parents through them. They weren't used to a young manager coming hanging around watching school games on a Saturday morning, but that was part of my job.

I learned all about scouting that way. About how to handle parents, about who is the important one. Then at Aberdeen it just carried on. It's always been in my make-up to produce players, and it's a great pleasure when you see somebody like Ryan Giggs coming through.

It's not very satisfying at the time because you are always asking yourself whether you are doing the right thing. When you're playing a young player, you wonder whether it will make them or kill them. It can kill them, particularly at this club. With Giggsy I remember Archie or Kiddo said:

"He's sixteen!"

But I said: "Ah, but he can bloody score, he's so quick."

Then we gave him his full debut against City and he scored. Well, his true debut was actually against Everton on a dirty day in February. We had a few problems with the pitch at that time and it was an absolute paddy field that day. But against City he got across the goalkeeper and just got a wee touch on the ball, deflecting it. Ryan's temperament was fantastic.

There are three or four youngsters here this week who we are very interested in. One is from Newcastle, and is in our School of Excellence in Durham. We've signed him now, so we don't need to worry about anyone else snatching him–the other clubs can't touch him. There's also

We think any boy coming to our club should come for the right reasons: will coming here give him the best chance of becoming a player? Is he going to be happy at the club? Is he going to be looked after?

If they do well, we do look after them. There is no young player who has ever left here voluntarily. We look after young players very well. We demonstrated that by giving the youth team four-year contracts.

By not offering them money to sign, everyone in the dressing-room knows that they are getting the same deal. From what I can gather, the jealousies and the squabbling in the junior dressing-rooms can be unbelievable. Players saying: "I got this to sign, and I got that." It creates envy and breaks up the camaraderie. I think it's amazing that clubs persist in doing it. They don't realise the damage they are doing in their own dressing room.

We tackled this issue head on when I arrived at the club. We sat down together to take a look at the youth system and how it should be run in the future, looking at the best interests of the club and the boys themselves. I was well aware of the trouble that can develop if young kids are being offered money or whatever. At that age they should be playing for love, not money, and anything that sets players against each other is bad for them, bad for the team, and bad for the club. So we just said right from the start: "If a boy wants to come to the club, he'll get the same deal as everyone else." That way, they join for the right reasons.

The youth programme is a hard road. I have a very hands-on approach to the youth programme, which also involves the parents. When I came to the club I think it was left to one or two people to get on with. Now I have regular meetings with my youth people and youth coaches and I involve everybody. That is because I believe it is important for everybody to be involved in deciding the young players' futures. But it is particularly important that I know who the young kids are and watch them play in their trials.

Tomorrow I'm having dinner with one of the young boys' families. We think it is important the family knows the manager as well. You always feel the mother might say: "I wonder if the manager even knows who John is," so we make sure that doesn't happen. I shall go over these points with them tomorrow night and then on Saturday we will take them to the game and maybe I'll have a cup of tea with them before the match. Hopefully the boy will sign this week.

We keep the families involved, make sure they know who everyone is. They come in on Saturday mornings, meet the landladies, go and see the digs, see just what's going on. We give them an educational video which we made a couple of years back, which explains how we run the whole operation: the School of Excellence; the kitchens; everything.

We also send it out to schools to show what United are about. Of course, everyone in Manchester knows United, but we send it to local schools as well as those outside the area.

We not only have a School of Excellence here, but we have them in Durham and Belfast, too. When I first came I thought that if we were going to make an impact, it had to be on a broad base, not just on our own turf. At the time our own area was really disappointing. We employed two or three people, but we weren't getting anything. When I employed Brian Kidd, I said to him: "Your mandate is to tie up this area. I don't want to hear any more about Manchester City getting all the best kids." In those days even Crewe Alexandra and Oldham were getting hold of the decent boys. Now we've got 19 scouts in the Manchester area. And they are great–all United supporters – and there are some great characters among them.

We started the Belfast School seven-and-a-half years ago and the Durham one seven years ago. We do well in Northern Ireland and Keith Gillespie went to our school in Belfast. The Durham school started up when we first got Bryan Robson (the other one!) involved. He started off doing some part-time scouting, then he set up the School of Excellence in Durham and now he is at Old Trafford full-time. Because the North East has produced so many good players it makes sense to have a school there. Quite a few clubs have followed our lead, for example Southampton, Leeds and Sheffield United.

But we've got two or three players out of the Durham school and they are doing quite well. There's always a bit about the Geordie which means you say you have to wait for the return. Brucie was a late developer, so was Peter Beardsley.

Southern Irish boys are very late developers in terms of football, one of the problems being that they don't leave school until 17 and you can't really touch them until they have left. But we deal with Southern Irish clubs, and they've jumped on this UEFA compensation thing. We've always made a donation to a club when we sign a boy, but when we wanted to sign one particular boy, the club wanted £50,000 compensation! For a kid who had only been with them one season and was 15 years old, to boot! I told them to forget it. If they want to run their club that way, looking for money that way, it's up to them, but asking £50,000 compensation for a youngster who is being offered the chance to go into full-time football is just ridiculous.

A youth system is a real commitment. It takes five or six years for a football is just ridiculous.

A youth system is a real commitment. It takes five or six years for a player to come through and a lot of clubs don't have five or six years to wait. We've now got 14, 15 and 16-year-olds all playing on a Sunday. We do coaching every night at The Cliff or Littleton Road from nine year olds up. We've got four part-time coaches and all my staff have to do one night a week. Up and down the country we've probably got forty scouts in total. It's a big operation.

If you look at our club now, we've only got 13 players over the age of 23 in the club. We've got 60 players for the four teams, so we are a really young club.

Our chief scout, Les Kershaw, is absolutely brilliant. He's been a dynamo since he joined the club. He's got endless energy, can't stop working, can't stop talking. He's activated by the game. He was a Professor of Physics at Manchester Polytechnic and gave up to come full-time with us. While he was a lecturer, he was always doing part-time work in football. He's worked with Terry Venables and George Graham. Eventually we offered him a full-time post and we've really had our money's worth.

Friday 28 October

I had a nightmare coming in today. The bridge at Wilmslow was flooded. I left home at 7.40am and I got across the bridge at 8.05–25 minutes!

I've got to think about Wednesday and the team I play tomorrow must be chosen with Wednesday in mind, too. Gary Neville did very well on Wednesday at Newcastle. But there'll probably be 120,000 in the stadium on Wednesday so I've got to be dead sure. You can always chance young forwards, but you've always got to be confident of their temperaments, because if they make a mistake as a defender it costs you. A midfield player has the back four and the goalie behind him. As a forward everyone's behind him, so a mistake doesn't really cost you. But when a young defender makes one, then everybody turns and looks at him.

I'll probably use Keane right back tomorrow to give him the easier game with his hernia. He was fantastic at right back on Sunday at Blackburn, really brilliant. He can play anywhere. He is also a magnificent centre half. I remember when we were trying to sign him, I was talking to Ron Fenton who said:

"Alex, he's the best centre half in Britain."

I said, "You're not going to..."

"Oh no," he said, "but if we're struggling at centre half, we'll put him in there. You want to see him play centre forward, he's brilliant."

I've played Keane wide right, I've played him centre midfield, I've played him right back and I've played him centre half. He's a fabulous player. I'll probably play him right back tomorrow with McClair in midfield.

I shall play Roy Keane at fullback to give him a run before the match in Barcelona, but not Paul Parker. I shall save him for Wednesday. Parks has got to work on the mental side of it. He's a great little player, but he's not the most confident. I said to him:

"You're always better when you're fresh. I've seen that time and time again. You come back from injury and you're brilliant!"

Jason phoned to tell me that Andy Cole is missing the game tomorrow. He'd just read it on the wire in the Sky sports department where he works.

"Aye," I said, "I knew that."

"Oh," he said, "you knew that. Did you know that Hitler had invaded Poland?" Then put the phone down.

That gave us a wee lift, because looking at Cole's goal-scoring record, he has managed almost a goal per game.

Saturday 29 October

United 2 Newcastle United 0

It was probably our best performance of the season. I think we caught Newcastle at the right time. We'd just got the result at Blackburn, we knew this was a big game for us and they had been at the top a long time. Perhaps they were beginning to feel the strain. Also, one or two of their key players were injured, which may have pushed them off course a little.

It was a great game, a credit to English football. Most teams have been putting a man in front of the back four, playing five in midfield, and frustrating us, but Newcastle went for the throat – just like we do. It was an open game. It embodied everything in the English game. What makes the English game so attractive is that it is so open, there is no calculation.

Andrei Kanchelskis had a fantastic game for us.

Ryan played for an hour. He's still got his ankle injury and was feeling a bit tight, but he wanted to play. I have to think about Wednesday, so an hour was about right, because it gave him a chance to get his match-sharpness up. He did all right; produced a good free kick for the goal. Then Keith Gillespie came on as sub and scored a great goal. I'd put Gillespie on the bench and left Scholes out to provide cover for Ryan.

We played the young ones on Wednesday while Newcastle had the full team out which meant they'd had another game. But I have a feeling they will win the League Cup. In fact I think they'll do well in the Cups.

It was a really uplifting performance for us and a great send off to Barcelona. The form of the team is beginning to emerge quite well now. We can look forward to going to Barcelona, confident of getting a result.

Venue: Old Trafford *Att:* 30,260

	Manchester United	*goals*		**Newcastle United**	*goals*
1	Peter Schmeichel		1	Pavel Smicel	
16	Roy Keane		12	Marc Hottiger	
3	Denis Irwin		6	Steve Howey	
4	Steve Bruce		15	Darren Peacock	
6	Gary Pallister	11	3	John Beresford	
8	Paul Ince		27	Phillipe Albert	
14	Andrei Kanchelskis		19	Steve Watson	
9	Brian McClair		11	Scott Sellars	
7	Eric Cantona		7	Robert Lee	
10	Mark Hughes		5	Ruel Fox	
11	Ryan Giggs		8	Peter Beardsley	
Substitutes					
19	Nicky Butt		10	Lee Clark (75 mins for Hottiger)	
13	Gary Walsh		30	Mike Hooper	
31	Keith Gillespie (66 mins for Giggs)	77	14	Alex Mathie (75 mins for Fox)	

5
Out of Europe

Sunday 30 October

We went to Old Trafford today rather than to The Cliff. We had the masseur in and used the jacuzzis. The main object at the moment is to get the players' bodies to recover after such a gruelling game. People just don't appreciate how physical the game is. And there's going to be another tough one on Wednesday.

Monday 31 October

I said to Kiddo: "Make it a really light session and we'll do free kicks against us because of Koeman."

On Mondays the goalkeepers train with Alan Hodgkinson, the old England international who is now a goalkeeping coach. Meanwhile, we did free kicks, just making sure the wall was right and who was in the wall in the areas where Koeman is usually dangerous. We also looked at areas in which Stoichkov is likely to take them.

We are confident: Saturday was our best performance of the season. The thing about the English game is that it is so open and free of calculation. It is completely the opposite of what we will get against Barcelona. The calculation and preparation that Barcelona put into a game is absolutely superb, but they have the time to put into a big game which we don't. And their weather helps them prepare.

After a particularly gruelling game we have to spend days getting the lads ready physically before even beginning to think about mental preparation.

Tuesday 1 November

We flew in to Barcelona this morning. Everybody is in great spirits. The hotel is excellent. We had a session on the pitch, which was superb, at 6pm.

My groundsman at Old Trafford says I am always on his back about the pitch. The groundsman here in Barcelona said: "I must have this pitch right. Mr Cruyff will be so angry if it is not right."

He had a meter which he puts in the ground to measure the density.

Then, before the game, he waters it so that the ball flies off the pitch.

Barcelona's organisation is absolutely magnificent. It's a big club operating in exactly the right way, not one of those clandestine operations where you haven't a clue what is happening. It is an absolutely open book: all the details; anything you want.

When a club is run like that, you know they are big and confident of beating anyone.

But perhaps it's better to encounter the sides you find in Greece, Turkey and Italy, or some of the other Spanish clubs, where they are always up to tricks–changing the time you are supposed to be training on the pitch and so on. Still, I always say that if they resort to that, we must have them worried.

My great problem is picking the team. I know that from the players we have available – May and Sharpe are out – the only answer is to leave out Schmeichel. Paul Parker will come back in for one game, at right back this time. I'd like to play him at centre half once more because he is the man to counter Romario, but with David May injured I shall have to play him as right back.

If Lee Sharpe had been available I might have left Giggs out. Sharpey would have given me balance down the left, but without him, I didn't have any alternative to leaving Peter out.

I didn't want to tell Peter I was leaving him out before the training session, because if Walshy was injured in the session, I'd have had to bring him back in. At the end I split the forces and we had a session at each end of the pitch. I went with Walshy and had him practising against people cutting in and shooting, mainly from the left, because I explained to him: "Stoichkov does that all the time."

It was just a detail I wanted to get into Walshy's thinking.

Wednesday 2 November

Barcelona 4 United 0

I went to Peter's room at 10am. He was still sleeping, so I said: "I'll catch you coming downstairs. There's no hurry."

I think he realised what it was.

He got up right away and came straight down. I was wandering around in reception, passing the time.

"This is a horrible thing to do, but I've got to leave you out of this game," I said.

"WHAT?"

"Yes, I'm going to have to leave you out."

"Oh Boss," he said. "Barcelona's the biggest game there is."

"Sit down and listen to me. You are playing your best football for us, the best form you've shown. But you have to pick a team. Andrei has been magnificent. I don't have an English left back with Sharpe and May out, so Denis Irwin has to play, right?"

"Right."

"I can't leave Sparky out, not with his experience of playing for Barcelona. Sparky is a big-game player. Andrei's form is fantastic. So who do I play wide left? Or do we play without a left-sided player? I've got to play Giggs."

"It's a stupid rule. Can't you do anything about it?"

We have been trying. It is a shame because he is at his best, but I just feel we have to get our best ten outfield players against Barcelona.

We had a team meeting at 11.30am. I warned the back four about diagonal balls in behind us to Romario. I spoke about it at length and said that if there was any problem, to go back and to try to keep the unit together as much as possible so there could be no space in between them.

Next we talked about where we think we can win the game. Andrei will be as much a threat to them here as he was at Old Trafford. And we think that runs from midfield are a problem for them. They didn't look as if they could handle that during the first game. We talked about how we played in the first game, the set up play on both sides to get our wingers in behind them because they defend so high.

I said to the lads before the game: "What you find is the suddenness of all the attacks. You think you are doing all right and then the roof falls in."

That's precisely what happened. Their first attack and they scored. The first three goals were like that.

Pally will probably have nightmares about Romario. If he thought he was the best player he had ever come across in the first leg, Romario's performance today was on a different plane. At Old Trafford he'd had a couple of thrusts. He kept getting himself against Pally, he had no interest in playing against Steve Bruce because Pally is six-foot-four, Romario is five-foot-six. Small, elusive, quick turns – he was always going to be a problem for Pally.

That's why I played Parker against him in the first leg. I got criticised for that. If Parker had played centre back tonight it might have been a different story. It's nothing to do with Brucey or Pallister, they are great players in our game, but we are talking about the best striker in the world, who can torture anyone. Parker is the best player we have in our country at handling that type of player. So what you have to do is eliminate the best player in the other team. If we had done that I don't think we would have lost, no matter how badly we played elsewhere.

It's all about defending. In the European Cup final against Hamburg, Forest were never out of the penalty box all night and people think they were a great team. If we played like that in a cup final we'd probably get slaughtered. But they won the European Cup. They had one or two injuries, so they cut their cloth and just decided to defend. John Robertson gave them a goal to win the game. I take my hat off to them. Resilience, determination, good defending. Good defending wins you games. So does preparation. Leaving Bruce out was the right thing to do at Old Trafford. We don't spend hours watching videos and discussing the opposition for nothing. Kiddo and I knew probably from last week, certainly from Saturday, that we would have to leave out Schmeichel for this game. I had to get my ten best available outfield players on that pitch.

There was no way you could point a finger at Walsh. Schmeichel would definitely have been beaten by three of the goals, anyway. He might have been able to save the one which went through Walshy's legs, but then Romario's goal at Old Trafford went through Peter's legs.

A few people wondered about the first goal, but I thought Walshy did well there, forcing the player wide. If there is a part of Walshy's game which is on a par or even better than Schmeichel's, it is one versus ones. I was confident that he made the right decision there, but Romario brought it back and played it to Cruyff. He did well and squared it instead of shooting, but it was going wide until it hit Pallister on the hip.

They were terrible goals for us to give away, but Romario is such a devastating player. One of those players you can't take your eyes off. For the second goal we were quite comfortable. We gave a throw-in away on the halfway line. It was one minute and ten seconds into injury time. Another minute and it was half time. Stoichkov hit a 60–yard ball which nobody spotted and suddenly they were in. We were all over the place. It's just that suddenness that takes your breath away and you're down 2-0. Make a mistake and you're murdered. Absolutely murdered.

For the third goal, we got a free kick. Brucey ran up to the back post and Pally played it short to Giggs, so we had a centre back out of the game right away. Ryan played it back towards where the free kick was taken, to Paul Ince, who tried to chip it into Giggs who was running through. It was unbelievable. From our own free kick when we'd sent the centre back up! It was agony. Absolute agony.

I'm sure they were thinking, but it makes me wonder how much they really listen. Perhaps they need these bitter lessons all the time. Keeping the ball is the name of the game in Europe and they just don't understand.

Although it's not much consolation, we did OK against Koeman's free kicks. They didn't have many within range. Koeman had one in the first half, but he didn't even try to put it over the wall because we had the tall players there. Instead, he went round the wall and it went past the post.

I said to Ryan in the team meeting: "Don't go running at them right away. Set them up, so you are running without the ball. Make sure you are passing it into the park and get hold of the ball in there, so that when they get tight on you, you've got space to run into."

But perhaps these are things about tactics that Ryan still has to learn. His natural instinct is to run at people, and when it came to it, he just went back to them and ended up crossing into the box when there was nobody there. He would have been better staying out and passing it inside and trying to pull opponents onto him.That was what we talked about, what we had down with Sharpey in the first match and what Sharpey did very well. But Lee is a bit older and more aware of tactics.

We started out reasonably well, without setting the place on fire. But you give players the chance of a part in a big game, on a great stage, and some fail. Some under-achieve. And you have to say to them: "You believe too much of your own publicity."

Venue: Nou Camp *Att:* 115,000

	Manchester United	*goals*		**Barcelona**	*goals*
1	Gary Walsh		1	Carlos Busquets	
2	Paul Parker		2	Albert Ferrer	88
3	Steve Bruce		3	Fernandez Abelardo	
4	Gary Pallister		4	Ronald Koeman	
5	Denis Irwin		5	Sergi Barjuan	
6	Andrei Kanchelskis		6	Guillermo Amor	
7	Nicky Butt		7	Josè Maria Bakero	
8	Roy Keane		8	Josè Guardiola	
9	Paul Ince		9	Hristo Stoichkov	9, 52
10	Mark Hughes		10	Romario de Souza Farla	45
11	Ryan Giggs		11	Jordi Cruyff	
Substitutes					
12	Paul Scholes (79 mins for Giggs)		12	Francisco Sanchez Jara (76 mins for Bakero)	
13	David Beckham		13	Angoy	
14	Gary Neville		14	Ivan Iglesias (62 mins for Jordi)	
15	Simon Davies		15	Aitor Beguiristain	
16	Kevin Pilkington		16	Luis Cembranos Martinez	

We did take one thing out of it. At half time we were losing 2-0. I thought to myself: "It's a long way back," but in the event I was forced to play 4-4-2, with two going through the middle. I put Andrei on the left-hand side to give us reasonable balance, with Ryan going through the centre. It didn't pay off, but at least it gave us some possession of the ball, and we weren't running all over the place in the second half. We lost two goals from counter-attacks – the fourth we should have cleared, the third, from our free kick, was just plain insanity.

But their preparation was good. What Barcelona did in the second half was to go back to their own 18-yard line, so there was no space for us to play in. They just drew us onto them. I was warned that they might do that, though they didn't start that way. They started off very positively and tried to unnerve us. Full marks to them; you hold up your hands when you are beaten tactically, too.

When I moved Andrei over to the left, they immediately moved Cruyff over to that side too. Obviously he was out there to cut off the supply to Andrei, who had destroyed them at Old Trafford. That's preparation.

We pride ourselves on our preparation too, but the problem is that we don't have a tactical game in England. I tended to get more benefit from doing tactical things at Aberdeen than I do now, because they were a young side and would listen. The problem at United is that a lot of them have their own profile and want to play their own way. It doesn't work in Europe, as we've discovered.

There has to be a better tactical discipline, which I got against Gothenburg and Galatasaray. This experience may help in the long run; they may realise they need to listen, that they can't just play their own game, because their own game is not good enough.

Thursday 3 November

We arrived back in Manchester at 3am.

I had a quiet day. One meeting at The Cliff, then a magnificent lunch at the Copthorne, which got *Cheshire Life's* "Hotel of the Year" award. I went on to Old Trafford to catch up on some letters and watched the reserves against Notts County.

That was disappointing. Several of the youngsters had travelled back from Spain and hadn't got to bed until four in the morning. It showed. They were not 100 per cent, they weren't sharp about their work. Notts County just defended, and scored a goal on the break.

I took Scholes off at half time because I have to think about Sunday. Mark picked up a neck injury in Barcelona and is in a collar, so he won't be playing at Aston Villa. Therefore, I might need Scholes.

Friday 4 November

The post-mortems on Barcelona continue. It was a reminder to me of the levels in Europe. There were some salutary lessons to be learnt there, but some of the coverage has been way over the top. I said to Kiddo that, in many ways, the chasing we were given when we were down paralleled our first 35 minutes against Barcelona at Old Trafford. If we had scored a second goal at that stage, we might have beaten them 4-0, because they might have folded. Would we then be going through all the breast-beating? But we didn't finish them off. Perhaps we lack that killing finisher.

But there were some hard lessons and I'm not going to hide away from them. I know the areas we have to improve in. I told my youth coaches yesterday that from now on we must practise possession in one half of the pitch, in a game situation, not in a box. We play possession games in a 40-yard box, which is not enough because you don't get the angles right. There is no target there's no forward, no back. It is all just spurts and spasmodic play. It is good for exercising your touch and control with people running around you, but it doesn't give you the big picture because you can't hit long balls. And the long balls killed us. Their short play was simple – just setting things up. But then there was the ball flying like an arrow in behind you.

Another of the real lessons for us was the contrast between the games with Newcastle and Barcelona. Newcastle was so open, and the thing about the English game is that we give the ball away and get it back quickly. There's no great concentration on keeping the ball. But you go into Europe and give the ball away and you can't get it back. At that level, passing, possession is the most important thing. That was emphasised in the game in Barcelona.

We can cope in games like that if we keep our group togetherness. If we can keep our tightness in the back four, if we can keep our tightness in midfield, we are all right. We have got the best players in England, but at that level possession is the most important thing. And special teams like Barcelona or AC Milan have a special player. They buy the best players in the world. Yes, they are restricted to three foreign players, but two of the three are the best in the world. Barcelona have four, because Hagi can't even get a game with them, and he was one of the outstanding players in the World Cup. Koeman is probably one of the best passers in the world; Romario the best striker.

That is our problem. I would say Peter Schmeichel is probably one of the best goalkeepers in the world. Cantona is unquestionably one of the best players in the world, because the weight and vision of his passing is in keeping with all the best players in the world. And that's what you really need – a passer who can open teams up. Unfortunately, Cantona was suspended.

We never competed in midfield because we were never anywhere near them. It must have been a chastening experience for Paul Ince, who has been hailed as the best midfield player in England, to realise how far there is to go in world terms.

Paul is a tremendous player and probably he is the best midfield player in England, but it is just a different game in Europe. Passing is vital. They calculate things better than us. They change round positions better. They don't worry if Koeman ends up centre forward. Someone fits in. Someone slides into the back and is comfortable. They all go back into a group and swamp you. They pressed the ball in the right areas against us; made us nervous.

Bakero has been the best midfielder over the two games and he can't get into the Spanish team. So it's a chastening experience and a horrible feeling to know that our game is built on giving the ball away and getting it back. They are so clever in midfield.

This isn't a nit-picking exercise after Wednesday. You have to identify the areas where we have to improve at that level. And I think all the talking I've done about not giving the ball away, about the importance of possession of the ball in Europe, came home to them. Because if you don't keep possession, you are chasing about all night. That is the whole point.

Sparky didn't come in today with his neck injury. It was a disappointing night for him, going back to Barcelona and getting beaten. He put a really good effort for us. One thing you can say about him is that he is a big game player.

Not only is Mark injured, but Schmeichel's done his ankle in. He just carried on at the end of his training. He was playing outfield for a while, taking a few strikes at goal, which all goalkeepers love. Fortunately, he came in right away, and it worked out all right – no permanent damage.

Saturday 5 November

We trained this morning, then went down to the Midlands. I travelled separately from the team because I wanted to watch the Wolves and Luton game. I must say, I was very impressed by Luton, they played Wolves off the pitch with their football. David Pleat always produced good footballers and now it looks like he's got another great bunch of players in the classic Pleat/Luton mould.

It was a blow to discover that Mark Hughes and Peter Schmeichel are not going to be fit for the game tomorrow. I phoned Sparky and said:

"Look, if you're feeling ill, don't bother coming in – there's no point.

You may as well rest."

Sparky has to drive in from Cheshire, which is a good 20-odd miles away. He was much the same as Friday: not bad, but nothing like ready, so we had to leave him behind and I decided that Scholes should get his chance.

Peter had treatment for his ankle yesterday afternoon, but this time he came out, did his own warm-up, but realised he was struggling. After a while he reported in to me, and said, "I'm struggliing, Boss." I told him to go back and get more treatment, but he was still feeling it, so we decided to leave him out. We don't want it to get to the stage it did last year, when he injured his ankle but let it get so bad that he couldn't train at all. A lot of people forget the standard of Walshy's goalkeeping, which means we don't have to take any risks with Peter's injuries.

When I give the team talk, I always do it on the basis that the other side will be at full strength – unless someone is suspended or has broken a leg or something. But it's hard to pick a team for Villa because they change it quite a lot. In their last three games the front three have changed every time. Away against QPR they played Lamptey outside right, Yorke outside left and Saunders through the middle. Then, during the week, they had Houghton and Staunton as the wide players and Atkinson and Saunders through the middle. The time before that – the game with Middlesbrough at home – they had Whittingham and Saunders through the middle and Yorke and Houghton as wingers.

When you keep changing the formation you definitely lose your consistency, which can be a problem when you're losing games. You change to try to get back your winning form, but in the process you lose that consistency. It's a wee bit like our own situation: we have had to change because of suspensions, injuries and European rules.

Big Ron's trying to find the thing that'll get them going again because they've got plenty of good players. Ron's obviously got to establish some consistency.

Sunday 6 November

Aston Villa 1 United 2

With just a few minutes to go, Kiddo turned to me and said:

"I'm more pleased for Walsh than anyone else."

"I know, that's exactly right," I said.

He had an outstanding game. After losing four goals on Wednesday there's no doubt the boy would be saying to himself: "I hope I won't let anyone down." He's bound to be thinking like that, but it was an unusual situation, because although you want to understand where you made the mistakes, I couldn't fault him on any of the four goals. He must also have been saying to himself, "Would Peter have saved any of them?" and that kind of self-analysis is paramount to a goalkeeper, for he, more than anyone, is an individual in a team game. But the great thing was, he answered all his own questions with his performance today. That was absolutely outstanding.

He had a difficult start. Andrei gave him a tough back pass in the first minute. I don't know what Andrei was thinking of. He should just have put it out for a throw-in. Gary tried to save the corner, slipped going for it, and hit it straight to Staunton. Fortunately it went to Staunton's right foot.

"That would have been a good start for us after Wednesday," I said.

They put big Ehiogu on top of him to ruffle him a bit. He's a big lad. If he developed his left foot he would be a really good player. He's just a bit one-sided, and the fact that he is playing on the left (because McGrath is the normal right-hand centre back) makes it just a bit more awkward for the lad. But he's definitely one to watch. He gave Walshy a few spots of bother. At that point, early in the game, Walshy lost his footing a few times and had to change his studs for the second half.

Every goalkeeper would like to have a save early in the match, and unfortunately, he was beaten by a deflected shot which gave him no chance whatsoever. This only increased his desperation to get a save, which fortunately arrived four minutes from half time, when he got a magnificent touch on another deflection, this time from Steve Staunton. It was an important save, and it set the standard for a magnificent second half by him.

A good performance and a good result. At times we had to dig in and at other times we got good possession, but in fairness to Villa, they pressed the ball really well. Teams lift themselves against us and they get helped by their supporters, whereas in other games they would be booing them. I really believe players' confidence is affected by their support. When their supporters start getting at them, it can be really tough.

It was a big effort by Villa. They realised they had to produce something, given the importance of their position. They completely ran themselves into the ground, and put up a great effort running-wise in the centre of the park. All credit to them. They realised they were in a difficult situation and they performed. That's why I think they've no chance of going down; they've too good an appetite to go down. I also think that Ron's got to get a bit of consistency out of his front players. Elsewhere they are comfortable. Ron stuck by his formula for Tuesday night and he played that against us, so maybe if he sticks to that he might get it back.

We got off to a bad start. Nicky Butt got a whack in the head and then we gave away a goal after only nine minutes. It was Dalian Atkinson's first goal since January 1st. Big Ron said it would take a goal like that for him to score!

I thought Ehiogu's challenge was a little rash. I don't think Nicky tried to avoid it one bit. That's the way he is. Kevin Moran was like that too – he saw it and he'd go for it, then end up with stitches all over his head. I thought it was a sore challenge because Nicky was through.

Butt did so well on Wednesday. But there was no way he could continue today – he was really groggy. I said to Kiddo that when you've got someone like McClair you have to put him on right away, he's such a great sub. You mustn't hesitate . It's going to take 20 minutes to get your boy round, in which time you could have lost the game. That's why I went straight down to the bench - but they had made the decision already.

In the early part of the game we didn't have any joy. Everyone was going through the midfield without much impact up front and I think Scholes needs someone close to him all the time. Scholes plays like Eric, that's the problem of having the two of them together. So we decided to put Ryan through the middle when we were 1-0 down. We put Scholes into midfield. He started getting on the ball then and hit a great shot for the goal. He's a good player, the boy, but we decided to play Ryan through the middle and just told him to enjoy it. When we put him up front I thought he looked a wee bit more like himself. He was lively and using him was a good option for us when we were under the cosh; it enabled us to stretch them a wee bit. We turned the ball behind them a few times and it got Ryan going.

McGrath was excellent. Big Ron was saying that it was his best game this season. I thought he was very convincing. When I came to the club I remember Jimmy McGregor saying he wouldn't last two years. That was eight years ago!

Venue: Villa Park *Att:* 32,136

Manchester United		*goals*	Aston Villa		*goals*
13	Gary Walsh		1	Nigel Spink	
16	Roy Keane		2	Earl Barrett	
4	Steve Bruce		5	Paul McGrath	
6	Gary Pallister		16	Ugo Ehiogu	
3	Denis Irwin		15	Phil King	
14	Andrei Kanchelskis	51	7	Ray Houghton	
19	Nicky Butt		6	Kevin Richardson	
8	Paul Ince	44	11	Andy Townsend	

7	Eric Cantona	3	Steve Staunton	
24	Paul Scholes	9	Dean Saunders	
11	Ryan Giggs	10	Dalian Atkinson	29
Substitutes				
9	Brian McClair (6 mins for Butt)	14	Garry Parker (78 mins for Houghton)	
25	Kevin Pilkington	13	Mark Bosnich	
31	Keith Gillespie (78 mins for Scholes)	18	Dwight Yorke (58 mins for Staunton)	

Monday 7 November

Nicky Butt's clash has left him really battered. He lost his front teeth, so we sent him to the dentist. It's a shame for the lad.

I was glad for Walshy more than anyone yesterday. It proved what we all know. Ron Atkinson was saying to people yesterday:

"I don't know why you are so surprised. At 19 he was the best thing I've ever seen as a young goalie."

And he is the manager who snatched Bosnich. At 19, Gary Walsh was magnificent, he really was. Definitely England's future goalkeeper. I've never known anyone so good in one-versus-ones. A game I'll always remember was when we played Tottenham at home. We scored an early penalty kick when Jesper Olsen was brought down and Walshy was absolutely brilliant. Five times in the second half against Ardiles, Hoddle and Falco – they were all through on one-versus-ones and he saved the lot. Then he got a string of injuries which stunted his career.

Roy Keane is excellent. I mean, he's so quick at the back, really amazing, which is particularly incredible considering his injury. The odd thing is he doesn't seem to feel it at the moment. So we'll keep on it.

I think I'll be forced to let him go with Ireland next week now. Jack's always been fair to me in the sense of not pressing for players for friendly matches, although some international managers would look on a friendly game as just as important as any other. I've said to Terry Venables, Graham Taylor and Bobby Robson that they shouldn't play friendly games. But all the FA love these matches, so the managers are beaten.

Managers think friendly games are important because they get so few games, and it gives them a chance to try things out, or bed people down into the team. But I told them you never get the team you want - there are always withdrawals in friendly games. That's why I said to Terry:

"You just frustrate yourself. You just get yourself all worked up about nothing. You may as well have a training session."

That was the idea I gave to him, to have training sessions. Get all the players down and have a combined team between ourselves and Arsenal, for example, and just have three half-hour practice games. If we did it on a Tuesday, they'd all be back at base on the Wednesday. We could do something like that – but whether he will or not I don't know.

Tuesday 8 November

A traumatic few days for football. Three managers – Ossie Ardiles, Mike Walker and Ron Atkinson – have been sacked, and there's a story going round that Bruce Grobbelaar took a bribe to throw matches.

With the internationals next week, there's virtually a two-week gap for most teams, although we're playing City on Thursday. So some clubs have taken the opportunity to get rid of their managers. That 14-day break is a death knell for managers.

Ron's departure was probably the most surprising. We played him last Sunday and had a chat with him before the game, and he asked me, "Are we that bad?"

"You know very well you are not that bad," I said. "It's the old story of when you get down there, it's how to get out of it. It'll need a deflection off somebody's arse that falls in the net to get you goal-scoring again."

Lo and behold the goal they got against us that day was an absolute freak and I thought maybe that would have carried them on to a change of fortune. If it does, Ron won't be around to benefit.

But I think he must have looked at the club and seen that there were one or two younger players he didn't fancy so he let them go. When you let younger players go, the average age of a team rises. They've brought Fashanu in and I don't think that went down well at all.

They say managers have always found Doug Ellis, "Deadly Doug", Villa's chairman, a bit of a handful. Because Ron's such a big personality, he was able to handle it, so long as he was doing well. But the minute he wasn't doing well all the hens came home to roost, as they say.

There's no doubt that Ron Atkinson will get another job. He's got a great rapport with the media. He may decide to stay with television, which seems to suit him. He's 55 or 56 now so he may have had enough of management.

I saw Spurs at City a couple of weeks ago, and looking at them, I could definitely see a fragility in them that wasn't healthy. You knew they were going to lose games, no matter what good, attractive football they were playing. When I watched them in that game, in every attack they ended up with six or seven players in the penalty box, and then they just jogged back. A team attacks together, but they must also defend together. Spurs have got to realise the consequences of losing the ball.

It's sad in a way because I think everybody recognises that every club Ardiles has been with have played lovely football. They've all had a freedom and a relaxation about their play. Watching Tottenham, even towards the end of Ossie's time, you couldn't see any pressure on them, nothing to say "we're bloody bottom!" They just played as if they were top of the League. That's credit to the manager, but the penalty of six points being deducted is hanging over them, and the media latched onto that and deducted the points at the start of the season rather than at the end, so all along they've looked much worse off than they are.

But it's a crazy spell. I think a lot of it is to do with the 14-day break. Everton haven't got a game until their Monday night Sky game and I think they looked at that situation and said: "Well we've got two weeks to get a manager in place and get a bit of work done with the players while we get to know him." Mike Walker had been under continuous pressure, anyway. He kept saying they'd get out of it, but eventually if you cry wolf people don't listen anymore.

I think Mike's problem was that a new board was appointed. I'm not saying they do it intentionally, but a new board always appears to want to disassociate itself from the previous regime.

During my first season down here they won the League. That was just seven years ago. That team has completely gone apart from Neville Southall, who is now in the last stage of his career, and Dave Watson. He'd just signed during that season.

How the mighty have fallen. It's a great reminder to ourselves. To make sure you keep that momentum going, to make sure that the players' ages are right, that the flow of new blood is coming into the first team all the time. If you stop you suffer the consequences.

Wednesday 9 November

We did a function today, playing Eric right forward because there is the doubt about Sparky. I played him and Ryan through the centre and Gillespie wide left.

Thursday 10 November

Sparky was OK. He came in and said "I don't have a problem", so we went along with it. I was tempted to put Gillespie in as a sub, but I left him out in the end, although I had a chat with him about it later. I was worried about Bruce.

Bruce and Pallister had doubts about their hamstrings for a few days so I decided to have Gary Neville as one of my subs, and if Sparky's neck did go I thought Scholes could score, so I left Gillespie out.

Joe Royle was appointed manager of Everton today. It's terrific that he's got a break at long last because I think it's the job he always wanted. And he's served his time. He more than served time at Oldham.

Thursday evening

United 5 Manchester City 0

Fantastic performance–really brilliant. Andrei scored the first hat trick for 34 years in a Derby game and it's the highest score we've had in 100 years so it really was a landmark.

Before the game I said to Kiddo:

"They are going to come and attack, they're not going to change. But if they do they're going to lose goals."

I just knew we'd score goals, but you just hope you don't let them in. We'd not had a goal against us at Old Trafford in the Premiership, so it would be just like us to start losing goals at home in the Derby game.

But it turned out well. I felt we were right from the first minute. It was pretty even in the first 15 to 20 minutes but I could see the sharpness about our play. They were fresh looking and their running power was terrific.

It could have been a big score but we missed a few. There was one during the second half which Sparky missed after our best move of the game. Denis teed it up for him and Sparky wanted to say that it bobbled. The interesting thing was that Denis could have scored himself, he was just making the easy option, and Sparky said to him after the game:

"What the hell did you pass it to me for?"

He wasn't expecting it!

It was smashing; the form of last year: the smoothness, the passing and movement, the quickness about the ground. And terrific for Andrei to get a hat trick. I've only had three players who've done that in my time at United: McClair; Hughes; and now Andrei.

The fans were obviously delighted with it. I don't think we can afford to go and get carried away, but I think it's terrific for the fans and I know how Brian Horton felt because I had a chat with him after the game.

"Look", I said,"when we got stuffed 5-1 at Maine Road, I went home to my bed, put a pillow over my head and I was lying there trying to get to sleep to shut it out".

But of course I couldn't sleep. It was almost 6pm, and the wife came in and said: 'What's wrong? What was the score?' I said:

"We were beaten 5-1."

She said: 'Oh Jesus, I can't believe it.' I just stayed in my bed the whole night. I was really down."

But Brian is in a difficult situation. A board has come in which didn't appoint him. I just hope it's going to go right because he's a decent lad.

The only blot on the game was that we lost Ryan. The referee blew for offside or something, Ryan half stopped and the young Edgehill clattered him. Had the referee been looking, it could have been a sending off. It was a hell of a clattering. He struggled on to half time, but I knew we were going to have to take him off because he was limping. The unfortunate thing is that I'll have to withdraw him from the Wales game again, which is something I've had to do two or three times. I get 100 letters a week from Wales blaming me, saying I'm a traitor to the Welsh cause. I am accused of everything in Wales. Fortunately Mike Smith was at the game, so it wasn't as bad as if it had just been me phoning that night saying I was sorry.

Paul Ince is going to have his sinuses done tomorrow. He's been having trouble with them, so he dropped out of the England squad.

Terry Venables came to me after the game and said, "Why didn't you tell me on Monday."

"Well, I thought he was going to be all right", I replied.

And Pally dropped out too. He was bothered with his hamstring before the game. I don't like doing it but when you think of our problems over recent weeks, the number of games we've had to play, something had to go. It's impossible to expect them to be 100 per cent all the time. So now we get a break. I know some are away at internationals, but it's a welcome break to get away from the rigours of our game and hopefully we can get players patched up. I've got Parker in for an operation, Keane needing an operation, Bruce is suspended and Sharpe and Giggs are out for Saturday. It's a hell of a toll. The young players have done fabulously, but you still need a break to get players patched up.

Venue: Old Trafford *Att:* 43,738

Manchester United	goals	Manchester City	goals
1 Peter Schmeichel		32 Simon Tracy	
16 Roy Keane		22 Richard Edgehill	
4 Steve Bruce		12 Ian Brightwell	
6 Gary Pallister		6 Michael Vonk	
3 Denis Irwin		3 Terry Phelan	
14 Andrei Kanchelskis	43, 47, 88	16 Nicky Summerbee	

9	Brian McClair		10	Gary Flitcroft
8	Paul Ince		21	Steve Lomas
7	Eric Cantona	24	11	Peter Beagrie
10	Mark Hughes	70	8	Paul Walsh
11	Ryan Giggs		9	Niall Quinn
Substitutes				
24	Paul Scholes (45 mins for Giggs)		18	David Brightwell
13	Gary Walsh		33	John Burridge
27	Gary Neville		24	Adie Mike

Friday 11 November

I went to a press lunch in Glasgow today. Tony Blair was the speaker and was excellent. His father was at Govan High, the same school as me, and his grandfather worked in the shipyards. I said to him:

"If your father's from Govan, you'll be all right. Most boys from Govan make it."

The organiser of the lunch is a famous character and ex-journalist, Jim Rodger, who probably has more contacts than any other in the whole of Britain. He devotes a lot of time to this particular lunch and he gets very uppity when he feels he's not getting the support he deserves from some quarters. This part of his character was very much brought home to one of the photographers at the photocall, when Jim turned on him and said straight to his face, "You're banned, your company wouldn't buy a table." So off trolled one truly disconsolate little photographer, with his tail well and truly between his legs.

My brother picked me up at the airport. As we had plenty of time we had a cup of tea at the hotel where the lunch was being held. Then, to break the peace and quiet, in comes the tornado Jim Rodger, and immediately informs my brother Martin, "You're coming to the lunch, that's an order." Despite having other things to do, Martin was compelled to obey.

While this was going on, I was busy on a mobile phone with Joe Jordan. Jim Rodger asked me who I was talking to; I told him Joe Jordan. He told me to tell him to come through from the foyer right away, because he had to come to the lunch too. Although he was busy with some journalists, Joe also felt compelled to obey the command.

The lunch was marvellous, and I was very impressed with Tony Blair's speech.

Saturday 12 November

I went to see our youth team in the morning. They won 5-0 against Crewe Alexandra. They played really well. I like to see the young ones and there are one or two we have high hopes for. Ronnie Wallwork played a fantastic game as centre half. If he grows he'll be a brilliant player.

Then I went up to Oldham in the afternoon to see them play Luton Town. It gave me another chance to look at David Pleat's good footballing team, but the pitch was against good football and it was a very difficult day for both teams.

At Oldham, Ian Stott came into Joe Royle's old office.

"I'm sorry you've not got the right credentials for this club, but do me a favour, sit beside me at the game," he said.

"Yeah, sure I'll sit beside you."

I had brought along a French coach with me, who was working for his accreditation with the French FA, so I asked if he could sit with us in the Directors' Box too. When the press and photographers saw us there was quite a stir. It was funny. It's a good wee club.

"We couldn't stand in Joe's way after all the service he's given us – 12 years," said Ian.

They've appointed Graeme Sharpe right away, which is good, and he's brought in Colin Harvey. The experience Colin's had over the past few years will help him enormously. Managers come in nowadays and they've no preparation. Only two weeks ago Graeme Sharpe was talking about coming back from his injury and saying he'd be fit soon. And the next minute he's the manager. What preparation has he had to be manager? Absolutely none. They are all the same. It's a good move from Graeme Sharpe's point of view to bring Colin Harvey in. He knows that he can trust him.

Sunday 13 November

Today I was supposed to go to a dinner held in honour of Alex Matthews, to mark his 25 years as a manager in Scotland, at Stenhousemuir, Albion, St Mirren, Aberdeen and Clyde. But after being up there on Friday, it was just too much for me.

Instead I decided to watch last year's school boys, our under 16s, play the England School of Excellence. We've got four players in it. England played very well. The score was 2-2; a really good game. England have some very good players: Branch of Everton has got a real chance. The Arsenal boy, Wickes, did very well. There was also a midfield player from Tottenham who was promising.

It's good to get a weekend when you can relax. I've seen three games and some potentially good players coming in to the club.

Monday 14 November

Apparently the dinner for Alex was terrific. All the managers from Scotland were there.

Tuesday 15 November

Butt had a tremendous game for the Under-21s. I was really pleased with him. Good, sensible, play, good composure. He's done very well; risen to every challenge we've set him. He's got better as his games have gone on, really grown up and given me terrific midfield strength.

He qualified to play for Scotland – his father is Scottish – but he said, "No way am I going to play for Scotland". They picked him a couple of years ago, and when the papers came in he said:

"I'm not going."

"I'll fine you!" I objected.

But now, with the new restrictions, it is good that he is English.

Wednesday 16 November

I travelled up to see Scotland versus Russia. It was a good result for Scotland but I thought Russia coasted a lot of the time. Their passing was terrific but the mentality baffles me. Twenty minutes into the second half and the adventure went from their game. The European mentality is amazing, they just shut up shop and say: "No more sales today." It was just so predictable - a 1-1 draw.

It's hard for Scotland to make an impact on any game like that. The commitment's terrific, the players worked their tails off and fought for every ball, which is typically Scottish. But you look at the new Hampden and think of the old Hampden with 120,000 capacity and what it must have done for the team. But with that kind of passion it perhaps inspired people to want to play there. But Hampden that day meant only 38,000, so the aspirations of younger players don't have to reach the same heights and they don't have the great events of Europe to cling on to; the likes of the Lisbon Lions or the other great heroes.

Denis Law is only a year older than me but he was still my hero. If you walk down the bloody street and you spoke to 1,000 Scotsmen, 999 would tell you Denis Law is the greatest Scot ever. The remarkable thing was that in the old system when Scotland lost a game, they used to blame Denis because he was an Anglo. I always remember after one defeat the Daily Record had four photographs and a headline that read something like: "These men must not be allowed near Scotland again." There was Denis, Bill Brown, Dave Mackay and Paddy Crerand, or someone like that.

But we've had some fabulous individuals. The last great players – Dalglish and Souness, maybe David Cooper and little Gordon Strachan – have all gone. We don't have anyone like them now. That's why you know that when you're watching Scotland toiling manfully to do their job, it's their attitude which is getting the result not their talent. In a recent article I did for the PFA in Scotland, talking about the fight we had to get our wages paid when you were suspended, I said the standard in Scottish football is going through a bad cycle because you reap what you sow in boys-club football.

Thursday 17 November

Roy Keane has come back from Belfast with a hamstring injury. I hope he's all right for Gothenburg on Wednesday. Parker's going in for an operation on Monday, so I have to forget all about him for the time being. Sharpe's got to go in, so that's two Englishmen out of the way. It looks as if I've got to look at young Neville. Walshy has an injury too, which is a bit of a sting.

Apart from the injury, Roy Keane and Denis Irwin were flying because Ireland won easily in Belfast. Poor Keith Gillespie didn't come back because there was some mix-up over flights, so the lads were saying afterwards that his body would be found face down in the river.

You get that, both sides of the coin. Some come back delighted. Eric Cantona had a 0-0 score in Poland, which is not a bad result, but he's still thinking that he could have done better.

I was speaking at a dinner for Jock Wallace who's got Parkinson's disease. There were 450 people there and it was great to see old Leicester City players coming to pay tribute to Jock: Mark Wallington; Eddie May; Alan Mauchlen; Martin Henderson; Gary McAllister; and Alan Young.

Brian Little was at the table. The commercial manager of Aston Villa was there too, and I said:

"You keep your thieving hands off him." Then when I got home I turned on the teletext and he'd been given the go ahead to speak to them.

He'd do well to consider it carefully; make sure the conditions are absolutely right, because you are never stronger than the day you arrive at a club. It's important that he establishes himself properly – what his role is and what Doug's role is.

I hope he does well, he's a nice lad. He's had the right upbringing, too. He did well at Darlington; he's been to Leicester and taken them out of the division. He's had disappointments which are good for a manager, about getting to the Wembley play-offs and failing. So that is great, that adversity, then coming back and eventually getting your promotion. But I think he'll do well if he accepts the job because he seems to have the right approach to it all.

Friday 18 November

Roy Keane's hamstring is a bad one. There is a big, dark brown bruise on the back of his leg. That's an indication of how bad it is. He could be out for five or six weeks. He stayed on ten minutes after doing it, which didn't help. But I'm not criticising him in any way. I understand why he wanted to stay on.

Apart from Roy's there are no new injuries. I've still got Giggsy and Sharpey out. I was tempted to play Keith Gillespie but I opted to play Simon Davies just because he's left-footed, plus I've got to think of an Englishman for Wednesday.

Mark Hughes had his autobiography launch at Old Trafford yesterday. His agent was there and all the press ran stories this morning about his demands for his new contract.

The headline on one read: "Set him up United or Hughes is on his way." They all said that he was quitting, that he won't see the rest of the season out – all that kind of nonsense, despite the fact that they know very well that he's on contract till the end of the season. And in the meantime we can negotiate. Dennis Roach, his agent, has asked us to put a price on Mark so he can start negotiating with clubs.

Mark Hughes is a United player until he actually walks out himself. In the meantime we'll do our best to get a compromise deal to keep Mark. But that's what negotiation is. You have to recognise the case of a talented footballer. You can't just say: "There you go, Mark. Take that," as in the days before freedom of contract.

They all go in with great strength nowadays because of agents and dealings with other managers. Some use a solicitor, some use their accountant. The most straightforward negotiator I've come across is Michael Kennedy, who dealt for Liam Brady and Frank Stapleton. If it wasn't for Michael Kennedy, I don't know whether we'd have got Roy Keane. He handled the whole thing with integrity.

Cathy has been going off her head because I've not been around while we've had new carpets laid and the floor tiled in the bathroom. Today I've got six visitors coming from Aberdeen and we're going out to dinner tonight.

Tomorrow night we've the ground stewards' dance at Old Trafford. It's a fabulous night. Some of them have been with the club for 50 years. Their fathers worked here. It's an honorary position. They're retired men but they still enjoy working at the club.

On Sunday night I've got the Italian dinner and dance at the Midland. I have to watch what I eat now because this is the time of year when you start to put on weight. I've been going to the gym almost every day, trying to do 30 to 35 minutes walking and spending time on the bicycle.

Saturday 19 November
United 3 Crystal Palace 0

We played really well. The passing was good. There was a buzz about the players and a terrific atmosphere in the ground. Palace came to have a go. They are young and athletic and they have dreams as young people do, but by having a go they left themselves exposed. It was a perfect situation for us. We knew we'd score. You just hope you don't lose any and in fairness to them, they could have scored one or two. They hit the bar and young Pilkington made a good save.

Peter came in after his warm up in real pain. He couldn't catch his breath. I knew right away.

"Just leave it. We'll make the change now," I told him.

"No, I'll go and try it," he said.

"Well, five minutes. I don't want to leave you hanging on because I've got Wednesday to think about."

Mind you, he'd no chance of playing on Wednesday the way he was. After his first kick of the ball I said:

"That's it."

I put Kevin Pilkington on after eight minutes but just as he came on they scored from the free kick. Great substitution that – inspirational!

But it was a good performance and I was quite impressed with Palace's attitude to it. And I've watched them a couple of times this season. I saw them at City and thought they should've won the game. They were enterprising and their attacking was good; very imaginative. They should do well this season.

It was a good result for us and it was a nice way to go to Europe. Simon Davies did well, Gary Neville was outstanding – particularly against Salako, because he's not the easiest opponent. He's such a positive player. He's always threatening behind you. He's got great pace, but Gary coped exceptionally well.

Venue: Old Trafford *Att:* 43, 738

Manchester United	*goals*	**Crystal Palace**	*goals*
1 Peter Schmeichel		1 Nigel Martyn	
27 Gary Neville		22 Darren Patterson	
6 Gary Pallister		6 Chris Coleman	

12	David May		14	Richard Shaw
3	Denis Irwin	8	3	Dean Gordon
14	Andrei Kanchelskis	50	2	John Humphrey
9	Brian McClair		4	Gareth Southgate
8	Paul Ince		23	Ricky Newman
7	Eric Cantona	34	11	John Salako
10	Mark Hughes		9	Chris Armstrong
18	Simon Davies		18	Andy Preece
Substitutes				
24	Paul Scholes (72 mins for 18)		15	Bobby Bowry
25	Kevin Pilkington (7 mins for 1)		16	Darren Pitcher
31	Keith Gillesspie (52 mins for 14)		19	Rhys Wilmot

Sunday 20 November

We came in and had massages. All we can do is get them as ready as possible physically, and then get their minds sharp.

Monday 21 November

A lot of thought about the side. After Saturday I know I'm going to be without Schmeichel. That means I can use McClair. He has been playing very well, and his experience was going to be important because the pitch will be bad. Gothenburg's has never been a good pitch and you don't know what kind of weather you're going to have to contend with.

I thought about Gary Neville after his display on Saturday, but experience is going to be vital. Also, if I don't play David May, it is sort of saying to him: "You've just never done it here." I couldn't really desert him that way. I had to give him support.

Wednesday 23 November

Gothenburg 3 United 1

All the plans went out of the bloody window in ten minutes. I've never been so shocked. I was speechless at the end of the game. Just lunacy. We gave a goal away by playing offside on the halfway line, which we never do. So we were then forced to chase the game all the time, keep the ball all the time which was completely against the plan to keep them running about.

I know the pitch was difficult. We did say to make sure that in our own half we would play the ball forward and build from there. But once we got into their half, the object was to keep possession. Instead once you go a goal down, you are chasing them.

Then you get to the equaliser and you say to yourself: "We'll be all right." At that point I thought we were going to win because we had them under the cosh. We were starting to close ourselves up a bit, but then we gave away another goal.

David knows himself that he should have done better at the cross - he had the winger in the corner. But when the cross came in, all the forwards stayed away on the back post, and one of them was completely free of all the defenders, and somehow we managed to get three defenders against one. To tell the truth, the boy took it very well, just side-footed it. It might have hit him, but he did the right thing by not trying to power it home.

I was so shocked. There are several differences in Europe. They're experienced and somewhere or other they try to get an extra man in. We knew they would play three in the middle of the park and they created a lot of problems for me in the sense of holding Eric and Sparky off. Andrei's not the best at coming in and being a midfield player – he's a natural wide player. We'd said:

"Make sure that the midfield comes in so you make up four very quickly and Simon Davies will come in a wee bit."

But losing a goal after ten minutes meant we had to go on to their wide players. They were throwing it to the full backs, so we had to push on them.

They didn't hold the ball in the middle of the park, so Incey never got to anybody. They just passed the ball by him. In Europe they pass to each other in midfield, they play in little triangles and keep it in there. They play one-twos against you in midfield. Whereas our midfield players service the wide players, the full backs, and the front men. In a lot of cases they run with the ball, giving you a chance to tackle them. That attitude that you can give the ball away and get it back within minutes is an indictment really. It doesn't apply in Europe: there it is the death sentence. If you lose it, you have to wait a long time to get it back.

To cap it all, Paul Ince got sent off for dissent. He knows it was wrong. In Europe you cannot argue with the referee. Paul was lucky he wasn't sent off in Barcelona for a display of dissent. Now he might miss two or three games.

The PFA have a tariff of permitted fines, and being booked for dissent is ten per cent of your salary. But I had a meeting at the start of the season in which I said I wasn't accepting that in Europe.

Venue: Ullevi Stadium *Att:* 36,350

	Gothenburg	*goals*		**Manchester United**	*goals*
1	Thomas Ravelli		1	Gary Walsh	
2	Pontus Kamark	71	2	David May	
3	Joachim Bjorkland		3	Denis Irwin	
4	Magnus Johansson		4	Steve Bruce	
5	Mikael Nilsson		5	Andrei Kanchelskis	
6	Mikael Martinsson		6	Gary Pallister	
7	Jesper Lindquist		7	Eric Cantona	
8	Stefan Rehn		8	Paul Ince	
9	Jesper Blomquist	10	9	Brian McClair	
10	Magnus Erlingmark	64	8	Mark Hughes	64
11	Stefan Pettersson		11	Simon Davies	
Substitutes					
12	Erik Wahlstedt (48 mins for 6)		12	Gary Neville (68 mins for 2)	
13	Dick Last		13	Kevin Pilkington	
14	Thomas Andersson (79 mins for 11)		14	Nicky Butt (76 mins for 11)	
15	Johan Anegrund		15	David Beckham	

16 Patrik Bengston	16 Paul Scholes

Thursday 24 November

It was a long journey home.

Looking back over our European disaster, one thing stands out: our speed of thought defensively was very, very poor. They froze on the big stage, they forgot how to defend. If you analyse the goals we lost, you shake your head and say, "There's no way my team could lose those goals in such a short space of time."

We've played five games in Europe and lost eleven goals – the worst in the whole Championship League. And when you analyse them! The first goal against Gothenburg at home was a cross into our box. Peter didn't want to come or go. He stayed, half came and lost a goal. We recovered, we got in front and then they had a free kick at 35 yards. The boy flicked it with his heel into the corner and the goalie had no chance. Bloody hell, that was bad luck.

Then we played Barcelona at home and they had two chances in the game and scored with both of them. The second time there was one Barcelona player in the penalty box against four red jerseys and he scored. He and Romario were the smallest men on the pitch. I said:

"What the hell is going on?"

Then we went to Barcelona and lost a goal in eight minutes through a catalogue of errors, compounded by the one right on half time – crazy bloody goals. In the third one we got a free kick which was played short – the ball through gets cut off. The score was 3-0. It was absolutely lunatic defending.

For the fourth goal, Andrei Kanchelskis was chasing back towards the goal. Instead of putting it out for a throw in, he tried to control it and lost it. Then on Wednesday in Gothenburg, we were playing offside on the halfway line after eight minutes. Absolute lunacy.

When I look back I say to myself:

"We don't deserve to be in Europe making these kind of mistakes. We don't give ourselves a chance."

Friday 25 November

I couldn't come to terms with it. I didn't go out training with the players today. I just couldn't muster the body strength to go and face it. You go over and over and over it in your mind. You think we'd have done better with the young players – the Nevilles and Casper would have gone back to their box instead of trying to play offside.

Joe Royle phoned this morning about the piece that appeared in the

Daily Mirror saying that he had bid for Mark Hughes. He was apologising and he thought maybe it was a director talking out of turn. But putting that in the press doesn't in any way help Joe's case because it just puts the supporters on edge. We have no intention of selling Hughes.

I don't usually talk to agents, but Dennis Roach wrote me a letter complaining that I'd been telling the press that he's been a problem. In the letter he said he had to inform the press what was happening because they were all asking. After receiving it I phoned him.

"You have no right to be informing the press abut what is happening to Mark Hughes. If you want to know, come to the club."

"I'd like to come up to see you and the chairman with Mark and his family," said Roach.

"No problem. We can sit down and try and reach a compromise," I said.

It's hard-going with agents because they're all well in with the press. The press know who to phone and which agents to pursue. When we signed one player we were in the chairman's office. The agent's phone went during the meeting and he said:

"There's nothing to report just now – there's no signing yet."

The press know exactly what's going on right through the deal. It's absolutely incredible. You're a manager and you pick up the paper and see you've made an enquiry about a player. Half the time it's come from agents.

There's so much intrigue when dealing with agents – that's why you try to avoid having any contract with them. It would be far better to have a system using the knowledge inside the game rather than having to go outside. The way we've operated with Sharpe and Giggs who are two young, emerging players, is to bring Bryan Robson and Brian McClair into it with the players' parents. We will be doing the same with the rest of the young players.

The managers – particularly at clubs of stature – should utilise the experienced players and make sure the younger ones don't get a raw deal. You're not taking them for granted because you brought them through as kids and they should be grateful to you for giving them a crust. Young players have to be recognised for their talent, not for their age.

We don't feel we need to use an agent to discuss the players, anyway. If a club of our size is interested in a player, we should negotiate with their club. This was a bone of contention with Alan Shearer who said that we had not spoken to him in the six months before leaving Southampton.

I told him my job was to be in contact with a player's manager, not to keep calling a player directly, unsettling him, taking his mind off the game. He mentioned that other managers had been talking direct, and from that comment I feel that maybe I lost the inside rail on the deal by talking solely with his manager. But that's the way we do things, the way I do things.

Saturday 26 November

Arsenal 0 United 0

Mark Hughes was sent off for two yellow cards. I'll need to look at the video, but I thought the referee was poor and very susceptible to the home crowd, who were screaming at every tackle. With every challenge Arsenal made in the air, elbows were flying, but he did nothing about it. And Paul Ince, who did make a bad tackle on John Jensen, got away with it.

I don't know where it is coming from, but last year in the 2-2 game, the support was fanatical which you don't always get at Arsenal. I can only assume it was because they were playing United. They screamed for every free kick, over the fence at the referee and linesman, so the referee had a lot to contend with. He was a real bundle of nerves. He booked Keith Gillespie after 23 seconds!

Not once did Arsenal look like beating us. They only had one move of any significance: Wright had a shot which was bundled clear by Gary Pallister. Other than that we defended well. In any game against Arsenal, the main thing is to stop Wright from scoring and we did that well.

David May had an excellent game. Full back is not his best position and his performance against Arsenal emphasised that he's a centre back. He was first class. And Gary did really well at right back. The back four all did very well – Gary Walsh only had one save in the whole match.

But the way they play the game, pushing up, condensing the game, playing offside, pressurising the referee and linesman for offside decisions, means it is never a pretty game with them. We never looked like scoring. We got into some good positions, but our finishing was poor. But I was quite pleased with the character of the side, because Arsenal are very aggressive and we stood up to it.

Venue: Highbury *Att:* 38,301

Arsenal		*goals*	**Manchester United**		*goals*
1	David Seaman		13	Gary Walsh	
22	Lee Dixon		27	Gary Neville	
12	Steve Bould		12	David May	
6	Tony Adams		6	Gary Pallister	
3	Nigel Winterburn		3	Denis Irwin	
21	Steve Morrow		14	Andrei Kanchelskis	
17	John Jensen		9	Brian McClair	
11	Eddie McGoldrick		8	Paul Ince	
19	Jimmy Carter		7	Eric Cantona	
8	Ian Wright		10	Mark Hughes	
9	Alan Smith		31	Keith Gillespie	
Substitues					

14 Martin Keown	18 Simon Davies (73 mins for 31)
13 Vince Bartram	25 Kevin Pilkington
27 Paul Dickov	19 Nicky Butt (56 minsfor 14)

Sunday 27 November

Maybe newspapers print different headlines in the North of England, but I got the London papers this morning and I was absolutely fuming at the reports on the game. Joe Melling, who I've never had any problems with, wrote: "United show their evil side!" There was one tackle in the whole game, when Paul Ince was outside the box. Admittedly it was a botched challenge but it happens time and again. A guy's going to shoot and a player goes in under his foot. Just one tackle in the whole game which merits discussion.

The Mark Hughes sending off was an absolute joke – he was knocked and he fell into the boy Jensen. He hardly touched him and he goes down bloody pole-axed. Bloody sickening. That's twice, two years in a row, with Arsenal that we've had someone sent off, and you have your doubts about the way the Arsenal player has gone down.

6
Back on the Trail

Monday 28 November

With us being out of the Coca-Cola Cup, we have got a free week for once. It will give us a chance to take stock.

We decided to let Sharpey go away for a week for a wee break to Tenerife. He's done a lot of work on getting back from his hairline fracture, and it's the time to say, "Right, take a break."

Tuesday 29 November

We released a young player, Gary Twynham, who lost interest in the game. You try to talk them out of it. He wants to go to college or something like that. I said: "What you should do is go away and think about what you're doing, what you're talking about, then come back and see me." I went to speak to his parents. His mother was going off her head, his father was going off his head, but he was adamant that's what he wants. He said, "I've no appetite for playing, mam, I don't enjoy it. I can't be bothered with it." He got an ankle injury and he was out for a wee bit and he lost it. It is sad, because he had ability.

There was another Welsh boy whom we also released, because his behaviour was not acceptable, but as a schoolboy he looked exceptional. Sixteen to nineteen are the vital years for the shaping of a boy's character: the shaping of their ambitions even. That is when you are giving them the platform which you hope will carry them out and through as a footballer, giving them that sort of an upbringing and discipline that's going to be needed to get on in life whether they are a footballer or a baker or a candlestick-maker, whatever he wants to be. You keep on telling the parents that between sixteen and nineteen they've really got to be hard on them, they've got to be strong on them so we can shape their destiny as best we can. The young boy Twynham has been honest about it but to lose the urge is sad, and difficult to explain. I hope that he rings up one day and says, "I want to go back playing," because he's got decent ability, he should get a career in the game really.

You couldn't explain that decision to anyone at the Stretford End.

Well I'm not trying to explain it, but I don't know the reasons, the answers myself to it. But people who haven't ever played but wanted to play, would shake their heads.

I remember when I first started, I did well with some young players. But this young boy, a boy named Sam Munroe, from Coatbridge, was really talented, but he didn't like training. I used to do some long distance stuff with him and he didn't like it at all. One day he came to me and asked me for two tickets to Wembley for a Scotland England game, and I said, "Aye, if you improve your bloody training."

He went out that night and he tried, but he couldn't make it. He couldn't do the long distance stuff, around the track. I think we may've been doing eight 800s or something like that. He came in to see me about two or three weeks after and said:

"I'm quitting, I'm going to be a tailor."

"A tailor!" I said, "A bloody tailor! Are you serious?"

He was only 18, so I went away up to his house. I said to myself there's somerthing wrong here, and I need to find out. And I did. His father had left his mother, and that was the reason. He couldn't face it. He couldn't handle the pressure of playing which is not a lot of pressure at 18. I kept his contract of course, which I could because it was before freedom of contracts came out.

About two years later I got a letter from him saying he wanted to come back. So I wrote back there and then, saying, "You come in to train next week, you'll be very welcome." But he never turned up. He must have had a fleeting moment of courage, of common sense, and then woken up the next morning and thought: 'what's the point?' Sad! But he would've made it. He had the talent to make it.

Wednesday 30 November

I went to see Forest play Millwall because we play Forest in a couple of weeks and also to give me a chance to look at one or two players Millwall have got coming through, including the young full back Thatcher.

I went with Bobby Charlton and we had a game of golf at Mottram Hall on the way down. You need that wee sort of a break away from it at times. The first time I'd played in ages and it was cold and it rained a bit, but I enjoyed it. David Herd and I played Bobby and a pal of Bobby's, Eddie Plimlott. Scotland versus England – on St Andrew's Day too. I refuse to name the score but it was a heavy defeat. Lucky England.

I left Forest ten minutes to go before time up, belted down that road, dropped Bobbie off at Mottram and was in the house in time for the start

Magpie turned Red Devil: Cole signs for us

Andy settles into a new training regime

Match day: nothing more I can do - just grimace and bear it

4th February 1995: Manchester United against Aston Villa at Old Trafford

Celebrating Cole's first United goal...

"Did you see that - I told you he'd score"

Back down to earth: Kiddo makes his point

Shouting instructions from the dug-out in Gothenburg

Highland fling!

22nd January 1995: Eric Cantona's winning goal against Blackburn Rovers

25th January 1995: feelings run high after Eric's sending off at Selhurst Park

of the football on Granada. Watching a game like Blackburn versus Liverpool or City against Newcastle, you are a bit envious, it's great being involved in that sort of cup tie, but having a week without a midweek match is a welcome break too.

Thursday 1 December

We made enquiries about Stan Collymore. I spoke to Frank Clark and there is absolutely no chance and I've not pursued it. I may go back to them but I just don't see it as a big concern just now. It may depend on their progress in the Cups. They owe a lot of money so that may help us. I've been interested in him and Ferdinand, but there's no joy with either at the moment. They are the two I'm really targetting. We made an enquiry for Sheringham but they wanted £5 million, which is crazy, so I had to forget about him.

Friday 2 December

We've used our free week to do some serious functional things, so it has been productive.

Roy Keane is starting to do some running. He's put himself to train for Galatasaray next Wednesday now, the thing being he's not played for three weeks. He's a strong lad and we'll maybe have to play him at right back to get the best out of him.

Saturday 3 December

United 1 Norwich City 0

Before the game I fancied us winning this with a bit of style, because I felt they'd got one or two players out after the hard cup tie on Wednesday against Notts County. We felt fresh and so you say you're expecting to see something, and the players didn't disapppoint me in terms of the quality of their play, particularly in the first half.

But you've got to give credit to Norwich. They do come to Old Trafford and enjoy themselves. When I first came to the club they used to have a hell of a record against us. I think they won three or four years in a row here. On Gary Pallister's debut they beat us 3-0 here. They've always been a good passing team. But since 1990 we've won all the games here apart from last year when we drew 2-2 in a terrific game. But they always come and play. John Deehan has taken over from Mike Walker as manager, they've lost Fox, they've lost Sutton and they've brought in a couple of players, but they still play the same way. It's almost like Nottingham Forest. They've set out a certain way of playing, and it becomes a tradition. Norwich are very much the same. It's always good to play against them, always refreshing. They come and have a go, they're not afraid to play and they have good experience in their team. I enjoyed the game to the point that, if they had equalised, I couldn't have denied them deserving the draw. They worked really hard in the second half.

But in terms of reaching the heights I thought some of the football in the first half was absolutely fantastic. Cantona was at his very, very best throughout the game. He kept screaming at them in the second half – to get up the pitch and keep playing up there to him because he was really on song. There were a couple of tackles which were intended to hack him in two, but he rode them as if they were nothing. And the goal was brilliant.

I said in the pre-match remarks, "Remember Mark Robins is about on the edge of the box, and if you are not alive to him then he'll score, as simple as that." And I thought he did well for them. I thought he was very bright looking and he led the line well. I think he's been taken off a lot recently and I thought that it was significant they took Newman off before they took Mark off because he didn't deserve to come off.

As a young player Mark was definitely better as a sub. When he got a prolonged spell on the team he didn't have an impact. He has always been a great finisher, and I'm just glad he didn't get any chances today. When you're leading 1-0 you are always worried and at one stage he put the ball in the net, but it was just offside. He took it well though he didn't even swing the leg back at it, he just guided it into the corner. A great finisher. I remember when he was coming through. I was at Tottenham watching the Under-21s and someone – it may have been Don Howe – asked me if he was quick.

"He's as quick as Lineker is in the box," I said, "And as quick as Norman Whiteside in the middle of the park!" He isn't as quick in his general play as he is in the box and that's just an instinct, a smell he's got. I just think if he'd waited, if he'd been patient to stay with us, he'd have turned into a better player. He started really well with Norwich but he just seems to have gone back a wee bit, he doesn't seem to be really in the picture now, although in fairness he had a couple of injuries.

Sunday 4 December

We had them in for a loosener, and looking around I said: "I haven't got Ince, I've not got Hughes, I've not got Giggs, I've not got Sharpe, I've not got Parker, I've not got Schmeichel." It's daunting. One principle of mine has always been never to talk about the players you haven't got. Every team has injuries, and you should just get on with it, and concentrate on the players you have got. But missing that group is daunting. You say to yourself, 'I've got to be really organised, I've got to make sure that the side which plays is going to be difficult to beat at least.'

The one gamble will be Roy Keane. He is on a really intensive training programme now, and he is doing well. I think it is a gamble worth taking.

I watched yesterday's goal on video. At the time it was a great goal but you should see the video! It was poetry, you could set it to music – or use it as a coaching video. You say, "Quicken the game up in the last third," and nothing could emphasize that point better than Eric's flick. It's: "Now you see it, now you don't." It's just a wee flick of his foot and he's flying away out the road of the game, away from his marker. McClair gets on to it, slips past one man and cuts it in and where's Cantona? In the space as usual. I keep saying that to players – you look up and in the last third of the pitch, he's always free, he's always available. He's marvellous at that. And he finished it really well. I think when you see goals like that it is fabulous to watch from the moment we get the free kick. Kanchelskis gets it down, touches it to McClair, McClair passes to Ince, Ince up to Cantona, into McClair, into Cantona – you're 1-0.

Some of the play in the first half was superb. Some of the press said we took the foot off the gas because of the European game. I don't think that's the case – I'd forgotten about the European tie to be honest with you, I think Norwich decided, 'Right, 1-0 down we may as well go for it. If we are going to lose we lose, but if we go for it we might get something.'

They might have done. The press this morning made a thing about Mark Robins' "offside" goal, and also about a penalty – they claimed it was inside, but it was awarded outside the box. For the first I was watching Robins peel off David May, and I was saying, "Watch it Dave, watch it," because Mark's good at that, but he went early and I thought 'offside'.

I asked David about it afterwards, and he said, "He was definitely offside. In fact Robins said to me he thought he was a bit off."

"He never said that to the press," I said, because Robins and John Deehan had gone in afterwards and had a word or two about the decisions. But after a game everybody wants to put their own case over, don't they?

The "penalty" was definitely outside the box, in fact it was a good yard outside the box when he was pulled down, but he fell in the box.

I wasn't too happy about the refereeing in the game. I support the new guidelines, but my only concern has been the lack of consistency. I think you're better with one who's over fussy rather than one who doesn't bother. I went to the TV studios to watch Wolves and Millwall, and there was this terrible tackle by Kelly. He's not that kind of player but it was a really bad tackle, the other boy was very, very lucky he was not seriously injured.

Graham Taylor used a new system: two centre backs; one in front of the centre backs; Darren playing right side; Emblem centre midfield and Thomas the lefthand side; the two full backs pushed on; and two up front. They were slaughtered. He took Darren off. I couldn't understand that.

Monday 5 December

We put out a roll call for the fit and healthy, and then we just did bits of possession. What I did with Galatasaray in mind was to get the midfield players practising their possession while being man-marked. I said to myself, 'My best chance is to make sure we're strong against them in midfield,' and they concentrated on that aspect. My tactic is to make sure there's going to be enough bodies in the middle of the park to be against them all the time.

Giggs is still in the treatment room having remedial treatment. The injury to Andrei Kanchelskis is a little bit worrying for me. So I've got to mull that over and look at it. It's not the easiest team to pick because you say to yourself, 'Well it's one thing playing two or three young players but in such an important game am I being fair to them?' We've never lost at home in Europe and you don't know if maintaining that record should be the biggest priority or going for broke and being gung-ho. In a way, perhaps, you are best playing the youngsters so they've got some experience, but you don't want any young players involved in a defeat, particularly with the record at Old Trafford. I'll probably settle for an experienced back four with the young ones in the middle of the park. That is a definite possibility, particularly if Kanchelskis is out. Gillespie can play in Andrei's place and we'll have McClair and Cantona and then you've got Butt, Davies and Scholes who could come in and young Beckham too.

But it's a very difficult one to call. I think the key to it is Kanchelskis because in a game like that he has the running power and pace to turn people. Without Sharpe or Giggs the penetration on the left side is lacking, so if you don't get it on your right side it's a struggle. Young Gillespie's got pace but he's not got the real power of Kanchelskis yet, or the understanding of the game that Kanchelskis has got. It'll come, hopefully, in time, but he hasn't got it at the moment.

The funny thing is I'm not bad for options at the back with Bruce back. Gary Neville's been doing great.

Tuesday 6 December

We had a practice match - three lots of 12 minutes. That's when I made my "booboo", playing Gillespie, thinking he was an assimilated player, in the first 12 minutes. In the second 12 minutes I brought Beckham in, and in the third 12 I used Butt on the right hand side with Scholes as the striker and McClair midfield. So I toyed between Beckham and Scholes and felt that McClair and Cantona would be better against the man-markers.

Gary Neville had done quite well at full back, so I didn't think any more about playing Keane there. I knew I was going to be short in midfield. It was either play McClair and Butt together, which is not the ideal combination – both are better at going forward, or put Keane in. Keane, although he's got the ability to go forward, is also a terrific defender and I had to get the balance right in there.

Roy Keane has been in a training programme for four or five days now. It has been really hard work and he has done very well. He is a powerful lad but when you are out fitness goes – it's amazing that when you've been out for only a couple of weeks you can drop your fitness so much. But I am prepared to gamble on that. Roy has done much better than Ryan Giggs. He tried to come back in training, he was hoping to be fit for the Wednesday – but he is further behind and has no chance.

We had the regular monthly board meeting.

Wednesday 7 December
United 4 Galatasaray 0

The players did really well tactically, but I think what set the pattern was Keane's first minute tackle on Tugay. Tugay had a look at Keane and said to himself, 'Phew, I'm not going to enjoy tonight – I know that.' And every time that Tugay got the ball Keane was right up his jersey. And I thought it was that determination which determined the outcome.

I think the experienced players knew they had to perform because of the young players that were playing. There was no hiding place for them, they had to do something to make an impact to help the young players but I think Roy is such an under-rated player. He can do anything you ask him to do because he has quite a disciplined mind. You say to him:

"Go and man-mark X," and he'll do it.

"Play centre half."

"Aye, no problem."

"Play right back."

"No problem." He has quite an easy-going temperament so far as playing positions. It doesn't bother him.

Brian McClair is the same. When you ask Brian to do different things he just laughs. "I've not played in goal yet, you know," he said this week when he was told Peter Schmeichel being out meant he would be included. And that's his attitude, whereas others say, "I never played there before," if you ask them to switch a position. Keane and McClair just say "When does the game start? What time's kick off? I'll be there." It's a marvellous attitude – they are tough mentally.

I said: "Get against them in the middle of the park. Now there's every chance they are going to play three in the middle of the park, be against them – no matter what. Forget the full backs." And they started off trying to play that lad Suat on the right hand side against Simon Davies without a right back. And we capitalised on that because we gave them a real problem down that side.

And to score an early goal helped the young players and they were able to go on and give a really terrific performance. I was really so proud of them – because it's not easy to go out and concentrate on the game knowing that we'd not much chance of getting through anyway, but they just ran about with really good enthusiasm and conviction that what they were doing was right.

The front players did fantastically well against the markers – they pulled them all over the place and it really was a first class performance.

Watching us get in front and then score a second, it was all set up for us and I said at half time, "If we score now, it's all over, there's no way they will ever come back." And we did get a quick goal early in the second half, and then you start to wonder about what's happening in Barcelona. There's a young girl who sits beside us with an earpiece and she has a computer in front of her, and she keys in all the scores. And she said, "Still nil-nil," and then the roar went up and in the excitement everybody thought that Gothenburg were winning and the rumour went round the ground just like wild fire. And we looked at her for confirmation and she said, "Nil-nil."

Maybe the rumour was just somebody with a taste for a bit of mischief making. But still that was exciting – I mean that wee buzz at that part of the game. The players must have said, "Christ!" Eric Cantona came and signed to the bench to ask, but we said: "No, no, no, it's nil-nil." Then afterwards we saw the goal Barcelona scored – that boy will never score another like it – he was perfectly placed. And then the goal Gothenburg got! They fought hard, they are an honest bunch of lads and I hope they go on and win it. No one can underestimate them because they set out their stall very well.

Venue: Old Trafford	*Att:* 38,301		
Manchester United	*goals*	**Galatasaray**	*goals*
1 Gary Walsh		1 Gintaras Stauce	
2 Gary Neville		2 Penbe Ergün	
3 Denis Irwin		3 Korkmaz Bulent	89 (o.g.)
4 Steve Bruce		4 Balkanli Sedat	
5 Roy Keane	49	5 Korkmaz Mert	
6 Gary Pallister		6 Kerimoglu Tugay	
7 Eric Cantona		7 Erdem Arif	
8 Nicky Butt		8 Hamzaoglu Hamza	
9 Brian McClair		9 Sukur Hamza	
10 David Beckham	37	10 Suat Kaya	
11 Simon Davies	2	11 Kubilay Türkyilmaz	
Substitues			
12 David May		12 Bologlu Nezihi	
13 Kevin Pilkington		13 Tütüneker Ugur	
14 Paul Scholes		14 Tepekule Yusuf	
15 John O'Kane		15 Sancakli Saffet	
16 David Johnson		16 Gür Bekir	

Thursday 8 December

I had to go to London to get that *Daily Express* award.

I watched the video again and I said to myself, 'Bloody hell!' The Danish Football Association were over studying our methods against English teams. They studied us against Norwich and they commented on the number of one-touch passes we had. We doubled the number against Galatasaray. They're going to send me the graph – but I found it really interesting. Last year we did a video of every player, videoing the number of runs he made in the game, the type of runs that he makes, the distance of runs he makes. We tried to get some concept of how you can alter that in their training, in pre-season particularly. And it was interesting reading – in the case of Paul Ince, the runs he makes are mainly between 10 and 20 yards, whereas the wingers and full backs tend to run longer distances. It's interesting reading.

Having watched the video I thought some of it was really good and some of it was excellent – the moving and passing were terrific. Looking back over the games, there have been some lessons for us. I must admit I certainly learned one or two things.

I think you've definitely got to play man for man in Europe. I think you've definitely got to get against opponents individually, and I think that, even defensively, you've got to be man for man and have a free player somewhere. Now the question is whether that free player is a libero or whether you can get someone sat in front of the back four, or make sure your full back's right in beside your centre backs all the time and not worry about the wide positions so much. I'm just beginning to think that that's the way to do it.

I've been fascinated looking at all the systems. Ajax play one through the centre and two out wide but they tend to play one centre back and one in front and take a risk. It's two versus two and one sat in front – the free player is always in front. And they take risks, but the width of their game and the possession they keep compensates. And they play one off the front – a lot of teams do. AC Milan do it with Savicevic. We can do with Eric in a free role off there.

The midfields are compact – its hard to play through their midfields – particularly Milan. And Ajax too – the wide men come in and kill off their width and the midfield group in there to make the old diamond. They don't get strung out. I think that's a way of playing in Europe.

We had our best moments against Barcelona through our wingers, and when attacking you want that width but I think as soon as you lose it you must all come right in there and stop the midfield.

But as I feared at the time, it was that draw which stopped us qualifying, as much as the defeats in Barcelona and Gothenburg. However, that's life as they say. Life in the busy street's not easy – you've got to watch for the oncoming traffic and we got hit by a few heavy vehicles, didn't we?

Our failure provoked a lot of critical analysis from the media, but I don't believe it reflected a lack of quality in our game. I was watching the Barcelona game there for the first time the other day, and some of the possession once we started to ease ourselves into the game in the first half wasn't bad and the possession in the second half wasn't bad. Our quality of control and ability to get on the ball was alright. The areas in which we failed were in both last thirds of the pitch. We really defended terribly – the third goal in Barcelona was incredible. They got a free kick and Gary Pallister took it and Steve Bruce ran up to the box and he put a short pass into Ryan Giggs. Ryan played it back to Incey who tried to chip it in behind him. Cut off! 3-0! While Steve Bruce was still in their penalty box and Gary Pallister was in midfield – can you believe it? I said, "What the hell is going on? God forgive me, what are you doing? You never do these things."

And the goal in Gothenburg! We tried to play offside on the half way line. We never do that!

And that type of thing tells you that maybe it was just a bit of freezing of the old brain cells and they made mistakes that you can never explain away. They couldn't explain them either. They hold their hands up afterwards. So you just wonder if it wasn't meant to be for us and that was the big lesson, saying, 'Look, you don't play that way in Europe and until you start to learn how to play in Europe you are going to get that.'

But finishing on such a high note we at least gave the fans something – the chance to say, "Well, we were unlucky." It's great to have fans able to say that. and I think we could say we were a bit unlucky. The good thing is we scored 11 goals in the section – our average was two a game which wasn't bad – so there are some positive things to be taken away from it.

But I did enjoy it and I think next year we'll be better for it.

Friday 9 December

Now we have to think about the Premiership and making sure we are in position to get back into the Champions League next year, by winning the Premiership. I said months ago that when the Champions League was over we would get a clear run. Now we're out of Europe, we're in the same situation as everyone else – apart from the ones who are still in the League Cup like Newcastle. We can only do what we are good at and that is winning games. We've got experience now. I feel they can handle going on the run, knowing they've won the last two championships and been involved in a third one which we lost. So we've got tremendous experience about handling run-ins and I just think we'll be there. I think the players sense it themselves – they've got to start getting their fingers out.

We have to go to QPR tomorrow without both Hughes and Cantona. But I'm confident. There's always a great Cup tie atmosphere there and I know they always play to beat us and they always score against us. But we've always managed to score goals ourselves.

Saturday 10 December

Queens Park Rangers 2 Manchester United 3

When they went 1-0 up, I thought there we go. No Sparky, no Eric and Andrei just wasn't quite right. But we dug the result out. The period when we scored the first goal until 15 minutes into the second half some of our football was really good. But the first half they really had us going, they really did. And the last 20 minutes, it was gung-ho. It was just, "Hang on and get the result," and at that stage you're heading them out yourself. The crosses are flying in and you're on tenterhooks in the dug out – going "oooh," and then, "aaahhh," as I jumped up and hit my head on the top of the dug out. The players had a right good laugh at it!

Walshy did great for us. I was pleased for him because you can see he's getting better – you can see he's got more conviction in himself. He's looking stronger and he's got confidence and he looks formidable now. He'd absolutely no chance with those two goals. I mean that thing that Ferdinand hit – it was more like a missile than a football. And as for the header, when the boy ran out towards the right position I couldn't believe him crossing so early. He just turned and crossed it and Ferdinand was in the right spot. We were caught off guard there.

I took Gary Neville off at that stage. He'd been caught at the goal with Ferdinand at the back post, and I thought that they were just going to bombard the ball in the box anyway. And he sometimes can just ball watch a little – any young player does. I felt that Keaney was tiring anyway and it was going to be crosses – and Keane's marvellous in the air, so I just decided to move Keaney back and secure the result, as they say.

It was just a matter of digging in at that point. I couldn't see us getting a grip in midfield again. You just have to recognise how the pattern of the game is going and they were in full throttle, getting the service to the full back Bardsley, when Simon Davies' legs had just gone a bit.

I put Scholes out there for a time, but having come from centre forward and then going out there, he worked hard but it was his first game for maybe ten days and he found it hard to keep pace with Bardsley. Maybe I'd have been better playing Choccy there but I put Choccy back in midfield and Nicky Butt in there with him. Incey hadn't been training all week because of a shoulder injury, so he tired a little a bit. And it was a dead pitch as there'd been a lot of rain on Friday.

It didn't stop little Scholesy. When they lined up and saw this wee ginger-haired lad there, they must have been saying to themselves, 'This'll be easy, this'll be all right – only 5'7", scrubby red hair.' But the first ball came up to him, he just got one touch to the side to Choccy and he was away. And Maddix dived in on him, missed him by about two feet and the wee lad was just scampering away, just one touch and away. He's got a great football brain – he's got great vision too. As we saw, he's got a goal touch about him. He can play midfield. He's not confined. He can play anywhere really because he can pass the ball. He'll do really well, the lad, but he's got to be on the right team, have the right type of players around him. He won't come towards the ball, so he may not play well with Eric.

Venue: Loftus Road	*Att:* 18,948		
Queens Park Rangers	*goals*	**Manchester United**	*goals*
13 Sieb Dykstra		13 Gary Walsh	
3 Clive Wilson		27 Gary Neville	
16 Danny Maddix		3 Denis Irwin	
2 David Bardsley		4 Steve Bruce	
6 Alan McDonald		6 Gary Pallister	
7 Andy Impey		16 Roy Keane	44
25 Steve Hodge		14 Andrei Kanchelskis	
14 Simon Barker		8 Paul Ince	
9 Les Ferdinand	23/65	9 Brian McClair	
20 Kevin Gallen		24 Paul Scholes	34/47
11 Trevor Sinclair		18 Simon Davies	
Substitutes			
8 Ian Holloway		19 Nicky Butt	
10 Bradley Allen		25 Kevin Pilkington	
23 Peter Caldwell		31 Keith Gillespie	

Sunday 11 December

I stayed down after the match yesterday for the BBC Sports Personality of the Year awards. The team award went to Wigan, who thoroughly deserved it. I was delighted for them. We knew we weren't going to win it, so the players didn't go. They needed a Christmas night out with the wives that night.

Saw my grandson today. Cathy and his mother went shopping so I had him all afternoon.

Tuesday 13 December

I had a meeting with Reebok about Ryan. Then a BBC interview with Ian Payne, who kept wanting to talk about commercialism, and Ryan.

Thursday 15 December

I went to a "Sportsman's Lunch" at the Moseley Street Royal Bank of Scotland in Edinburgh.

We've had a lot of talk about injuries recently, but it is not just the celebrated players who suffer, although they get all the attention. There's always great attention paid to Lee Sharpe's and Ryan Giggs' injuries, and Peter Schmeichel's and Paul Parker's. And they are bad injuries and you don't want to see that with any player. But we've got a young boy, Stephen Hall, who joined us a year and half ago straight from school, and I think he's only played one game because of injury. He's the nicest kid you could ever me, an absolutely belting boy. He does all the staff's boots.

He comes in in the morning and says, "Does anybody need their boots cleaning? How's yours boss?" He couldn't be a nicer boy. Now how does he handle knowing he's not played for a year and a half? It is tragic.

At Aberdeen I never really had a young player who had to quit the game. But United have had several. The air's not as good down here, that's what it must be. But you've had Nicky Wood who quit the game and he looked as though he was going to be a real player too, and Billy Garton, and Remi and Gary Bailey.

I've never had that before. It just seems that during the last decade there's been a change in the physical part of the game. The number of cruciate knee ligament injuries is not coincidental, it's to do with the speed of the game. That's why we spend a lot of time with the three physiotherapists and the nutritionists and we try to give them the best chance they can get, physically. It's become more and more of a physical game.

I'll always remember watching at Wimbledon when I first came down, the day my mother died, and we lost 1-0. And we had a back four with Sivebaek right back, Mick Duxbury left back, Kevin Moran and Paul McGrath in central defence. We had Jesper Olsen, Remi Moses, Clayton Blackmore and Peter Barnes in midfield and upfront we'd Peter Davenport and Frank Stapleton. They'd no chance! Wimbledon would get these long throw-ins and we couldn't get out of our box all day. Bryan Robson had been injured, so I'd played him the night before at Northwich Victoria just to get him a game. And I brought him on as sub with half an hour to go. It made no difference. Physique comes into it nowadays, whether you like it or not.

You look around Europe and the players are powerful – the Scandinavians, even the Romanians have really solid bodies. You never see a frail German international do you? Possibly Sammer and Moeller are lightweights in relation to their team. All their strikers like Uwe Seeler ,Voeller, Muller, Riedle are well made lads. Even Littbarski may be small with slightish legs, but he has good shoulders on him.

But you compare English people to Scots. The English are a much bigger race than the Scots. They haven't got any big centre halves up there. You could name a dozen big centre halves down here. People who don't think that they are good in the air down here would be good up in Scotland because they are just a smaller race.

The Scottish race has changed a wee bit. We don't have so many manual workers and workers in the pits. We used to have big centre halves – George Young, Willie Woodburn after the war. Maybe it changed when things like mining stopped. I had a good friend who died a couple of years ago, Andy Matthew, who played in the successful East Fife team just after the war. And I remember one night round his house he got out his scrapbook and he showed me a photograph of the East Fife team and the shoulders on them! They were all miners doing physical work all the time, so they'd got shoulders like a bloody ox. The difference now is amazing. That's maybe why weight-training has had to come into it.

Saturday 17 December

United 1 Nottingham Forest 2

They suck you in, and then they hit you on the break. The players have changed over the last 8 years since I came down, the manager's changed, but Forest have never changed. The two games against us everybody was back, behind the ball, all the time. Whenever they had the ball they just passed it and passed it and passed it. It wasn't going anywhere really. You have to get in front of them.

But we started slowly and they settled, they deepened right away which was good tactics. They had two centre midfield players deep in front of their back four so we couldn't get the service up to Hughes and Cantona as easily as normal. So McClair and Ince were always left with the ball. You start off with that tempo, giving them a foot in the game and of course, you are going to lose a goal. And now you are chasing shadows a bit.

But I thought the commitment was good in the second half, I thought they had a right go at it and were a bit unlucky really. It was a disappointing performance, but I don't think it was a bad one. It was an untidy, bitty game. How long did Crossley keep the ball in his hands after his saves? He must have been keeping it in his hands for 20 seconds at a time. And the referee didn't bother about adding time on. He kept tapping his watch but he never bothered. It's annoying, that. Some teams will come here, like Chelsea last year, and always want to have a go at you and be positive about it. But Forest have been playing this way for years, yet they've always got a great press. They've had a better press than they really deserved.

You've got to lose at home sometime and the good thing was that it didn't do us a great deal of damage – only one point damage because Blackburn only drew at Leicester in Mark McGhee's first game. I thought Mark would've got the result.

We want all the advantage of points we can get but it's a wee bit early to start thinking like that, one goal, one point. There is so much ground to cover before you can start talking that way.

There was an incident between Incey and Stuart Pearce. Ince went down, Pearce claimed that he had dived, which he doesn't do, and they had an exchange of views. Nothing unusual in that, except that Pearce made some racist remarks, and Ince, understandably, reacted angrily.

Ryan, Sparky and Eric were all back. I took Ryan off, I should have kept him on actually. I should've kept him and taken off Andrei, as Pearce was having one of his aggressive, intimidating days and we weren't getting much joy on that side of the pitch. But Ryan was tiring. He was starting to run to inside a lot and not go back out to keep the shape. That was all the time the concern and that's why I did take him off. Ryan was knackered, but I thought he did quite well for his first game back.

Match of the Day was very selective. They didn't show the Pearce - Ince incident; they hardly showed any of the bookings. And they never showed the incident when Brucey was elbowed. His teeth went right through the gum. I couldn't see, and the linesman didn't flag, but the players said Stone hit him with the elbow. A good wee player, Stone, but he can be really difficult. He's had three broken legs himself. A tough wee bugger but difficult as well.

Tony Blair, the leader of the Labour party, was at the game.

Venue: Old Trafford	*Att:* 43,744		
Manchester United	*goals*	**Nottingham Forest**	*goals*
13 Gary Walsh		1 Mark Crossley	
16 Roy Keane		2 Des Lyttle	
3 Denis Irwin		18 Alf-Inge Haaland	
4 Steve Bruce		6 Steve Chettle	
14 Andrei Kanchelskis		3 Stuart Pearce	62
6 Gary Pallister		7 David Phillips	
7 Eric Cantona	68	11 Steve Stone	
8 Paul Ince		8 Scott Gemmill	
9 Brian McClair		14 Ian Woan	
10 Mark Hughes		10 Stan Collymore	35
11 Ryan Giggs		22 Bryan Roy	
Substitutes			
19 Nicky Butt (75 mins for 11)		20 Paul McGregor	
25 Kevin Pilkington		9 Lars Bohinen	
27 Gary Neville (87 mins for 14)		13 Tommy Wrigh	

Sunday 18 December

I went down to the Granada studio to watch Reading versus Wolves. A great day – a big screen, Reading versus Wolves, and Middlesbrough and Burnley on that screen. Brilliant. Then I went home, taped Liverpool and Chelsea and watched Scotland and Greece, then went out for a meal. Four games in the afternoon, great eh?

Chelsea have moved the pitch in five yards. Glenn Hoddle was complaining about that. Must be for the building – it's the only thing I can think of. It won't help us, that's for sure.

Monday 19 December

Today I had a great day. I had I had to go to the UMIST campus to make a presentation to the principal, H. Hankis, who retired. Big United fan. Then I had to come back here for the invalids' Christmas party. I had a meeting with Maurice Watkins and Paul McGuinness over his contract at 2.30; the carol service at 5.30, and then I had to be at the Acton Court for Paul Doherty's surprise leaving dinner tonight. My wife's always saying, "Why don't you grow up?" and I say, "Why should I? I'm enjoying myself being silly and young."

We might be changing our venue for pre-match meals. It's just all the hassle on Saturdays. We try to be accommodating to supporters, and if you get one lad on his own you don't mind, but when you get a dozen coming round it is not fair on the players. They can't concentrate on having their meal when they are having to stop all the time for photographs and autographs.

Then they go down to the players' lounge and all of a sudden there are 30 posters and 20 balls to be signed, and autograph books and photographs. I'm not against players signing autographs, but not when they should be thinking about football.

You're expected to put up with anything here. Running this club is like the Grand National. You take it a hurdle at a time, a fence at a time. The players are fantastic at remembering all their duties towards the kids at the training ground and all that. Last week I sent eight of them to the children's hospital, and they were there for two or three hours. They don't get any recognition for that. I've said to the chairman many times that we should have a PR department furnishing the papers with all this stuff.

I noticed the players were distracted on Saturday, though, so they didn't concentrate on the game. It's very difficult for them at times.

Tuesday 20 December

The Carol Service went well. It was started by Jonathan Boyars, our chaplain. It's terrific because it gets all the people from different departments together, and they all bring their family. It's got bigger and bigger every year. I think there were about 200 at it this time – and Sky television.

The chaplain is a terrific guy. He's got a great manner with the players, and is there if you need him. He comes into the club maybe once a week. "Has anyone got a problem? Is there anyone I can talk to?" he'll say to me.

Ken Merrett, the club's secretary, is a lay preacher, and when he first suggested that we should have a chaplain, I wasn't entirely sure. It needs a particular type of person to be accepted by football people – particularly by footballers. We had two young lads to start with. Nice lads, but they were young. Jonathan has the right experience behind him. He has a good open manner and he isn't intrusive. When Andrei's baby died a couple of years ago he did the service for him, and he was very good.

I think I never quite realised the importance of that kind of thing. But he helps the other staff members with family problems, deaths in the family and that type of thing, and the young person nowadays doesn't always have the stable family life of decades ago. I'm not being disparaging to any parent, I just think that we've lost a lot of the family discipline and the strength of the father in the family. What you hear now is, "Let them go out, they'll be back in at 12."

I remember quite vividly when I was 28 coming home at New Year with the wife, my dad saying to Cath, "Happy New Year! Do you want a wee dram?"

And when I said I wanted a drink he said, "What you bloody wanting? It's a bloody disgrace drinking at your age." I was 28! All I wanted was a beer or a sweet stout or something. I was terrified out of my bloody mind.

When I was 21, on a Saturday night he'd say, "You get in here at midnight or you'll have me to answer to." But it's different now. There's a softness.

I had to put up with it if I went to play cards in the back. My ma was shouting, "Alex, Our Alex, Our Martin!" And the windows went up one by one, "Our Tommy there? Our Stephen there? Our Malcolm there? Stephen, up you get! Michael, up you get!" And you wait. You'd wait another couple of times and then you'd get, "Alex! GET UP HERE." I used to scamper up those stairs. Then all the fathers would come out one at a time. That was the end of the card school.

Today I went up to Glasgow with David Sainsbury and Sir Richard Greenbury. Sainsbury's and Marks and Spencer are doing this new development in Govan. I haven't been that heavily involved, but I've kept in touch with it through the Govan Initiative. There's been a lot happening on Clydeside since the shipyards have gone. This development is going to be right on the banks of the Clyde, with leisure facilities and restaurants. It'll be absolutely brilliant. Every time you go to Glasgow now something is happening. There is a real buzz about the place.

I went to do some photographs at the site, and also to receive an award from the City Council – the Lord Provost's Medal for Sport and Achievement. It is nice to be honoured by your home city. It's the first time, so it was a lovely day for me.

Cathy came up too, and stayed on with her mother. I came back because we have our staff Christmas bash tonight at the Portland Hotel – the football staff that is. We have a meal, and we all stay the night, so it gives us a chance to relax and have a good chat. The players are having their night out too, because we don't play until Monday.

Wednesday 21 December

We had an excellent meal, so the party was great.

We had a day off today after the parties. I had lunch at the Midland with the Royal Bank of Scotland, then I went shopping trying to find a present for Cathy. Absolutely hopeless. Nothing in Manchester. Then I went into Hale. Nothing! In the end I found a jacket in Wilmslow which I just hope she likes.

I've always been hopeless at picking presents. You just hope that you will get inspired. Two Christmasses ago we were down in London playing Chelsea – Eric's first goal for the club – and I jumped into Harrods and picked up a nice suit, which Cathy has still got. That was bingo, that was winning the lottery!

I was assessing players with my staff, with Kiddo and Eric Harrison, with Jim Ryan, Bryan Robson and Les Kershaw and discussing who we should go for. I said I fancied Collymore.

Some of them fancy Sheringham because he's the best link player. I said, "But Collymore can link."

They said, "We don't think he can." Now after seeing him on Saturday they're saying, "You're bloody right he can link."

Cole is another one I rate really highly. I think he's a good player.

There are always those question marks about players, critics saying he can't do this or that, but you have to try and be positive. I'm saying to myself, 'Well what can he do that would improve us?' At the moment we don't know how Collymore or Cole would cope against packed defences, but how would anybody? We don't know, because they're not faced with that. Maybe if Newcastle become successful, they might face that. You don't know how Cole would react, nor how Sheringham would act. Would he have enough pace to bother anyone?

Ferdinand's another one I fancy. But how would he handle it? Would we have to change our style because of Ferdinand? And you go through all the question marks of the players and at the end of the day, they're all good players. They're all good at what they can do.

The problem with Sheringham is his age. Ferdinand's the right age, he's 28. Get him at a right mature age, a right peak. If we can get him for the next years he'll be very good. Collymore and Cole are younger. Sheringham's too old for my liking. So its all these questions putting doubts in your mind. When you're going to spend money, and it is big money, you have to try to make sure you've got all parts right.

I look at Collymore, I think he'd do well in Europe. He kept us on tenterhooks all day on Saturday. It was very difficult for me to assess him, to talk about him in the press conference after the game with all the speculation going on, so I just said how good the goal was and left it at that. But he made us nervous; every time the ball was played up there he was a constant threat. And he can link. He's got good vision, he can spot players.

In the evening I went to watch the Youth team play Charlton in the FA Youth Cup. We drew 1-1, so we've got to go to the Valley for a replay. I'm quite confident that they'll win now, but it was a disappointing performance. I think some of the young ones, knowing it's a big game and they are playing at Old Trafford tend to get a wee bit nervous.

Charlton got an early goal, which gave them something to hang on to, and the refereeing was poor. The game never really got started. It was foul after foul, and the trainers were on all the time.

The FA Youth Cup is special for young players. Usually they are confined to local opposition, and I can understand that they get, not apprehensive, but excited and sometimes nervous on the wider stage. We've had a great run getting to two finals and a semi-final in three years, and the present team should go quite far, but they've got to calm themselves down at games.

Thursday 22 December

There's a cold snap. We had to train indoors because the pitches at The

Cliff were frozen, and tonight's reserve game at Bury was called off, which is frustrating, because you want to keep the young players ticking over, keep them match fit.

I think that there's a case for the argument that Giggs has been used too much at the commercial end. Jimmy Greaves has done a good article on it. I think the souvenir shop has got an important part in financing the club and it made £14 million last year. They reckon they're going to do £20 million this year. There are twenty girls working in the mail order department. Never stops! But it can only grow through about sixteen components: i.e. Schmeichel, Walsh, Parker, Irwin, etc. And this club is full of heroes. We're great at building up heroes for supporters. Build 'em up and they come back as a legend. Sparky is a legend. This club is probably very vulnerable to that kind of supporter participation, supporter mania. Ryan has such a photogenic face that you can understand how easy it is to sell photographs upon photographs and posters upon posters. And it's not been without problems. His agent's not been happy about a lot of things, Ryan's not been happy, his mother's not been happy about a lot of things. The club has to be sensitive about how he's going to be used. They just forget he's only 21. And it's not right. You shouldn't over-expose the boy at that age. I think there have been a few lessons learned in the past year with Ryan Giggs. The freelance photographers are making a fortune out of the kid and we can't do a thing about it. Or I pick up a magazine and read an article about Ryan Giggs.

"What's this? When did you do this interview?" I ask him.

"I've not done any interview," he says.

They take a bit off one magazine and other bits off papers and put the whole story together. They've got the photographs there so where did they get them? Where do they get all the photographs? The guy who did his book always swears that somebody made a killing out there because the photographs are everywhere. So who gets them? If I come back to this world, I'll come back as a photographer I think.

I say sometimes to Brian Kidd: "Who could you get in to do the job here now, the way it is now?" What would their first opinion be if they walked in this place and saw all that goes on here – the autographs, the posters, the balls? Every Thursday they have to sign 40-50 balls. Every day there are queues of young bairns stood with autograph books, photographs, posters, everything. And if a new manager walked in he'd chase them all out. But you have to understand the club. You have to understand that commitment to the support because that support waited 26 years for anything worth talking about. And that loyalty is worth rewarding. The horrible thing about signing autographs is that it's hard to be personal when you sign so many. You don't even know who you're signing for because your head is down signing. You can only put a scribble because you're trying to get them all done very quickly. The signatures are all scribbled or fudged because somebody shoves you as you are writing and somebody you've just signed for tramps on your shoe. You come away and you've got ink all over your hands. But you can't do without it. You must have that.

But Kiddo and I often say, "I wonder what they would do if a manager came in here for the first time?" People say, "How do you manage to cope with it all?" I've been here eight years and I think you just get an immunity to it. You just become woven into the fabric of the club, and all these things become peripheral because you are managing the biggest club in the game and you know that every game you go to is going to be a full house, and you know you're watching good football.

I was a supporter too. I used to stand outside Ibrox and wait for autographs. I always remember it was a big game, Rangers and Clyde, three or four players sent off, a real battle and Sammy Cox, one of my heroes, was standing there, and I think it was his brother he was talking to and he swore. And I went home and said, "Dad! Sammy Cox swore, I heard him swearing."

And my dad said, "You're joking. Terrible."

I couldn't believe it. I was only about seven. Round our road I was telling everyone that I heard Sammy Cox swearing. I have been a supporter all my life, and I don't think you ever lose that. I can go to a game of football and I'll take sides. I always go for the underdog. Ironic – because that's why everybody hates United. Everybody's the underdog against us.

Friday 23 December

The pitches were still frozen, so we put on the heating at Old Trafford and it turned out it wasn't working. So we were restricted to two corners of the pitch where the heating got through. We had to have a limited session. Kiddo gave them a bit of running in the confined space – which was adequate – but no more than that.

I'm going to need the strong ones who can handle it down at Chelsea. I know what it's like there. So I'd better just stick Keane in near the back. I probably won't play Andrei there, he's not at his best.

There's been a lot in the papers this week again about "sleaze" in football, and particularly about the accusations that George Graham took money for buying John Jensen and another Scandinavian player. Now there are queries about all the Scandinavian players who have come over here. Some people are inferring that £25,000 had found it's way back to someone in United on the Schmeichel deal. I said to the chairman, "You need to kill that one." It was for a tour in Sweden. I didn't even know we were going! But they always bring United's name into it. It was the same a few years ago when they were talking about schoolboys. We were as clean as a whistle. We don't give schoolboys a penny.

With George it is a different league. It's a lot of money being talked about. And people will be wondering whether he is buying a player because he's making money or because the player is good.

I've watched a lot of Scandinavian players who were with Rune Hauge, the Norwegian agent who has been involved in the George Graham allegations. Rune has a good knowledge of the game. He was a coach at Nuremburg. And everybody got to know him because he's a good opinion of players and was sending us dossiers on every player in Scandinavia. When I was looking at Patrick Andersson, Bobby Charlton and I went across to Hauge, and he met us and took us to the game. I didn't think that Patrick Andersson was what I was looking for and it would never enter my mind to buy a player who I didn't think was good enough.

We always involve Maurice Watkins, who is the club solicitor, in any transfers. When we bought Peter Schmeichel, the chairman and Maurice Watkins went across to Denmark, and Brondby wouldn't let Rune Hauge in the room.

Maurice was always at our side because you need him with foreign players. They always want to talk "nett". Maurice says, "Sorry, we can't do nett. It's got to be gross and taxable. It's very complicated now with foreign players, because they get all these things in other countries. In Portugal, apparently, they can deal in net value, and in Italy they always talk the net figures.

I've never seen a deal done as quickly as Eric Cantona's. We met at a hotel in Manchester. He came with Jean-Jacques Bertrand from the PFA in France. So we had a cup of tea there, and Jean-Jacques went to the table with the chairman. The chairman got his calculator out and said, "We'll do that." Eric and I were just having a cup of tea. Eric doesn't speak much English, and I was practising my French.

And the chairman said, "Right, that's that, can we shake on that?"

Jean-Jacques said, "Yes!"

"Eric, you've haven't told Eric," I said.

And Jean-Jacques never even asked Eric if he was happy with it. Eric always trusts him to do the deal. But that must have all been done in half an hour at the most, because I'd left Peter Reid and Bob Cass and Joe Melling at a lunch. It was before the second derby game against City. I said: "I need to go, I'll be back in about two hours, if you're still here, fine. Have a good lunch." So I went down there, signed it, and took Jean-Jacques to the airport. When we were at the airport my secretary phoned and said, "I've got Joe Melling on the phone. Have you stolen his recorder?"

I had it, I took it as I went away. He was looking for it all over the hotel. Cassy said, "That bugger Ferguson's stolen it".

I said, "Tell him I'm coming back and we'll look for it when I come in."

And I came in and they were still sitting there.

"Where were you?" Cass asked.

"I had a bit of a meeting," I said.

"How did your meeting go?"

"Fantastic, brilliant. In fact one of the best bits of business I've done I think, for a long, long time."

"You've not been buying, have you?" asked Cass. We were sitting smoking a few cigars.

"Yeh, I bought Eric Cantona today."

"Bugger off," Peter Reid said, "Bugger off!"

"Honestly, I bought Eric."

"Oh bugger off, do me a favour, wait until next Saturday."

"I've already waited two weeks," I said.

That was quick. Andrei was a very difficult one because he didn't speak English. There was a Russian there and a German, and the German had a Swiss guy who spoke English. That took two or three days. On different days there was the Chairman, Maurice and myself. The Chairman went out to Frankfurt and started the thing going. Then they had to bring him over here and Maurice came in and the interpreter. And we had to get George Scanlon.

Saturday 24 December

The grounds were still frozen, so we went back into the gym, and had a game of head-tennis.

Sunday 25 December

The players came in at tea time. Old Trafford was OK, and we did a wee session, had a bit of box, a bit of finishing practice, and then we travelled down to London.

At least with it being Christmas day, the roads were clear. We did it in three hours. We got to the hotel, had a sandwich and went to bed – we've a 12 midday kick off tomorrow.

Monday 26 December

Chelsea 2 United 3

The midday kick off is the hardest to prepare for. We've got a few players who don't eat breakfast – Schmeichel, Bruce, Cantona and McClair do, Ince and Giggs don't – and they would normally just have the pre-game lunch. We put out a breakfast buffet – cereals and yoghurts, poached eggs, scrambled eggs, beans and some spaghetti – and kept it as basic as that. For a normal match there is usually fish, chicken, spaghetti, soup, potatoes, beans, a selection of things to give them the carbohydrates and protein they need for a match.

And yet, despite having had a poor week's preparation, and a difficult pre-match, we probably played our best 45 minutes of football for some weeks in the first half. The passing was magnificent.

I said to them, "It's a tight pitch, so make early passes, don't let them get to you, don't have a congested game. If there are clashes all the time, and it's up in the air, get the ball down and pass it early."

It was 1-0 at half-time, and I was saying to myself, 'There's still a job to do, because it should have been two or three.' And we got an early goal after the interval, and then we just got careless. You could see them thinking, 'That's it, this game's done, we've won this.' I think it may be because of the number of games they have to play which are of cup tie intensity. Everybody wants to beat them, so when they get into a winning position they tend to cruise, to take the foot off the pedal.

And you can understand it, but it can cost you. It nearly did so today. Chelsea got back to 2-2, although we went straight up and got the winner.

Roy Keane has been playing marvellously. He made a great run for a goal at QPR and again today for our second goal. Neville played the ball up for Cantona. You could see Keane saying, 'There's a space, there's Cantona, I'm off.' And he was off like a missile. Cantona just touched it, and he was away. Such power. Anyone who even half attempts to get in his road is going to be steam-rollered. He flew by them all, and Sinclair ended up bringing him down. A marvellous run.

It's timing. We coach our teams, and you can coach a lot of things in the game, but there are some things you can't coach. It's a point I used to make about Bryan Robson. You can coach third man runs until your eyes come out of your head, but unless a player has a sense of timing then it will never work.

People used to ask what Bryan's greatest asset was. I always said, "Timing." I know he had this fantastic courage and presence and all the rest of it, but his timing was his greatest attribute. When two players went up to head the ball, and it was dropping, Robbo was always there first. When the ball came into that penalty box, Robbo was always there. He'd come flying in late, or sometimes he'd come in early, but his timing was incredible. Just being there at the right time. And Keane's got that.

McClair's got it too. He has good timing on his runs. It's a wonderful asset, and it's very difficult to coach. The player has to be born with it.

The first goal was a good one too. It was a terrific ball from McClair in behind them. Ryan delivered a good cross and Sparky finished well. We talked about getting in behind Chelsea before the game and it is always pleasing to see something that we've talked about work. They play offside and push up, so you've got to get players in deep positions to run all the time. We said that we must get people running by Eric and Sparky in this game, and hitting the spaces, which we did well in the first half.

We might have been a wee bit lucky with the third goal because the ball broke for Choccy, but he finished it well and I think we deserved to win.

The referee had a great game in the first half. At Chelsea it can be difficult, because the crowd are right on top of you, but he wasn't swayed, he got his decisions right. We went 2-0 up and you could almost see him thinking: 'Oh, this is boring, let's make a drama out of it.' He ended up booking five players and there wasn't a bad tackle in sight! He booked Eric because the crowd wanted him booked. Some referees are so easily influenced by crowds at some grounds – Leeds, Chelsea, West Ham and Liverpool. We had four players booked for nothing

Incey ended up with a hamstring. I wondered whether the preparation for the game was wrong – if we should have taken them for a walk last night when we got to London. I don't know, but a walk wouldn't have done him any harm after a three-hour journey.

Our diligent secretary, Ken Merrett, informs me that us playing at Chelsea on Boxing Day was his idea – he thought that doing it in two-and-three-quarter hours instead of four was a bright idea. He said it would be Southampton at Christmas next year!

Venue: Stamford Bridge	*Att:* 31,161			
Chelsea		*goals*	**Manchester United**	*goals*
1	Dmitri Kharine		13 Gary Walsh	
2	Steve Clarke		16 Roy Keane	
5	Erland Johnsen		6 Gary Pallister	
6	Frank Sinclair		4 Steve Bruce	
15	Andy Myers		3 Denis Irwin	
12	Craig Burley		19 Nicky Butt	
20	Glenn Hoddle		9 Brian McClair	78
17	Nigel Spackman		8 Paul Ince	
10	Gavin Peacock		11 Ryan Giggs	
7	John Spencer	58	10 Mark Hughes	21
8	Paul Furlong		7 Eric Cantona	46
Substitutes				
9	Mark Stein (54 mins for 12)		14 Andrei Kanchelskis (76 mins for 19)	
13	Kevin Hitchcock		25 Kevin Pilkington	
18	Eddie Newton (73 mins for 20)	77	27 Gary Neville (45 mins for 8)	

Tuesday 27 December

We just had the players in to loosen off. I had to think about whether to freshen things up by making changes for tomorrow. It's something you always think about when you've got games on top of one another like this. Andrei will be back, but he is still suffering a wee bit with his groin injury.

Wednesday 28 December

Manchester United 1 Leicester City 1

You've got to give Leicester credit. Since Mark McGhee arrived there's been a resurgence in spirit and determination. They kept the ball well and passed it really well at times.

I played Andrei on the left, partly because I thought it might help his groin, partly because they were unbalanced down the right because of their formation. They didn't have tremendous cover on that side. We took our time to exploit it, but at least Pallister and Irwin got forward a bit in the second half. They got to the by-line a few times and I thought it might win us the game.

I took Sparky off, partly because I was worried that he was going to get sent off after being booked. It was disappointing the way their players all sprinted to the referee, but Sparky wasn't playing well anyway. I'm worried about him. I think the contract negotiations are affecting him. He is a very insecure person. He is either in heaven or right down in the toils – there's no middle of the road with him.

We'll have to find a solution, because at 31 I can't play him four times in seven days. We are going to have to rest him sometime.

Dennis Roach, Sparky's agent, had a meeting with the chairman just before Christmas, and the chairman said to me that it looks as if they are coming round to the idea that a one-year contract is sensible for the club and the player. I certainly hope he accepts it. It will give me a chance to change things round a bit. Also, another year's contract will take Mark to 32 years and eight months, which is not bad. Not many strikers are still in the top flight at that age. Peter Beardsley is, but he isn't an out-and-out striker anyway, he drops into the hole behind the front man. Ian Rush is 31 and he is beginning to show signs of waning; Dean Saunders has reached that age too and hasn't been in the Villa side recently.

Mark has been at the sharp end of the game for more than a decade now and I have to be sure how long he can go on. You need a tremendous amount of energy to be able to play here all the time, and when players get to 30 you have to look closely at them. Last year we played 63 games; this year we'll be approaching that – we've played 21 Premiership games and six European matches already and there's the FA Cup to come. It's a lot of football year after year after year.

The problem at this club is that they have great heroes and the supporters are very reluctant to accept that their hero has died or gone away. But my job is to maintain a high level of success.

Mark has been a fabulous player for United. He embodies a sort of British warrior. Anybody who sees himself as a centre forward of the old type should come and watch Mark Hughes. He has always scored marvellous goals, so you can understand why he is such a hero. The other thing about Mark is that, no matter who you are playing, he always gives a hundred per cent.

Mark's situation has probably fuelled a lot more of the stories that keep cropping up about us signing Collymore. They aren't coming from here and I don't think they are coming from Forest, either. I don't know whether he is for sale or not – the last time I enquired, he wasn't. Maybe they want to sell him now because there are rumours that they need the money. We'll have to wait and see. But in the game against us, he was the difference between the sides. He beat us – nobody else did. They sat in there wasting time all day, and whenever they needed him he was there to give them a breather or to keep us on tenterhooks.

There are one or two good strikers around at the moment. I like Les Ferdinand and Andy Cole too. Malcolm Allison was reported as saying that Cole isn't good enough, but I don't agree. He makes great little runs in the penalty box. I think he is European material.

If you look at the British strikers who have gone to Italy, the only one to have been a real success was John Charles. Hitchens did all right, but the great players – Greaves, Law, Rush – none of them did it. I think Cole is the one British player who could do well in Europe, though. He could succeed in Italy because he makes great runs across the face of people and he is so quick. That will always give him a chance to get a shot in. But you never know, because Italian football is completely different from British football.

Venue: Old Trafford *Att:* 43,789

Manchester United	*goals*	**Leicester City**	*goals*
13 Gary Walsh		33 Kevin Poole	
27 Gary Neville		4 Jimmy Willis	
6 Gary Pallister		2 Simon Grayson	
4 Steve Bruce		19 Colin Hill	
3 Denis Irwin		3 Mike Whitlow	65
14 Andrei Kanchelskis	61	6 Steve Agnew	
9 Brian McClair		17 Steve Thompson	
16 Roy Keane		21 Lee Philpott	
11 Ryan Giggs		10 Mark Draper	
10 Mark Hughes		20 David Oldfield	
7 Eric Cantona		9 Iwan Roberts	
Substitutes			
12 David May		8 M Blake	
25 Kevin Pilkington		1 Gavin Ward	
24 Paul Scholes		18 David Lowe	

Thursday 29 December

We just had the players in for massages today. It is very difficult to try and organise the usual routine over the Christmas period. Our masseur will come in again a week tomorrow. We're playing on Saturday, but it is not entirely fair to get him in on Sunday, which is New Year's Day. Then we play again on Tuesday, but after that the players are having two days off because there isn't another match until the following Monday. We will have them back in again a week tomorrow for a massage and to loosen off.

At this stage, getting the training right is crucial. Kiddo and I spend a bit of time on it. Kiddo is excellent at judging what is needed. He knows from his own experience how much to give them, when to rest them. That is invaluable. Kiddo has to set a programme, then we chat about it. You don't overdo it, but it is important that they loosen off, that they get their stretches, and that they get their massages at the right time. Plus, of course, their wee tinkle on the ball, which we'll do tomorrow.

I sat down with Gary Walsh and looked at the video of the game against Leicester. He had come in for a bit of criticism, but the video showed that Gary Neville had him with his knee as Walshy came out, so it wasn't entirely his fault. But there was no doubt he was to blame for the Chelsea goal.

Friday 30 December

Today we did boxes. A loosen up, boxes and nothing more.

Denis Irwin wasn't in today. His wife lost their baby. It has been touch and go for a few days and I asked him coming back on the bus if he wanted to play on Wednesday. He said it was OK and he did want to play, but he was obviously feeling it a bit after the game. He phoned this morning to tell me the sad news. Losing a baby is traumatic, and they are a very close family. We will not consider him for tomorrow.

Andrei is still feeling his groin. Ryan is also feeling a bit tentative, so they both need watching. I think Ryan's is tiredness after playing twice in three days so soon after coming back.

The news about my CBE was released to the press today, so it was the topic in my regular Friday press conference. I said that the award is for everyone at Manchester United and for my family, who have to put up with so much because of the demands of the job. It's a nice birthday present.

Saturday 31 December

Southampton 2 United 2

We are getting caught up in these cup ties, and the referees are not coping. We had some silly bookings today, just because the crowd reacted to a tackle, nothing more.

It is affecting us, too. This was another game we should have won – snatched a draw from the jaws of victory, as they say. We made hard work of it. We aren't taking our chances, which is a recurring problem, so we aren't winning games we should and that could cost us dear at the end of the season.

Alan Ball's sides are always passionate. He cares, and he communicates it. Watching him on the bench was riveting entertainment.

I asked Kiddo at one stage: "Did we get that carried away?"

Bally was wearing this bonnet and, at one stage, he snatched it off and threw it down in disgust, shouting: "That's the most stupid bit of football

I've ever seen in my life." I said to him at the end: "Thanks for the entertainment."

We flew back from Southampton and arrived back in Manchester by 7.30pm, so we were able to enjoy our New Year's Eve.

Venue: The Dell	*Att:* 15,204		
Southampton	*goals*	**Manchester United**	*goals*
1 Bruce Grobbelaar		13 Gary Walsh	
2 Jeff Kenna		27 Gary Neville	
3 Francis Benali		6 Gary Pallister	78
4 Jim Magilton	44	4 Steve Bruce	
6 Ken Monkou		12 David May	
7 Matthew Le Tissier		19 Nicky Butt	51
9 Iain Dowie		9 Brian McClair	
18 David Hughes	74	16 Roy Keane	
21 Tommy Widdrington		11 Ryan Giggs	
24 Ronnie Ekelund		10 Mark Hughes	
15 Jason Dodd		7 Eric Cantona	
Substitutes			
8 Craig Maskell		24 Paul Scholes	
13 Dave Beasant		25 Kevin Pilkington	
12 Neil Heaney (66 mins for 24)		31 Keith Gillespie (79 mins for 9)	

Sunday 1 January

We had them in for a loosen-off. A quiet day with not too many hangovers.

Monday 2 January

Another quiet day. Boxes.

Tuesday 3 January

United 2 Coventry 0

We started the new year with a win. It was all a bit low key, but probably the game we wanted after the battles of the past couple of weeks. Coventry had a weak side and although Dion battled well, they didn't threaten us much – certainly not once we scored. Then they had the boy Pressley sent off. He's a young Scottish centre half they bought from Rangers, and he was a bit impulsive and kept diving in.

Venue: Old Trafford	*Att:* 43,789		
Manchester United	*goals*	**Coventry City**	*goals*
13 Gary Walsh		1 Steve Ogrizovic	
27 Gary Neville		17 Ally Pickering	
4 Steve Bruce		6 Steve Pressley	
6 Gary Pallister		3 Steve Morgan	
3 Denis Irwin		16 Paul Williams	
31 Keith Gillespie		7 Sean Flynn	
16 Roy Keane		25 Mike Marsh	
19 Nicky Butt		15 Paul Cook	
7 Eric Cantona	49	14 Leigh Jenkinson	
24 Paul Scholes	29	8 Roy Wegerle	
Substitutes			
9 Brian McClair (63 mins for 16)		24 Cobi Jones (82 mins for 7)	
25 Kevin Pilkington		13 Jonathan Gould	
12 David May		4 Julian Darby (53 mins for 8)	

7
Andy Arrives

Wednesday 4 January

Kiddo and I had a talk and decided that we really have to get another striker because we've been missing too many points recently. We've been discussing it for some weeks, but the games with Southampton and Leicester decided me. The team needs freshening up, we need an injection, a lift. The lads have worked hard for three years now, they've seen us let Dion, McKee and Whitworth go and they deserve to see that we are ambitious. The only signing we have made was David May, who cost us £1.2 million (we'd got £2.5 million for Dion and the two young lads who went up North). We are drawing games that we should be winning.

We've discussed who we should go for. Unfortunately QPR won't sell Ferdinand until the end of the season and we need someone right now. There are indications that Forest might let Collymore go, but the most interesting thing was that Kevin Keegan phoned to ask about Keith Gillespie. I said no, but then asked about Andy Cole in passing, and he didn't dismiss it like he had earlier in the season. I detected just a little uncertainty about Cole so I told Kiddo and we agreed to should target him.

Thursday 5 January

Joe Royle phoned today to ask about Sparky.

"We're not in a position to let anyone go," I said. "The only problem is how Mark would react if we bought a striker. But we are trying to get someone in at the moment."

"Who is it?" he said. "Cole?"

"No, why Cole? Why do you say Cole?"

"Oh," he said, "I heard there's a bit of unrest."

Friday 6 January

We might be signing a striker – not Collymore, as all the press have been saying for weeks, but Andy Cole. I can hardly believe it.

I tried to get hold of Frank Clark today because I was led to believe that they might be prepared to do business for Collymore. I phoned three times but he didn't call back. Then, about 3pm, Alan Hill phoned. He said: "Frank's not well, he's off home to his digs for a rest. He'll phone you Monday or Tuesday."

'Oh, here we go,' I said to myself. 'They're going to mess us about.'

I've always a feeling that Nottingham Forest want to stitch us up, I don't know why. My dealings with Cloughie were always fraught with uncertainty. The only way to get a player from Forest is when he's out of contract, as we did with Webb and, in a way, with Keane, who had it written into his contract that he could leave if they were relegated.

So I thought, 'I wonder if Kevin would sell me Cole before I go any further down the line on this one. After what Joe said, I wonder if it is worth another crack. I'll try and see if I can get Cole.'

I phoned Kevin and said: "I may be being a bit over-adventurous here, but I'm in the process of buying a striker. I just want to check that there definitely is no way that you'd sell Andy Cole to me."

He said: "You've really handed me a beauty there, Alex. I wouldn't say there's no chance, but we'd really need to think about it. If you're serious, I don't know how I would respond. I sometimes feel the club isn't getting to the place I want."

"Well, have a think about it and come back to me," I said.

He rang back at about 4pm and said: "We could be interested in a deal, but it would need to involve Keith Gillespie. I've spoken to you before about Gillespie and you wouldn't sell. If that was a possibility, I'd look at the Cole thing more seriously." I knew that he rated Gillespie highly.

"Well, that's something I'd need to think about myself," I said.

So I went away to think about it with Kiddo.

"You've got to do it," he said. "If that's the only way you're going to get the deal done. You've got to let Gillespie go."

There were two factors that made me go for it: one, the fact Keith's Irish; and two, he's not in my first team every week at the moment because of Kanchelskis. I've got Kanchelskis, Beckham and I've got a young boy, Cooke, coming through, who's a wide-right player in the youth team and who looks excellent. I've got two left-sided players, Giggs and Sharpe, and I've got young Davies. So my balance in the squad is adequate on the right hand side. I thought about it and then phoned Kevin back.

We began discussing the price and Kevin said: "You know what the market is. If you go for Ferdinand, Collymore, or anyone of that calibre, it's going to cost you £6 million."

"That's a lot of money," I said.

"Cole is gold," he replied. "Sutton cost £5 million and he never scored the goals that Cole does."

He was going on those lines, so I offered him £5 million plus Gillespie. He turned it down. Then I offered £5.5 million and he said: "No, I need a bit more."

Finally, we agreed on £6 million, and he said: "I need a bit of time to try and sign a player, so we'll have to keep it on hold."

Now the ball is in his court.

Scholesy was coughing and spluttering right through the reserve game on Wednesday. Afterwards, I told him to go home to bed and to stay there all the following day. Today Butty was feeling like that, too.

I hoped Peter Schmeichel would be ready to play in the A-team game tomorrow, but after training this morning he said he needed more training.

Saturday 7 January

Two days before a cup tie and we've got a flu epidemic. We had to send four home today: Walsh; Pallister; Hughes; and McClair. Butty was still a bit hangdog and Scholesy was still coughing and spluttering. I think the worst is over for those two, though.

I phoned Kevin again. It was in the papers this morning that they had been turned down for Armstrong, so now I know who it was they were after. But Kevin still said he needed a bit more time. Newcastle are playing Blackburn tomorrow.

I said: "Are you going to cup tie Cole?"

He said: "Oh aye, I'm not interested in anything other than doing my job, and I'm sure that you aren't going to drop the deal just because he's cup tied."

"Well, what about Gillespie," I said.

"It's the same thing. I can't ask you not to cup tie him."

Sunday 8 January

The flu thing is getting to be a worry. Hughes and McClair were a bit better and came in. Pallister and Walsh were still off but they'd been joined by May, Giggs and Gillespie.

I was worried about Walshy, which made me think about using Peter Schmeichel, because the big man's presence would be a great asset at Sheffield. He had turned down the A-team game because he said he needed to train, and yesterday he trained like mad. Today he was really stiff as a result. We had to massage him all day.

I went up to Newcastle to watch their match with Blackburn, so on the way up Kiddo was keeping me informed. I spoke to Schmeichel on the phone and had to turn it on.

"Don't you worry, Peter. If I play you tomorrow, don't worry about not being ready. All I'm interested in is that you've got experience and presence and there is no-one better than you in a situation like this."

"Okay, okay", he said. "As long as you know that I'm not one hundred per cent."

"We know you're not a hundred per cent, you never have been, so why worry?" I said, "there's always something up, mental or physical."

"You're cheeky!" he said in that big booming voice. "You're so cheeky."

I humoured him the right way. It was just a matter of patter. I treated it lightly, as if it was just another game. He wanted to play, but needed somebody to reassure him that it would be alright.

I took Les Kershaw up with me and told him about Cole. He was excited. "Are you kidding? You're certain to win the league if you get him," he said.

So far, I've only told the Brian Kidd and the chairman – and now Les. The other person who knows is my son Jason. He was in my car when I had a call from Kevin on Friday. He works for *Sky*, so I said: "Not a word." But later I phoned Darren, who said: "What's this about Cole?"

"Did that so-and-so Jason tell you?"

"Aye."

The twins tell each other everything.

There was no word from Newcastle while I was up there. It was strange, because they looked after me well. I had a lovely lunch, at which I talked to Sir John Hall, their chairman, and it was obvious that he didn't know about the transfer.

Monday 9 January

Sheffield United 0 Manchester United 2

We had a ring round on Sunday night and again first thing this morning. Brian and I split the calls between us, then we took a roll call. May was out, Walsh was out, Bruce was struggling, Pally was struggling. I sent the doctor round to Pallister this morning. I phoned him at 8.45am and he was sounding really rough. But the doctor phoned and said: "There's no temperature now, I think he's over the worst, but the trouble is he hasn't been out and he's living on tablets. He's been taking eight paracetamols a day and he feels groggy. He needs to get some fresh air. I suggest you take him to Sheffield with you at lunchtime and see how he is."

Giggs was the same and at first Pally was worse. At lunchtime he still wasn't looking too good. I picked a team at that stage and my centre backs were Keane and Casper. I thought: 'Bloody hell, they've got that Jostein Flo who's six-foot ten.' But fortunately Bruce and Pally made it in the end.

Schmeichel came up to me and said: "I wish I'd recorded what you said to me last night."

"Why?"

"Because it was the best grovelling, pleading case I've ever heard in my life."

"What? What do you want me to say? You're playing and that's it!"

In the event, I thought Peter's presence was good. He looked fresh and I had a feeling that he was happy to be back. His throws are marvellous at times. When he gets the ball you see players sprinting to forward positions, because they know he's capable of finding them. That's an unbelievable asset.

At 3.30pm I was having a sleep in my room in the hotel when the phone rang. It was Kevin with his final answer.

"Yes," he said.

"What?" I asked

"Yes. It's on. We'll do the deal!"

"Great. Terrific." It's £6 million plus Gillespie. It's a lot, but I think that it'll be worth it. We want to win the Championship again and we want to be better in Europe. I can't think of a player who would suit our needs better in the penalty box; someone who can operate in the last third of the pitch. Good feet, great turns, really quick. I think we really need him.

So then it was a question of the timetable. Kevin said: "I'm going to come down right away." The whole bunch were coming down: Kevin, Freddie Fletcher, Freddie Shepherd and Sir John Hall, so I thought they definitely meant business.

So I was then left with the problem of whether it was fair to cup tie Keith Gillespie. Cole played for Newcastle yesterday. But as it was a cup tie away from home I'd decided to put Butt on the right anyway, and I wondered whether it was fair to put him on the bench and perhaps deny him a cup medal. I decided it wasn't and left him out.

I spoke to Keith before the game and told him about the deal. I took him into the toilets and told him it was a swap deal, but didn't tell him who the other player was. I said: "Don't say anything now, just think about it, let it seep in, and I'll talk to you after the game. Don't breathe a word. It's important it doesn't get out."

Then the game went on. During the first half I thought we'd got a tough one, I really did. But they lost Charlie Hartfield early on for tangling with Eric and that finished them off. There are some games when ten men can prove a real problem, but I felt that provided we got to half time with a score of 0-0 we could improve. It was so wild and windy, the ball was swirling about everywhere. Sheffield had the same problem in the second half. Because of the wind, they just couldn't get it into the areas to trouble us.

At half time I said: "You're just not stretching them enough. You are passing in the air and you're not keeping the ball. Get that ball on the ground and work your way through them. If you do that, you'll create chances."

But as the second half went on we missed a lot of chances. In a league game you never think it could be catastrophic the way you do in a cup tie. Going into the last ten minutes of a cup tie when the score is 0-0 you say to yourself: 'One mistake and we're out.' It's as final as that. With ten minutes to go we missed a couple of chances: Nicky Butt put one past the goalkeeper as he came out, but just wide of the post; and then Eric put one back across goal and past the post when he should have scored.

I took off Choccy and put on Scholes. Choccy had done well, but I thought a change was needed. We had the wind with us, and I said: "Scholesy, if you get any chance at all, just have a shot."

Scholes was involved in the goal, although not in the way I'd expected – he passed to Giggs who lobbed it in to Sparky. Then Eric got a great goal. A measured lob from thirty yards over the keeper and just under the bar. It was sheer genius. People can talk all day about goals blasted from 35 or 40 yards as "Goal of the Season", but that's power. This was complete precision, awareness, judgement – absolute genius. You saw all the years of practice in that goal, it was fantastic. If anybody other than Eric had scored it, it would have to be goal of the year. Possibly the goal Matt le Tissier scored at Blackburn could beat it because there was fantastic skill in that goal, and if it does, fine, but if Eric's doesn't get in the first three you will know it is because his name is Eric Cantona and he plays for Manchester United.

There were great celebrations in the dressing room after the game, then I went to see the press. Then I took Keith into the toilets again with Brucey and Choccy and I told them what had happened – not that it was Andy Cole, though. Keith told me he was happy about it. I told the other two that I would represent Keith in his talks with Kevin, and the salary I would try to secure for him.

I wasn't getting on the bus with the lads, I was going off to the Hallam Towers hotel with Keith, but when I got alongside the bus, Brucey and Choccy were interrogating Kiddo, trying to find out who we were signing. They said, "It must be Andy Cole."

Kiddo said: "Well, Steve Howey's playing well. It might be him, you never know."

Brucey snapped: "Bugger off!"

Of course, all sorts of rumours were flying around the bus by then. Kiddo told the team I wasn't on the bus because I thought I'd contracted the flu and didn't want to risk spreading it. I was astonished no-one found out, because Newcastle had brought such a large party down.

We contacted Keith's mother to tell her the news. She couldn't understand at first why we were letting him go or why he should move. But I explained that it would give him first-team football, and said: "I'll look after the boy," and in the end she was happy.

Kevin was great. It all went very smoothly in terms of the deal we negotiated for Keith, and we arranged for him to fly to Newcastle the next day.

The next task was to make contact with Andy. Kevin gave me his agent's carphone number, and I finally got hold of him while we were on the way back to Manchester. I finally had a long chat with Andy on the phone at about 2am and arranged for him to come down to Manchester.

I didn't even bother to go home, but went straight to the Manchester hotel we use for meetings, because I thought that if I went home to Wilmslow and then had to come back, I wouldn't have time for any sleep.

Venue: Bramall Lane *Att:* 22,322

	Sheffield United	*goals*		**Manchester United**	*goals*
1	Alan Kelly		1	Peter Schmeichel	
2	Kevin Gage		2	John O'Kane	
3	Brian Gayle		3	Denis Irwin	
4	Roland Nilsen		4	Steve Bruce	
5	Andy Scott		6	Gary Pallister	
6	Paul Rogers		7	Eric Cantona	82
7	Charles Hartfield		16	Roy Keane	
8	Glynn Hodges		19	Nicky Butt	
9	Dane Whitehouse		9	Brian McClair	
10	Carl Veart		10	Mark Hughes	79
11	Nathan Blake		11	Ryan Giggs	
Substitutes					
12	Philip Starbuck (75 mins for 8)		5	Lee Sharpe (54 mins for 2)	
13	William Mercer		13	Kevin Pilkington	
14	Jostein Flo (85 mins for 9)		14	Paul Scholes	

Tuesday 10 January

I didn't sleep anyway, I was too excited. Today we signed Andy Cole. Most of the day was taken up with the transfer, discussing terms with the chairman, doing medicals, and so on, but it was one of those days when you get half a dozen different things demanding your time.

I keep getting phone calls from a film company and the guy who rings me is absolute agony. Eric's doing a big television advertising campaign for a French company called Bic. It's been going on for absolutely ages. They need two days to shoot it and this guy thinks I can say, "Yes, we've got a game, but you can have Eric the day before." Just incredible.

While the transfer was going on, I was also having to think about the youngsters on schoolboy forms – getting Eric Harrison to talk to Brian about their insurance, and which ones we will sign.

There's always a problem with young kids: you've really got to be hard, because they've been here since they were 13 and have built up their hopes. There are four or five who have not progressed quite as well as we thought they would. But because they're local kids, you feel you've got to give them a chance. And if you were to go back five years, say, you'd sign them up immediately, because the standards in playing have risen dramatically during the past few years. So I'll speak to the boys' parents tonight and explain the situation; how we're going to give them a bit more time. We should notify them before the end of January as to what we're doing, but some know they're going to be called up because they're outstanding. Word gets around and it filters through to the parents, so I'll have to give them plenty of consideration.

Andy arrived at about 11am from Newcastle. These negotiations are never easy, but I had nothing to do with it – I just said to the chairman: "On you go." So the meeting was between Martin Edwards, Maurice Watkins and Andy's agent Paul Stretford, who is Kevin Moran's partner.

Meanwhile, Andy and I just sat and had a chat. I told him about our training methods and he was quite impressed. He'd had a call from Incey, who he is quite pally with, and Incey told him everyone was looking forward to having him at the club. Cole said to me: "I hope my agent doesn't get too daft," which made me think it might be a bit tricky. But then added: "I won't let this deal go." So it was obviously going to be alright.

Funnily enough, I saw Paul Stretford at St James's Park on Sunday. He's also Stan Collymore's agent. He asked me whether I'd managed to get hold of Frank Clark.

"No, he never returned my call, they said he wasn't well," I said.

He said: "Well, he was in training on Friday morning."

Of course, I couldn't say anything about this then. Paul had stayed with Andy on Sunday night, drove back to Manchester yesterday morning and then had to turn round and drive back to Newcastle when Kevin phoned him at 5pm.

Yesterday morning Jason said: "Can we do the story?"

I said: "You can't do anything until Andy Cole agrees to join Manchester United. But you'll be the first to know because you've held it since Friday."

Then the story broke in Newcastle, so Jason had to go and tell Vic Wakeling, *Sky*'s head of sport. Vic said: "You can't break your word, you've done the right thing." But Jason said he thought he could get an exclusive interview at 3.15pm, when Andy was having his medical. I thought he deserved that after sitting on the story for two or three days.

The medicals were all fine, although we don't get the results of the scans until tomorrow. When such a huge amount of money is involved you obviously have to have fairly tight medicals. Finally, we had a press conference at Old Trafford about 4.30pm. It was packed. As far as the media was concerned it was a sensation. It isn't every day you spend that kind of money.

We'd set out to buy Collymore and got Cole. Andy is a totally different player to Stan: he operates within the penalty box, whereas Collymore drifts. I think that away from home Collymore's a real threat to anyone, but I think Cole is better at home against packed defences, which we are facing quite a lot now. I think Andy'll be vital to us. He's the best around without doubt.

Everyone was amazed that Cole was leaving Newcastle. He is a Nottingham lad and I think two years in the Northeast eventually gets to you. Newcastle have never been able to keep a big star for long. I think Kevin summed it up last night when we were talking. "Our local derby is Leeds United," he said. "You miss not being in the centre of football."

That may be the answer. At Aberdeen I had to travel two-and-a-half hours down to Glasgow to see the big games, which can really wear you down. You feel shut off, not being right in the hotbed of football. There is fantastic passion up there in the Northeast, but maybe it's just too isolated. And all their stars eventually wander south.

Kevin meets the press every day. I said to him, "That sounds like a film I saw with Laurence Harvey and Frank Sinatra. It's about an American GI who gets caught by the Chinese and tortured. They dripped water very slowly onto his forehead, which sends him round the bend. That's what'll happen to you. You'll end up going mad. Tell them everything they want to know."

My problem now is Mark Hughes and how he handles the signing.

There are one or two clubs which want to talk to him. I'll probably let him do that, because with Andy here it's not going to be the same for him. He is the obvious person to make way for Andy, but after the service he's given us he certainly doesn't deserve to be sitting on the sidelines.

So it is a momentous day in a great career. Yesterday, Sparky scored the goal which took us into the FA Cup fourth round; the next day, Andy is brought in, hopefully to take us through to the next century.

It's entirely up to Mark what he does, but if I keep him there are three things to consider: first, he's not going to be happy and he deserves first-team football. I wonder if he's the right type to play with Cole. You can see Cantona doing what Beardsley does for him now. Or Scholes could play with Cole. I'm looking ahead because Eric will not be here for ever. You never know how long we'll have him. So I've always got to think about alternatives.

The second thing is that, without a doubt, Mark's going to be soured by not being in the team.

Third is the fans. I don't want to have a situation where Andy is trying to settle in and they are screaming for Mark Hughes. It's better that it is a clean break. Mark's 31 and probably has three good years ahead of him in football, but he's Welsh. He has flogged his guts off for this club and he's been a fantastic player, but progress is progress, we can't stop it. It's unfortunate. But for us, this would be a good time to sell.

We have to change the whole structure of our pool of players. With Keith gone, if Mark goes we will have reduced our quota to seven foreign players instead of nine. We can play five foreigners in Europe but in three years' time it's got to be down to three in English football. So I'm starting to prepare the ground for that. Also, with Brian McClair now 31, he'll be phased out in a couple of years' time, although I expect he'll play until he's 36 because he's very fit and looks after himself. I wouldn't want to let Brian go because he's such a versatile player. That leaves me with Kanchelskis, Cantona, Giggs, Keane and Schmeichel. In two years' time Denis Irwin will also reach 31. That'll be the time to look seriously at it all, although at the moment he's a fit wee so-and-so.

Joe Royle rang to enquire about Mark. I told him I would have to talk to the chairman and first to Mark. "As far as I'm concerned, I'm happy to let you talk to the lad," I said. "But obviously we'll need to give it consideration and we'll have to explain it to the player." That I am not looking forward to, but I will call him in tomorrow.

Wednesday 11 January

Andy wasn't in today because he was attending his grandmother's funeral. We got the results of the scans and there were no problems, but a number of players these days have signs of operations or knocks and damage to joints. The only two we've had who were totally clear were Andrei and Cantona, which was interesting because they hadn't been brought up in British football.

When we were contemplating signing Steve Bruce, we sat at a reserve game discussing his knee with the specialist. In the end the chairman came to me in the stand and said: "Well, it's up to you. How much do you want him? There is a risk he could be bothered with his knees in future years."

I said: "Chairman, everybody is a risk. But his playing record is good, he never misses a game." If we had been really strict about the medical record, we wouldn't have taken Brucey and what we would have missed! When you look at the service he has given us, it would have been the biggest mistake ever.

My mind goes back to Asa Harford and his move to Leeds breaking down because he had a hole in the heart. I could never understand that, because a hole in the heart is quite common. Mark, my eldest, had one, and it isn't a serious problem for young people. Asa went on to get about 50 caps for Scotland. So while you've got to be cautious about the x-rays, you've also got to trust the playing record.

You can be unlucky, though. When he was at Arsenal, Viv Anderson missed only three games in four years – and they were suspensions. Then he came to us and got nothing but injuries. When he left us, he was never injured again. It's just the luck of the draw.

Thursday 12 January

Andy's first session – mainly with the reserves. I'd told everyone with flu not to come in, so there weren't many players there. We had to train at Old Trafford because we're in a cold snap and The Cliff was frozen hard.

We did a session with Andy on attacks. It was a good session – all sharp stuff. I think he quite enjoyed it. He said it was different to Newcastle's training.

Eric failed to get the message about the change of venue and, turned up about ten minutes late . When he arrived, he came onto the pitch, went straight across to Andy, shook his hand and then patted him on the head as if to say: "I'll look after you."

Andy said to Kiddo afterwards: "Bloody hell, that Cantona, he's some player. He kept passing the ball to me all the time."

It was as if Eric was welcoming Andy to United. He is a big man,

Cantona. He has been absolutely brilliant in the last six or seven games. He has got the bit between his teeth. Eric is desperate to win this league, absolutely desperate. It would be a record – four championships in a row, one with Leeds, three with us.

There has been a lot of speculation in the press about why Newcastle let Cole go. It's a typical case of modern journalism, with reporters continually searching around for negative answers.

Always assuming we could get them, there were three possible targets for us: Les Ferdinand, Stan Collymore and Andy. Les is 28 or 29, a Londoner who might not settle outside London and get three hamstring injuries a year plus an ankle injury. They wanted £5 million so it's a question mark. Stan gets two hamstrings a year plus an ankle injury. They say he's a bit of a lad off the pitch. So again there is a question mark. Then there's Andy. There's nothing said about him. When we signed Andy, it took everybody unawares. But now that we've signed him we read he's a strange lad, likes to be on his own – all that sort of thing. The only way to judge it is work out what all these negative things add up to. But they don't really add up to anything that stops you scoring a goal.

You have to dismiss all the negative stuff, all the rumour and innuendo. Alan Hansen says we've thrown the league away; John Giles is saying that Newcastle have got the better deal. But, if we win the Premiership, if I then sell Andy for £1 I'll have made a profit, because it will have got us into the Champions League, in the big pool, in a competition that will test us to the full.

That is how I judge myself. If I look at my career, I would say: "What did I do in Europe?" I would have to admit that I have had a disappointing record in the European Cup, both at Aberdeen and here, so I've got to stretch myself, the players and the club to the maximum by going into the European Cup again. We threw away our chance of going further this time. When you look at our home form and our away form, they are like night and day. But with Andy we will get goals, and we will just have to take a wee bit more care away from home.

The only speculation in the press that troubles me is about Mark Hughes' future. He isn't as confident as people might think from seeing him on the field, so I brought him in for a chat.

I said: "I know all the speculation and I can't avoid it, that's out of my hands. All I can control is what I do for the club. And I could not let that transfer go."

He asked me what would happen to him now.

I said: "What do you want? We're in your hands. The service you've given us deserves that consideration. I don't want you sitting in the stand, kicking your heels and turning sour. I don't want a situation like last year's, when I brought Roy Keane in. I had to tell Brian McClair, who I thought was one of our best players the previous season and was at the prime of his life, that I was bringing in a replacement for him. But I just could not let Keane go."

"I know," he said.

"Brian only played six games last season, which made him very unhappy. Now he's back and he's doing really well for us. These things happen, but it's how you handle yourself that matters."

Joe Royle has been on to me wanting Mark, and there is no doubt that Dennis Roach has been working hard on Mark's behalf. I'm sure he will have spoken to Joe.

So I said: "What do we do? We would let you go for £2.5 million."

"That's not very fair to me."

"In what way?"

"How am I going to get a deal?"

I said: "Bloody hell, Mark. They'll give you what you are looking for. What they'll pay us is what they can afford to pay. If they can't match what we want, then the deal won't happen. What I'm saying is that we are not interested in selling you, but in the situation as it is, I don't want you feeling that we aren't recognising your contribution to the club. You've been a fantastic player here. We've got the FA Cup – which Andy is cup tied for – and we've got a lot of big games coming up that you'll play in. France have got games on Saturdays, so Eric won't be here. You can still be a great player for this club."

And so it was left that we will see what happens. We don't want him feeling that we are saying: "Bye, sit in the stand for the rest of your life," but my own feelings are that a transfer might be the best thing for him.

They are unfortunate, these things, but what do you do? People were writing to the chairman and to myself saying: "Give him a three-year contract, give him what he wants." But it's just not as simple as that. You can't just give great players, who have been first team players all their life a three-year contract, knowing that they will just sit in the stand.

I always remember Bryan Robson, aged 37, raging at not playing in a game. He handled it well, but he was not happy. You could see that stubbornness that comes across Robbo, that defiant streak in his face. I said: "It's not easy for me, Bryan, I'm not enjoying doing this. You'll play in plenty of games for us, but obviously you want to play in the big ones and I've got to pick what I think is the best team. You'd do the same if you were in my position." Although he didn't agree, he handled it well, but not everyone can handle it well. Bryan was 37, but Mark's only 31 – a completely different kettle of fish.

Mark could play three years at another club quite easily. But could he accept a different role for us when he's always played on a Saturday? And he's a big lad. If he doesn't play every week, he could "go" quite quickly. I don't know when he last played in a reserve game. He's not played one in my time, so you're talking ten years, at least. Imagine asking him to play at Bury on a Thursday night. How would he feel? People don't understand that. They don't think about when a player gets to the point where he is told he's playing in the reserves at Prenton Park, for example, and has to travel with the young boys, half of whom he doesn't know. How does he feel sitting on that bus?

That is why I think that if another club comes in, it may be better for Mark to go. At the end of the day, we've had our money's worth out of him – and he's had his money's worth out of us. He had a great testimonial, has been paid a lot of money and is set for life. He never needs to work again. So we've not disgraced ourselves in any way.

When it comes to things like that, my job can be pretty horrible. Some people say it's no way to treat a loyal servant, but what else can I do?

After training we went down to Charlton for the FA Youth Cup tie. After that I took Brian Kidd, Les Kershaw, and Jim Ryan into London for a meal. It was a smashing day, a wee break from it all.

I love going to watch reserve or youth teams. I find it very relaxing. I'm able to just look at them objectively and say, "Right, he'll be a United player." that is a pre-requisite at our club. You must want the ball. Others you look at and think they're going to struggle. It's all down to being able to play, wanting to play, having the bottle to play, wanting the ball all the time.

I always feel there is an anxiety about United youth teams. They want to do well in the FA Youth Cup. They won it the first five times, so that cup's always had some significance for the young lads.

This time they played a little apprehensively. At half time I said to Kiddo: "Bloody hell, they're just a bundle of nerves."

Eric Harrison, our coach, laid into them at half time and said: "Look, we're not interested in whether you win this or not. We're interested in whether you're good enough to play for the club. We want to see that you have real belief in yourself and the presence to wear a United jersey. Not for this team – for the first team. But in the first half you did yourselves no justice whatsoever."

God, the second half was unbelievable, a fabulous performance. We brought on a young boy, Curtis, a School of Excellence boy. He came on as right back and did brilliantly. He's told everybody he's a United player. He had listened to Eric Harrison and said: "Give me the ball, I'll show you how to play." We put Philip Neville at left back and he just transformed the game.

I enjoyed it, and there was a good crowd – they said 4,000 but it looked more. They used to have about 30,000 on the big hill, but now they've built a new stand on it, which I think holds 7,500. They've got a bit of work to do on the main stand, but it'll be really smart when it's finished.

There's a little prefabricated hospitality suite, which houses a fantastic photograph of Charlton coming home through the streets when they won the Cup in 1947. All the little kids are chasing after the team bus on their bikes and running through the streets. The housewives are all standing at their doors watching the procession go by. On top of the bus are Don Welch and Sam Bartram with the Cup. It seems very spontaneous, as if they weren't really prepared for winning.

Friday January 13

We did a bit of work with Andy, Paul Ince and the ones who had just returned after injury. It was amazing how the young ones were all standing off Andy Cole, making sure they didn't get alongside him because of his pace. The young ones are thinking about it.

There has been a lot of ludicrous speculation about Andy's salary. One paper suggested he was earning £24,000 a week. It is ridiculous that editors allow such stupidly inflated figures to be published. Of course, if you come out and deny it, it only serves to give them another story. We have a ceiling salary and there are about eight players on it.

I think the lads know how stupid these stories are, because they've all negotiated in the same way and found the chairman reluctant to go above the ceiling. Incey tried hard for a while, as did Schmeichel but, at the end of the day, they know he won't budge.

The other factor is that maybe Newcastle United don't pay as big a basic as we do, although their bonuses are enormous which redresses the balance.

Our top wage is not bad. In fact, I wish I was on it myself. If the top players maintain their success at the club, over the next five years they will be millionaires, which is pretty good for a five-year span. And they're not even halfway through their lives. Some people can work all their life and not have a penny. Even successful people work all their life and have to live on their pension at the end of it. We are not unfair to the players, but they deserve it. They're pulling 43,000 people into the ground.

Then there's all the outside business of the club: the commercial ventures, the book deals and all the other bits and pieces. They have the players' pool which earns them a lot of money; last year they made a record which sold really well.

They do all right. Take Darren, for example. The season they won the league, Darren played in seventeen games, got injured in November and didn't get back into the game until the February. Then he left to go to Wolves. Choccy sent him a cheque for two-and-a-half grand, and he was only really one of the younger pool members. It was very good of Choccy and Darren appreciated it.

Kevin has been under pressure since selling Andy. We agreed when we did the transfer that Andy and Keith wouldn't play on Sunday, but we decided today that Andy shouldn't go to the game either.

Saturday 14 January

I watched the youth team in the morning and we travelled up to Newcastle this evening. We're staying at Lyndon Hall in Morpeth, a very well kept family hotel. It's a very peaceful place.

I called Kevin to see if he was alright. Then I phoned Freddy Fletcher to see how things were. "We'll get over it, it's not a problem," he said.

I thought Kevin has handled the transfer very well. He's got a marvellous way with the media – he's an open book.

I remember once at Aberdeen we had all the kids in for coaching during the school holidays. And we were promoting a youth a tournament at Pittodrie involving West Ham, Southampton and Man United. Kevin, Phil Parkes of West Ham and Mick Brown, Ron's assistant at Man United, came up to promote the tournament. We had a promotion day.

So I said to the kids in the morning, once I knew Kevin was actually there:

"Look, if you really do well in your technical exercises or your controls this morning I'll give you a big surprise at lunchtime."

"What is it?" they asked.

"Just have a good day or you'll never know."

So we were all in the dressing room before it started, and I said to Kevin, "How would you like to do us a favour? I've got all these kids from all over Scotland, you know, 13-year-olds and that type of thing. Would you go down and meet them?"

No problem! Brilliant! He went round everyone, signed their autographs, and sat and chatted to them for about 20 minutes.

"I remember when I was a kid and you never got opportunities like this at Scunthorpe," he said. "And you had to fight for everything."

He was excellent. A great pro. He's walking out that door and there are 40 kids in that dressing room who idolise him because of the way he's handled them. Absolutely superb.

Kevin is so positive. He learnt that from Bill Shankly, I'm certain of it. I think if you get influenced by great people, that influence should show through. I'll always remember Scot Symon, Rangers' great manager, signing me. I only had Scot as manager for about six months because I was his last signing and eventually the hounds got him. But he was a man of real substance. He never bowed to the press and he never criticised his players. That's something I've never forgotten. He'd always defend his players to the death, even though he was under pressure. Unfair, but that's the way the modern media is. You could see the strength in his eyes, so nobody messed with him too much.

Everybody's got a Shankly story. When Bobby Charlton lived in Lymm, Liverpool used to stay at the Lymm Hotel when they played United. Bobby's daughter Suzanne, who was only four or five, once said to him: "Daddy, there's somebody prowling about the garden." It was only 8am on a Saturday morning. So Bobby jumped up, looked out and there was Shanks. Bloody Shanks was in the garden! So Bobby put on his dressing gown, went downstairs and opened the door.

"Bobby," he said, "You know there's a bloody game on today." After that Bill used to come in to see him every time Liverpool played United. "I just wondered whether it was to freak me out," Bobby said afterwards.

That's one of Bobby's stories, but I've got my own: I had a chance to sign for Shankly's brother Bob at Hibernian – Rangers wanted me to go on a swap for Colin Stein. I didn't want to, because I loved playing for Rangers, but I was told to at least go and talk to them.

I thought that if they really wanted to sign me why wouldn't Bob come to see me at Rangers? But rather than being ungracious about it I decided to travel to Edinburgh. When I arrived at Bob's flat, his wife said: "I'm going to go out for a wee walk and let you two chat." So she made a cup of tea and disappeared. Bob sat at a wee table with a phone beside him, and I was maybe about three or four yards from him on the settee. We were chatting away when the phone rang. Bob picked up the phone and started talking:

"How are you doing, great to talk to you yesterday… Ach, we were going to play that… play that way… Yeh?… Oh did he?… Aye." Then he put the phone down. Just put the receiver down on the desk. Didn't hang up. So I continued talking to Bob, but I could hear this crackle and a faint voice coming out of the receiver, which was distracting me. I said: "Excuse me, Mr Shankly, but I think there's somebody still on that line."

"Oh, it's Bill," he said. "He rattles on for hours. I just pick it up now and again and say 'aye' then put it back down again." It's absolutely true!

Sunday 15 January

Newcastle United 1 Manchester United 1

Well, we got buried, but I expected it. Before the game I said: "I can't see us having much joy here." I thought a draw was predictable, but the unfortunate thing is that Sparky was injured quite badly.

Sparky was lying down, not moving, for so long that I began to fear the worst. I really thought it was his cruciates. I got down from the directors' box and told them to get him off.

It was clearly his ball when he scored, but the goalie hit him as he came out. It was a clatter, a right good clatter, but it could have been much worse.

As a result, we lost our shape a little. I didn't know whether they were going to play with one up or with two up because they overload in the middle of the pitch. We just couldn't get going at all during the game.

There comes a point when a team commits themselves, when they're prepared to go man for man everywhere on the pitch and surround the ball. Newcastle were like that for most of the game. We had two great chances in the last 15 minutes after they'd run themselves out. It wasn't that they were tired, but they'd run themselves to a point at which they didn't think we could come back at them. Then we started playing. They relaxed a little and we played the three centre backs, stopping their strikers. Our full backs started getting into the game, which the opposition didn't handle too well. In those last 15 minutes, we started to run over the top of them, so at least we got something out of the game. But the whole thing was pretty predictable.

We're still having problems with the flu bug. At half time Brucey was off – he'd actually taken his boots off. We also had to get the doctor in to look at Nicky Butt who had double vision again. Nicky said he was all right but the doctor said that if he couldn't see, we couldn't put him on, so he had to stay in the dressing room. It's really weird, Nicky's had all kinds of investigations – brain scans, the lot – but the doctors can find absolutely nothing wrong with him. It's not only worrying for Nicky, but it stops him from playing, which is a problem for everyone.

And then Keaney's hamstring went. I said: "Well, just sit in front of the back four." I put Ryan through the middle to try and stop their flow, to ensure there was somebody quick round about them, but it didn't make any difference, really. In fact, it got worse. I changed it round a few times to try and improve matters, and I was ready to play three centre backs when they got the goal. If I'd done that, I think we would have got away with it. But that's football, that's decision-making. I waited too long.

Pally perhaps could have done a bit better for their goal, but Brucey was struggling beside him and he had a tough job on his hands in terms of how far up the pitch he was defending as a result of Brucey struggling so badly. I really should have put three centre backs through to help Brucey.

David May did very well when I did put him on. He's a good player, but he just needs to get past the difficult first season.

With all the emotion of the occasion, it was good to get the game over with. We went up to the hospital to see Sparky afterwards, to make sure he was settled in. He'll be allowed to come back to Manchester tomorrow.

Venue: St. James' Park *Att:* 31,161

	Newcastle United	*goals*		**Manchester United**	*goals*
1	Pavel Srnicek		1	Peter Schmeichel	
12	Marc Hottiger		3	Denis Irwin	
15	Darren Peacock		4	Steve Bruce	
6	Steve Howey		6	Gary Pallister	
3	John Beresford		5	Lee Sharpe	
2	Barry Venison		19	Nicky Butt	
5	Ruel Fox		16	Roy Keane	
10	Lee Clark		9	Brian McClair	
7	Robert Lee		11	Ryan Giggs	
26	Robbie Elliot		10	Mark Hughes	13
28	Paul Kitson	67	7	Eric Cantona	
Substitutes					
14	Alex Mathie		12	David May (45 mins for 4)	
19	Steve Watson		24	Paul Scholes (13 mins for 10)	
30	Mike Hooper		13	Gary Walsh	

Monday 16 January

For once we have a clear week, so I caught up with some admin.

Tuesday 17 January

Not having Eric, we used Scholesy in the functions instead, because he can play in the same way.

Wednesday 18 January

The lad who comes in to massage the players – which he did today – is from Wigan and he does the Wigan lads as well. He has a problem with his eyesight, so when he comes into a room and the light is different from the last, it changes the focus of his eyes and it takes a while before he can adjust. Because of this he can't drive, so he has a guy who drives him in. He's extremely good at his job and the players really love it.

In the evening I went with Bobby Charlton to watch the Blackburn-Newcastle FA Cup replay. I didn't know whether to go, because sometimes you get a bit of abuse going up there, but Bobby really wanted to. It's usually fine once you are inside, but sometimes there's a wee bit of hassle going into the ground. This time there was none and I really enjoyed the game.

Newcastle were really lively. They all wanted the ball just like against us. Even though they only drew with us, it seems to have given them a great lift. Perhaps that's gone against Blackburn in a way.

The supporters were right behind their team all the time and kept chanting, "Kevin Keegan, Kevin Keegan." Blackburn had their chances, mainly on the counter-attack, but then with just five minutes to go Newcastle scored the winner, just as we were leaving. With Sunday in mind, I said to Bobby, "Extra-time will do us no harm", but it didn't happen.

Thursday 19 January

This evening I was invited to the premiere of the film Interview with the Vampire, because it was in aid of the charity Help Adolescents With Cancer, of which I am patron. I was really pleased that the proceeds were going to HAWC and I made a wee speech before the start, but oh, what a terrible movie!

Friday 20 January

They kept Mark in hospital until today in case of any infection. He's got young kids at home so maybe it's not such a bad idea, because his leg is in plaster and it wouldn't be good for him if they jumped on it. We went up to see him. Pop Robson said: "He must be the hardest man ever."

"Why?"

"Well, he's got this gash and I can't look at it because it goes right down to the bone. The doctor came to look at the damage and Sparky just sat there without flinching. I was nearly sick but Sparky didn't bat an eyelid. I don't know what he's made of, but it's not human flesh."

The Premier League was honouring me with a lunch at the Portland Hotel to celebrate my CBE. It was organised by Keith Pinner and lunch started at 12.30pm. I didn't get home until 11pm though, because I got talking to Joe Melling from the Mail on Sunday, Hugh McIlvanney and Kiddo. We talked football for hours. Cathy is not pleased with me.

Saturday 21 January

The great thing about the Blackburn game is that we have had seven days to prepare! You have to watch what the workload's like because the grounds are a bit soft at the moment, but we had a really good, full week.

Today we did the set pieces as Andy was there. We decided to leave two up the pitch for the corner kicks, just for a change.

Ripley has been missing recently and he is one of Blackburn's stronger players. There were stories today that he might be fit, though. It's always this cat and mouse thing – what the team is going to be. Feeds come out that this one's got a problem and that one's got a problem, it's just all gimmickry. Gamesmanship is maybe the better word. I do my team talk with their best team, that's what I always do. When you hear teams talk about, "Ach, he might be fit and that", I always pick their best team against us and make my stall out that way, so that mentally the players are prepared to play against the best team. And if there's a change then fine. You've still given them that extra boost.

Kenny has been trying to put pressure on the referee for tomorrow, harking back to the penalty at Ewood Park in the first game and saying that they want a fair crack of the whip tomorrow – a referee who isn't swayed at Old Trafford, that is.

I went to see Bolton this afternoon. A dirty, wet day. McGinley does pretty well for them; he's got a sense about the goal. And that little boy Lee. We watched him as a kid at Bury. To my mind, he is not what you call a top-drawer player, but what enthusiasm he's got for the game. He always wants the ball and always wants to take people on. What a buy he's been for Bolton.

Hugh McIlvanney is staying with us for the weekend. He and I go back a long way. I was really winding him up and said: "You'll not believe what I got for my Christmas."

He said: "No. What did you get?"

"A portrait of your brother." (His brother William is a novelist.)

"A portrait of my brother? Why the hell did you get that?"

"My son got it for me. He saw it in a gallery, and he knows that I'm friendly with you."

"I suppose it's a good one."

"Christ, you've got so gracious in your old age," I said.

It's a fabulous picture. But he still said, "What the bloody hell do you want that for?"

Sunday 22 January

Manchester United 1 Blackburn Rovers 0

An engrossing game and quite controversial, I suppose. I was pleased with the performance. Blackburn had a "goal" disallowed in the last couple of minutes, so they weren't happy at all. But if Andy had scored in the first couple of minutes, we might have had a good score. It would have been a travesty if we hadn't won.

At least our goal was very clear-cut, because their "equaliser" in the final moments was controversial. Shearer got up above Keane and headed the ball back across for Sherwood to fling himself in front of Pallister and head it home. The referee disallowed it for a push on Keane. There was a slight touch, but nothing much. Just enough to give Shearer a good header. It was the sort of thing that he usually gets away with. But Blackburn wanted a perfect referee. I don't think Shearer would have got a good header in if he hadn't have got in the position that he did. Keaney's brilliant in the air. He wouldn't have lost that one.

But it was a soft one, although I didn't admit that at the time. Last year, before we played Blackburn, they came out with a lot of nonsense about our discipline on the day of the game – or our lack of discipline. Now we've got the next thing – referees. So we're not going to yield on any controversy about the goal.

I think the referee was out to prove that he could come to Old Trafford, and Kenny's obviously made his point. Kenny seems to forget he was at Liverpool for so long. And that's where the disappointment comes in. Has he ever come out and said that when Liverpool got penalty kicks other teams were getting robbed? No. That's why I didn't want them to be singing all the songs about the goal.

But I don't see the need for referees to come and prove themselves. Why are they appointed for the game in the first place?

Blackburn got every decision in the first half. There was a pass back that Flowers palmed away, and he didn't give a free kick. Then Ince was brought down by Wilcox when he was right through, and although we got the break of the ball, the ref didn't book the player.

During the second half we got a few decisions and he booked Wright for nothing really. I thought it was a soft one, but the referee had been put under pressure by Kenny, so he was bound to react to tackles.

To be fair, in the second half Blackburn defended well. I never rated Hendry all that highly, but he's got determination and he had a marvellous game. He's always diving under people and getting away with murder, actually. There's a funny thing about defenders who dive in. As long as they're on the ground they tend to give less fouls away, whereas, if you keep your feet and go through people from a standing position, they give the fouls.

Nobody noticed Cantona running for the goal because Hendry was left undecided, then took the middle position. He did the right thing, but with Giggs' cross he was never going to get to it. And if he'd put it in the front post he would never have made that either. So he had to take the middle. And whether they saw Cantona, I don't know. But they seemed to just stand.

We did everything we set out to do. We made sure in the tactical part that Ince and McClair were close to the two centre backs and tried to draw them on to us. But they didn't come, they just stayed put, which meant Incey and McClair were always on the ball in the first half and at least we got some passing continuity going.

During the game Cantona went up and patted Andy Cole on the back as if to say, "You're doing all right." All the lads are keen for Andy to do well. Watching him in the game today, I could see the number of times he was looking along the line to run in. In his last chance he did brilliantly, because the ball was right under his feet. He's so quick on his feet. He certainly gives us a great option now, but we've got to find the spaces, we've got to work it into the inside forward positions and feed him in, not from the centre or wide.

Venue: Old Trafford *Att:* 43,742

Manchester United	*goals*	**Blackburn Rovers**	*goals*
1 Peter Schmeichel		1 Tim Flowers	
3 Denis Irwin		20 Henning Berg	
4 Steve Bruce		24 Paul Warhurst	
6 Gary Pallister		5 Colin Hendry	
16 Roy Keane		6 Graeme Le Saux	
8 Paul Ince		11 Jason Wilcox	
9 Brian McClair		4 Tim Sherwood	
5 Lee Sharpe		22 Mark Atkins	
7 Eric Cantona	80	3 Alan Wright	
17 Andy Cole		9 Alan Shearer	
11 Ryan Giggs		16 Chris Sutton	
Substitutes			
14 Andrei Kanchelskis (77 mins for 5)		10 Mike Newell (90 mins for 11)	
25 Gary Walsh		13 Bobby Mimms	
12 David May		25 Ian Pearce (90 mins for 22)	

Monday 23 January

The problem with these big games is the number of people you have coming to watch it. I had about 30 people in my office today, which was pretty hard going. It's an added strain and the game's hard enough. I was exhausted.

After the match, Kiddo, Norman and an old friend of mine went out for a meal with our wives. But I was tired, so we left at eleven. When you get to 53 things don't get any easier. It's the tension.

So we got the result we needed, but now we have to do it again on Wednesday at Crystal Palace. They are an athletic and enthusiastic young team who get stuck into us. We have just got to make sure that we realise that Sunday's game was only part of the job. We've got to now complete it, and that means winning on Wednesday. Then we can say, "Well it's been a good week for us." And we must not give Blackburn any more encouragement. We don't know whether they're good enough, but they're strong enough. They're a big, powerful team, and they certainly can score a goal. But there are other things that'll come into being. They've still to hit a wobble. And a wobble means you're drawing games and maybe losing the odd one in maybe a three or four game spell. Which we've had, Newcastle have, Liverpool have, but Blackburn have not had. So that'll be the big test for them. And when that happens, hopefully we're there and ready to take advantage.

I had a call this morning from Alex McCleish, my former centre half at Aberdeen. He is manager of Motherwell and they lost 6-1 last Saturday to Dundee United. It was his first big defeat.

Keith Gillespie made his debut for Newcastle on Saturday and did really well. He'll be a good player in a couple of years.

Bruce is suspended again and will miss Wednesday's game. He's had a hard time this season. He always seems to be the one being singled out. The rate he's going he'll be *sine die* by the end of the season. He gets booked for every flipping tackle. I'd like to know what he was booked for yesterday.

Eric was booked, too. That was a bookable offence. He lifted his foot, although he never touched the guy, but I think it was more of a show than actual intent, trying to convince you that he can tackle – but he can't. I said, "What are you doing? Just run alongside him."

Andrei was on the bench and he did alright when he came on. That was quite pleasing. He still feels a bit below par, so maybe we'll have to send him back to the specialist on Thursday. I think he's the type of person who really needs to feel perfect when he plays a game of football.

There have been a lot of resilient teams like Blackburn over the years.

So long as they've got something to hang on to, they'll work away hanging on to it. They'll keep their shape and pattern. But if you score first, it is a different problem for them, and a test of their flexibility which teams like that sometimes lack.

Today is the *Manchester Evening News* "Sportsman of the Year" lunch. Andrei is supposed to go but I can't, because we're talking to Cantona's agent, Jean-Jacques Bertrand, about a new contract. They approached us, which is good. Cantona worked his nuts off yesterday. The six-month period from last March right through to September has been a bad six months for him in terms of the number of times he's been sent off and all the controversy surrounding him. But now he's playing all the time and is totally fit. He seems to have settled down and knows where his destination is now. His last six performances have been magnificent for us.

8
L'Affaire Cantona

Tuesday 24 January

Negotiations with players are protracted affairs these days. For a first meeting, yesterday's discussions with Jean-Jacques Bertrand went quite well, but there's a long way to go. There's never an easy solution; it's all about haggling and banter and bartering. It reminds me of the old tribal rituals in which warriors did a dance with one stepping forward and pretending he was going to throw his spear; and then the other one did the same until they were face to face, then they stepped back.

Every time you meet for player negotiations there is a spear being waved, but the demands from one party get less and the other side relents a bit, and in the end you come to a sort of happy medium – at least you hope you do. That's how it was with Eric. He and his agent have gone to think it over. We have things to think about too - the chairman also has to go to the plc about various points.

But there is plenty of time; Eric has 18 months left on this contract. A new three-year contract would take him to 32, but we don't see that being a problem. Kiddo and I assess players the whole time and Eric is playing really well. He is working his tail off in games and his goal ratio is better than one every two matches. On top of that he wants to stay, so everything should be fine.

Mark Hughes is more of a problem. He won't play for a month now, so there is no urgency, but Joe Royle has been on the phone again about him and we had a meeting with Dennis Roach, Mark's agent, about it. Dennis always wants something you can never really match. He always starts off at something ridiculous and then you have to knock him down to just common sense.

But with Mark's injury we'll have to see how it all settles down. We may need him, anyway. I hope he signs a new contract, but first he needs to accept the whole situation.

This club has always had heroes, legendary figures, and the last few years have created some more legends, new heroes for a new generation.

There used to be Law, Best and Charlton; now we have had Bryan Robson and Sparky. One of the problems of being the manager of this club is that it is always down to you to tell them when their career is over, when they have to be left out or it is simply time for them to move on. People are full of advice, but they don't have to tell Mark Hughes or Bryan Robson that they are leaving them out. Neither my assistants, nor the chairman, nor any supporter ever had to go to Bryan and say:

"Oh, Bryan, you're not playing in the cup final."

That's my job, and you sometimes get pilloried for it. But I have to do what I think is best for Manchester United in terms of winning matches. Of course there are times when you are wrong, but successful management means being right far more often than you are wrong.

In Mark's case, I've bought a player for £6 million and I've got to tell Mark that he is the one to be replaced. It's a decision which may be misunderstood, but some will realise that the United bus has to keep moving.

One of the reasons I signed Andy Cole was that I felt that we needed an injection. All the time I've been here, this club has never had a penalty-box player, which is what Andy Cole will give us. The problem at Old Trafford is that teams come and just sit there with 8 or 9 bodies back, mainly because we've not had the real threat to make them wary. But Andy has that quickness, those really fast turns and really quick feet and he will be able to unlock doors for us.

But it means that we will have to play differently, though. At Newcastle, when Mark went off, we missed him. When they really went gung-ho and pressed the ball all over the pitch, we couldn't get it forwards. We missed knowing that we could look up and find Mark, and he could take it on his thigh or on his chest and use his power to hold people off, enabling us to keep possession.

We just did boxes today – possession games. We are flying to Crystal Palace, so we don't need to travel until tomorrow. It gave me the opportunity to go to see Darren. He is really down at the moment because he is out of the Wolves side. I told him I had a managers' meeting in Birmingham, which gave me an excuse to go down and see him, take him out for a bite to eat and try to cheer him up. He is different from his brothers – the other two are really open and more emotional; Darren keeps everything bottled up.

He said he was fed up and didn't enjoy the style of football they were playing. Graham Taylor admitted to Darren that he was probably being a bit unfair to him, having told him that he had been their best midfield player all season, and then making changes, but said that he had to because they just weren't getting any results.

I told Darren to keep plugging away, and if he still isn't happy in a few weeks' time, then someone may want to buy him and he might be able to go to another club where he could enjoy his football more. He is suspended now, anyway.

"Regard this as a sabbatical," I said. "You're out of the team, so practise the things you need to improve: your finishing and your strength and pace. Work at them, because you've only got the one career. But you are only 22. At 25, when you are approaching maturity, you can decide whether the frustration is too much. But you've a long way to go, so work on these things so that you can carve out a career for yourself until you are 35 or 36."

I felt happier having seen him.

Wednesday 25 January

United 1 Crystal Palace 1

At 5.35pm on Sunday Eric took us to heaven with that wonderful goal to beat Blackburn. Three days later we have been taken to hell without any hint that there was anything wrong. He was sent off for kicking out at Richard Shaw, then, on his way to the tunnel, launched himself at a fan, with a kung fu kick in the chest. I just could not believe it – or understand it. And all hell has broken loose.

I felt bad enough about him being sent off in the first place. I said to him: "Why do you get involved with that Shaw fellow, because he's just an ordinary player?"

It's not as if he's a top player. OK, he was niggling at him, but that happens all the time. He was not a player who was going to influence the game in any way and not the type to give you problems. I think Shaw had a wee niggle at him after half time, and he reacted. It wasn't a vicious foul by Eric, but it was a silly foul for no reason. Shaw had blocked his run forward, but that happens all the time.

When he was sent off he came towards the dugout and stopped. I wondered afterwards whether he had stopped for a reason, but you just don't know. Then he carried on walking towards the tunnel. I said to Norman:

"You'd better go with him."

I saw Eric walking towards the tunnel and turned my attention back to the field. Then I heard this commotion and turned to see Eric spread-eagled across the hoarding.

I didn't go towards him, but stayed back so I could watch for a minute. All the players were over there, everyone was involved. But I didn't know what caused it. I thought that a fan had pulled him across the boards and into the crowd as he walked past. There was a lot going on in that crowd, it wasn't just one or two sounding off, it was really unpleasant. When I went out after half time, a kid standing at the front had asked me for my autograph. I was going towards the kid when the verbals started, so I turned away and went along the path to the dugout. As I have already said, we get terrible abuse away from home these days.

At the time I was mainly concerned about the sending off because I assumed that Eric had been protecting himself. That would have been bad enough, but at least it's answerable. If someone attacks you, you hit back.

When the game was over, I went into the dressing room and said to Eric:

"What the bloody hell were you doing getting involved with Shaw? It's not worth it. You've let your team down and you've let yourself down."

He just sat there and didn't say a word.

Then I asked Norman what all that scene was about. and he said:

"I don't know what happened, but I think someone threw something at Eric."

"What?"

"I think it was a can of beer."

"Before or after the incident?"

"I'm not sure."

We didn't have a clear picture about what had happened. Next we were called into the referee's room to talk to the police. The inspector said:

"I'll tell you what we are going to do: we are not going to get hysterical about this. We are going to interview everybody we can. There are a lot of allegations flying around and it is our job to investigate them thoroughly. But we are not going to be doing anything tonight, so why don't you go home. Emotions are running high."

He was quite good, actually, but next he was doing interviews with the press and television, which I was a bit upset about.

I had a meeting with the directors in the corridor. The chairman asked me if I had seen what happened and I said no. I told them what I knew and Maurice Watkins, the club's solicitor, said:

"Are you sure that Norman said there was something thrown?"

I relayed what Norman had said to me, that he thought it was a cup of tea or a can of beer. We agreed to say nothing and leave it until tomorrow.

The police said they would want statements from both myself and

What Eric does best: playing football

Vow of silence: Eric sits impassively at the press conference as his FA ban is announced

Happy days are here again: Cantona signs a new United contract

Sideline instructions in the dying moments at Upton Park: "It's 1-1 at Anfield!"

Frustration for Cole as inspired Miklosko foils us again

Thoughts of what might have been... agony is etched all over the lads' faces

Old pals: Joe Royle and I greet each other on Cup Final day

United's bench boys look on anxiously as Rideout gets Everton's winner

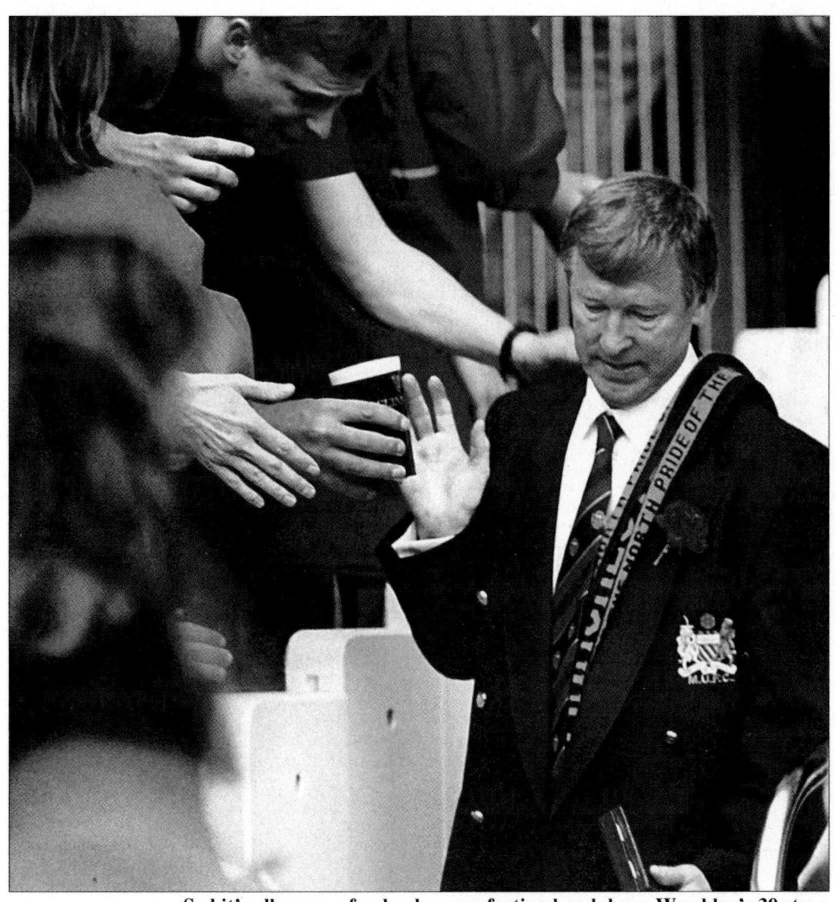

Sad it's all over: a fan lends a comforting hand down Wembley's 39 steps

OOR
FERGIE
UMBRO

Norman, and from the players.

"There's been an allegation against Paul Ince," one officer said to me.

"Against Ince? What for?"

He said it was for allegedly assaulting someone, but the way he said it, it looked as if he knew what that was all about.

When we flew home, the police at the airport were really excellent. The coach came out to meet the plane and Eric was given a police escort home.

Venue: Selhurst Park	*Att:* 18,224		
Crystal Palace	*goals*	**Manchester United**	*goals*
1 Nigel Martyn		1 Peter Schmeichel	
3 Dean Gordon		3 Denis Irwin	
4 Gareth Southgate	79	12 David May	56
6 Chris Coleman		6 Gary Pallister	
8 Iain Dowie		16 Roy Keane	
9 Chris Armstrong		8 Paul Ince	
11 John Salako		9 Brian McClair	
14 Richard Shaw		5 Lee Sharpe	
16 Darren Pitcher		7 Eric Cantona	
22 Darren Patterson		17 Andy Cole	
23 Ricky Newman		11 Ryan Giggs	
Substitutes			
17 Andy Preece (75 mins for 8)	24	Paul Scholes	
15 Bobby Bowry		25 Gary Walsh	
19 Rhys Wilmot		14 Andrei Kanchelskis (83 mins for 5)	

Thursday 26 January

I got home about 1am this morning. Jason and Tanya were up with my grandson, Jake, waiting for me. When I first went in they said:

"Do you want to watch it?"

I said no.

"You'll not believe it," Jason said. "He karate-kicked the guy."

"Karate-kicked him? Are you sure?"

"I'm telling you. He karate-kicked him."

Having Jake there took my mind off it for a bit. Then he fell asleep and we all went to bed about 2am. I couldn't sleep, I just lay there wondering what he had done. At 5.25am I got up and put the video on. I couldn't believe what I saw.

Today was a nightmare. I am gutted, devastated; the players were devastated; everybody connected to the club was devastated. It was just a case of getting through the day. There were hoards of press hanging round and we had to shut the gates at The Cliff to keep people out. The phone didn't stop ringing. Eric came in. Maurice Watkins came in to see him. Brian McClair fixed up a meeting for Eric with the PFA and Brendan Batson came in with the PFA lawyer. There was endless coming and going and the air was filled with an overriding sense of doom.

The chairman had stayed in London to talk to the FA. We arranged a meeting at the Edge Hotel at Alderley Edge at 8pm to decide what to do – we couldn't hold it at Old Trafford because we knew we'd be besieged. The chairman, Sir Roland Smith, chairman of the plc, Maurice Watkins and I were present. When we arrived at the hotel there was already a table of three journalists in the restaurant. I wonder how the hell they found out where we were going.

My initial feeling was for letting Eric go and Sir Roland felt the same because although we appreciated his qualities, we couldn't imagine him being able to play for the club again. I have supported Eric solidly through thick and thin, but I felt that this time the good name of Manchester United demanded strong action. The club is bigger than any individual. I related that to the board and they agreed.

On the way to the meeting, Sir Richard Greenbury phoned me and we discussed Eric. He said that Eric reminded him of John McEnroe. "Off the court, John's a splendid chap, but on court, his temper gets the better of him."

Cath had said to me: "You cannot let him off with that. Never let it be said that you put winning the championship above doing the right thing."

I agreed with her. I wouldn't want anyone to think for a minute that we had considered putting winning above our good name. If we do not do the right thing, that will be the charge levelled against us - and some people cannot wait to criticise United.

There's the practical side of the matter, too. I fear it will be impossible for Eric to operate in our game after what happened. We've seen how the media are reacting and I don't think that will go away. Eric will be under terrible pressure from the media now. I think that will make his position untenable. And the provocation on away grounds will be even worse now.

I felt for Eric's wife, who is pregnant and will be going through agony over this. I am sure Eric is haunted by it all now – I hope he is, anyway. But I really felt we had to let him go.

Maurice took a legal stand and counselled caution because of the police investigation and also because of the terms of the player's contract.

The chairman put forward the FA's view because he had had two meetings with David Davies during the day. We went through the entire thing, eliminating what we couldn't do and what we shouldn't do. Maurice emphasised the legal issues.

Then we discussed suspending him but again there were legal matters to consider and there had to be consultation with the PFA and their advisors. All this happened during the evening and the phone was hot.

The debate see-sawed on what the correct length of suspension should be. The FA had given the message that action had to be taken, but we also had to demonstrate that United were concerned with upholding standards.

I am nervous about the future; about how Eric will be able to operate in our game, but we will cross that bridge when we come to it. They say that time is a great healer and I hope the suspension does the trick, but I've got my doubts. When we came to our decision, Eric and the PFA accepted.

Friday 27 January

There's a problem with Nicky Butt. I was thinking about playing him tomorrow, but this morning he couldn't move his neck. This is on top of his intermittent double vision. We can't find anything wrong. I hope he doesn't go through his whole life like this, with neck problems and seeing double every few weeks.

The Cantona situation is dominating everything. It was the lead story on News At Ten again last night. Surely there are more important things in the world? There are cameras outside his house, cameras outside The Cliff. The press – and I don't just mean the tabloids – are having a field day. There were endless articles in papers this morning criticising us for acting slowly and not suspending or sacking Eric immediately. It took us 24 hours, which I don't really call taking our time.

I held a meeting to tell the players of the club's decision. I didn't handle it very well and a lot of the players thought the club had overreacted. Before the meeting there was the usual banter – "Alcatraz this time, Eric," "four years' hard labour" – but the players were very subdued afterwards.

Maurice and the chairman held a meeting to tell the press. I was happy to miss that one.

Saturday 28 January

United 5 Wrexham 2

The game came as a welcome relief. In a way it was the perfect match for us to have because Wrexham were a credit to the game. They played really good football and tried to win, but it was an open game and we were too good for them once we got into gear. They took the lead, though, so there were a few nervous moments until we equalised.

Their manager, Bryan Flynn, said afterwards that the one thing they didn't want was a draw because they are committed in the Welsh Cup and they still hope to get into the second division promotion race.

The Wrexham fans were tremendous. They filled their end and really enjoyed their day. The atmosphere is always so much better when the away support is good.

But inevitably Eric's absence cast a long shadow. There was some hysterical reaction in a few papers today saying that we had only suspended him instead of sacking him for financial reasons. Money was not mentioned once at the meeting.

There was also some criticism of me, saying that I had indulged him. But that is not true. People believe such things because I never criticise any of my players publicly. Eric is punished when he steps out of line, just as they all are. We've tried to bring him into the development of the club and hope that the longer he is here and the more he understands what the club is about, the better he will become. I also talk to him all the time. Before some games we warn him that certain players are going to try and wind him up. But you can't say for certain that that is going to work, because you don't know what is ticking inside him.

Eric is the type who doesn't say anything in training. He is very quiet, just practises and practises. He is the perfect pro. He is the first on the training field and virtually the last off it.

There are no indications that he is any bother to us at all until he does something really crazy. Things you can't understand. The incident with Goss at Norwich, for example. I couldn't understand that. Or the incident with Moncur at Swindon - although I think Sanchez had elbowed him on the touchline just prior to that and the referee didn't give a foul.

But people say we let him get away with murder. We don't any more than we do Mark Hughes. Mark has been sent off four times in the last two or three years. Once was for allegedly head-butting David Burrows in the Liverpool game, when it was proved he never touched him. He kicked a ball away in Moscow; he kicked a boy up the backside at Sheffield; he was sent off for a second bookable offence at Arsenal. That's four sendings off and sometimes he produces tackles that make you turn your head away. People say: "You're not controlling your players." But Mark was like that at 16.

I do discipline the players, it's just that, unlike some clubs, I don't do it in public. I think that's unacceptable. Competitive players will get booked and we play cup finals every week because everyone wants to beat Manchester United. The critics don't make allowances for that, but I do.

There were petitions being circulated outside the ground demanding that we keep Eric. Whatever the papers say, there is no doubt about how our fans feel.

Venue: Old Trafford	*Att.* 43,222		
Manchester United	*goals*	**Wrexham**	*goals*
1 Peter Schmeichel		1 Andrew Marriot	
23 Gary Neville		2 Barry Jones	
12 David May		3 Barry Hunter	
6 Gary Pallister		4 Tony Humes	80 (o.g.)
3 Denis Irwin	17/73	5 Phil Hardy	
8 Paul Ince		6 Kieron Durkan	9
16 Roy Keane		7 Bryan Hughes	
9 Brian McClair	67	8 Karl Connolly	
5 Lee Sharpe		9 ?	
24 Paul Scholes		10 Gary Bennett	
11 Ryan Giggs	26	11 Steve Watkin	
Substitutes			
14 Andrei Kanchelskis (69 mins for 16)		12 Wayne Philips	
13 Gary Walsh		13 Mark Cartwright	
28 David Beckham (73 mins for 9)		14 Jonathan Cross (71 mins for 9)	89

Monday 30 January

The chairman told me:

"I haven't had a wink of sleep since this happened."

"Join the club," I said.

Tuesday 31 January

Eric's lawyer is coming over tomorrow. Last week we discussed Eric making a public apology, but he didn't think it was right because Eric was still too upset about it. He thought it might be better to do it this week, so we will see.

One thing we will pursue is that Eric's problems always occur in the second half. His sendings off against Rangers, Swindon and Arsenal, and this one against Palace, all came in the second half, and there are suggestions that that might reflect a diet problem - low blood-sugar, which could be solved by a supplement at half time. We will carry out some tests.

Wednesday 1 February

The meeting with Jean-Jacques was inconclusive. We are still not issuing an apology because of legal fears that it is inappropriate before the court case. Eric is going on holiday for a couple of weeks, which is probably the best thing.

George Graham phoned. He said, "Thanks for keeping me out of the headlines!"

Thursday 2 February

I went to a dinner in honour of Sir Stanley Matthews last night – a really great occasion. It was wonderful to meet so many of the game's greats.

I thought it might help me to sleep going there and having a relaxing evening with a glass of wine and some good company, but even that didn't work. I have not had a night's sleep since it happened. There is no escape during the day and my mind is just racing, thinking about it at night, turning it over time and time again.

Everyone deserves a second chance and Eric has had a terrible punishment – the unprecedented suspension by the club and the public humiliation. But I am convinced of one thing: the good name of the club is paramount. My concern is that it should never be considered that we put winning above our good name.

The second thing that worries me is that it is going to be impossible for the lad to operate in our game again.

The third thing that I'm worried about is the consequences if he returned to Old Trafford after his suspension and did something like this again. It would destroy my credibility and the club's good name, and it would finish him as a player. The whole thing is very hard to come to terms with.

9
The Affair Lingers On

Friday 3 February

In spite of all the interference, we've done a lot of work this week, much of it with Andy - things such as movement in the last third; different types of finishing. Andy has remarked that the training here is harder. He's found that he's having to push himself to keep up with the standard physically, with the type of things we do.

A lot of clubs play wee games. It's a syndrome. They've copied teams who have done well over the years, like Leeds and Liverpool who always play little games. We don't do that at all. We give them a wee game to end the session sometimes, but I'm more into technical training: finishing; possession; and things that'll crop up all the time in games. And we try to repeat these things. That's my belief about football. Because I always feel that whatever you do with the players during the week will surface on Saturday – if you do them well, that is.

Andy has found it particularly difficult getting to grips with the amount of work we do on possession and finishing. We don't just do finishing, we do movement and finishing. There has to be passing, movement, control, position and finish. Or cross, position and finish. It involves him running all the time. In many ways it will improve him technically, though. A lot of players find that they have to improve technically when they arrive here in order to reach the level we play at.

I've been very impressed with Andy in training. He has a good football brain. He takes care in his passing. When I first came to the club all the people used to say that Robbo was a great passer. His simple passes were good because he concentrated on them. He was always positioned right and he was always making sure that the pass got there.

And Andy is a wee bit like Robbo. A lot of people have been saying that Kevin's struck gold, getting £7 million for him. But only two months before that, Kevin was saying he wasn't going to sell him for £20 million. Something must have happened, but you cannot concern yourself with that and Andy provides some great raw material to work with.

We decided to go to Spain on Sunday for a short break, to get some sun and to get away from all the problems. We told the players this morning - we'd kept it as a surprise for them. Their wives weren't happy with me.

Dennis Roach insisted on a meeting with the chairman and I at 2pm. He came in and gave us four options: one was that he felt the offer was derisory considering the service Mark had given us. I suppose a lot of supporters would see it that way too. We've always tried to explain the situation regarding Europe. Second, he's prepared to stay until the end of the season if he gets a free transfer. Third, he goes now, and if he doesn't go now then the fourth option comes in, which is him asking for a transfer.

I don't know how much of this Mark agrees to because he never says anything, he just sits there. He's such a quiet lad. Roach has got a bit of a nerve, so it wouldn't be any hassle to him to ask for the Moon and expect to get Mars too. The chairman and I said we'd have to discuss all this.

There were options that we obviously could not agree to. He has to stay, so we couldn't release him. And we had to avoid him asking for a transfer because that would get the supporters on our back at a very sensitive time. So you have to evaluate just what the situation is. I said to the chairman:

"OK, let's delete what is not possible and work with what's left: One, we can't let him go; two, it's out of the question giving him a free transfer at the end of the season; three, we can't afford for him to ask for a transfer."

This left the last one - offering him a new two-year contract.

So I said to the chairman, "There's no way we can let him go. We've had a bad press. The support is really down over the Cantona thing. We've got to give them good news. I think we've got to offer him a two-year contract. We don't know what's going to happen with Eric at this point."

The chairman said he'd always supported me, but if we were offered £2 million for Mark, it's a lot of money to consider.

"Of course it's a lot of money," I said, "but remember that you've got to fill the stadium. You want to build a new stadium and you want to fill that. I think you'd be crazy to let him go."

So we got them in and gave them the offer. Mark was delighted.

I then left them at about 3.45pm because I had to have another meeting at Mottram Hall with Paul Clayton, the manager, about Darren's wedding, which is soon. They went on until about 6pm, apparently, because then Dennis got a giant screw and tried to screw the chairman into the wall. I don't know how it transpired in terms of the contract moneywise – I wasn't really interested. I thought that resolving the situation and keeping Mark was the important thing to do. Mark was delighted and we want to make an announcement to give the good news to the fans tomorrow.

There has been a complaint against Paul Ince. A Palace fan accused him of assault in the aftermath of the incident with Eric. The police want him to go and see them next week.

Saturday 4 February

United 1 Aston Villa 0

The day got off to a great start when we told the fans that Mark had agreed a new contract. It was also good because The Sun ran a story this morning saying he was going. Then Andy Cole got his first goal for the club. A magnificent goal! But then it all went a little flat.

For 25 minutes during the second half Villa dominated us. They deserved something out of the game, didn't get it and we were fortunate to get away with three points.

I've watched Andy's goal two or three times on video but at the time I couldn't see it. Bang! I suppose that's what you pay such a huge sum of money for, that reaction. Quickness of feet, quickness of movement, positioning. Brilliant! I think it'll take away the strain a little bit, make him relax and get on with enjoying the game now.

He worked really hard. I thought he did very well for us, particularly in the last third of the pitch. In the second half he was the one who kept them on edge. We got things played into him a few times and you always felt there was something going to happen when he was involved. It was a terrific start for Andy.

In the first 20 to 25 minutes we played very well. There was good linking play with Cole and Scholes and Giggsy was looking terrific. Then Giggs got done in a clash with Fashanu, a really ugly challenge. Fashanu ended up getting injured himself and Giggs had to come off after a further five minutes with a badly bruised knee, right on the bone. From that point on we just never seemed to get any flow to our game whatsoever.

Villa played very well. At the start of the season they were one of my dark horses to be in trouble - they simply looked like a team who were getting old. But since Brian Little arrived they have performed like any team will under a new man, running all over the place and their fitness seemed really good. I thought they'd die in the last 20 minutes, but they were running all over the place. So when they're in form and their experienced players are playing well, they're a decent side.

When we're planning for games we look at who the opposition's influential player is. Steve Staunton has been the key for Villa, so we were conscious of the need to stop him. It didn't work. Gary Neville's inexperience showed. He was always just a half yard off Staunton; he never got to grips with him. And then when he tried to get tight, he started diving in and missing by yards. It was creating a problem and Staunton controlled the game.

Taylor also did very well for them. He was out running in the middle of the park, making those long surging runs, and he's very quick.

But there are some performances when you know you're never going to get it all right. Our form at home has been excellent this season. We lost to Nottingham Forest at home but played twice as well as we did against Villa today. So one balances out the other, really. Villa are the first team who have come to Old Trafford and actually dominated us for a long period. Its a game where you start to think, 'we're going to have to defend properly here.'

Schmeichel and the centre-backs did very well and got us through. Pally is hitting an outstanding period now. He is such a laid-back lad but you know at some point he's going to take real responsibility and say to himself: 'I really should be the best centre half in Europe.'

He's starting to look as if he is beginning to take that step. He's been in marvellous form this season, I'm really pleased with him.

Pally is also starting to come out from the back and make a contribution to the attack. He had some impressive moments today. He used to run into crowded areas, but we said, "Don't run into crowded areas. If you break forward, break into space. And if you go into crowded areas you've got to use it early."

In the main, his perception is much better than it used to be, which is down to experience. You've got to remember with Pally that he didn't really start until he was 22. People forget these things. And being such a big, coltish lad, his physique never really materialised until he was 25 or 26, so there's still an immaturity about him in many ways. At 30 years of age you'd think it would be impossible for him to still be realising his potential, but there's evidence this season that he's now taking that responsibility and having that grip that makes a great centre half. He's been a power for us this year.

Venue: Old Trafford	*Att:* 43,795		
Manchester United	*goals*	**Aston Villa**	*goals*
1 Peter Schmeichel		13 Mark Bosnich	
3 Denis Irwin		22 Gary Charles	

4	Steve Bruce		5	Paul McGrath
6	Gary Pallister		4	Shaun Teale
27	Gary Neville		20	Bryan Small
8	Paul Ince		18	Dwight Yorke
5	Lee Sharpe		11	Andy Townsend
9	Brian McClair		17	Ian Taylor
24	Paul Scholes		3	Steve Staunton
17	Andy Cole	18	8	John Fashanu
11	Ryan Giggs		9	Dean Saunders
Substitutes				
12	David May (64 mins for 27)		7	Ray Houghton (61 mins for 18)
14	Andrei Kanchelskis (44 mins for 11)		1	Nigel Spink
13	Gary Walsh		25	Tommy Johnson (43 mins for 8)

Sunday 5 February

We went to Marbella this morning. Paul Ince stayed at home because he has to see the police; Kanchelskis because of his stomach injury; Mark because he is in the throes of moving house, plus his knee injury needed some treatment; and Ryan Giggs didn't come because of his bruised knee. But we've got 11 of the players out. It was a long trip because we left first thing – 7.45am – and went via Zurich. We got there in time to watch Blackburn lose at Tottenham on Sky. I watched it at Mr Midani's place, the Marbella Club. I fancied Tottenham before the game, but Blackburn actually did quite well in the second half .

They keep you hemmed in because of the way they play and their pressing game, with everything played forward, tends to suffocate you. They are always looking to turn you back towards your own goal. But I always thought that when Tottenham got out to play they looked very, very good. I thought they looked like a real threat. And Blackburn, to me, looked nervous at the back, too. They didn't know how to handle it.

I thought Spurs could've scored more. I don't think Blackburn could've scored any more than they did, although Shearer hit a post and Sutton had one chance. But Tottenham could have scored a lot of goals. It was a nice lift for us, knowing we are in there two points behind with 15 games left to go.

Monday 6 February

The weather is fabulous. We played golf.

Tuesday 7 February

We did a little training and then played golf. The players love it here. It is great just sitting by the pool. It's great relaxation and nobody knows who you are, nobody can get you. I sat by the pool with Kiddo and Norman and a couple of the players sleeping, talking and relaxing.

Mr Midani has looked after us fantastically. He put on a superb buffet for us tonight at his club on the beach.

Wednesday 8 February

We came home after training in the sun this morning. It was a great trip, with a bit of golf and a couple of good training sessions in the sun. The players' behaviour was great and we had a good laugh with them.

Thursday 9 February

Back to normality. We did little bits of finishing, just a regular training session. Mark was back in training.

There was a fuss because the police were annoyed that Eric had not gone to be interviewed with Incey, because he was out of the country. But there had been no suggestion that they wanted to interview him this week.

Friday 10 February

We had a surprise visit. Robbo came in to train with us because his team are at Oldham tomorrow and rather than going all the way up to Middlesbrough, he stayed behind. It was good to see him and we had a good chat. We did the function in relation to how we were going to play against City. Robbo stood at the side and watched the function with me. We stood discussing management and it was good to see how much confidence he has.

I said: "You're having a bit of a hard time."

"Aye, but we're playing all right," he said. "We're playing well. We're just not finishing off the way we did earlier on. If we get that back we're okay."

"It's good to hear that," I said. He was facing his first test as a manager, and he wasn't saying: "I don't know what to do here." He was positive about it. I think they'll win the League.

Mark played in the practice match. I spoke to him before and said, "What do you think about tomorrow?"

"I'm still feeling it a bit," he said." I think sub is the best I can do."

"I thought that," I said and I knew that really. But Andy Cole had to go to hospital with his girlfriend - she is pregnant and had to go for a check up, so I'd given him the day off. I played Mark in Andy's place and he did a function in relation to how we were going to play with three in the middle of the park, with Ryan wide left, Andy wide right and the support running through from midfield. It gives them a picture of how we're going to operate the next day.

Philip Neville will come in for his first Premiership game tomorrow. He is an outstanding prospect.

I've got a cracked rib. It must have been that big Schmeichel when we were doing the boxes yesterday. I thought that I'd got a torn muscle or something, but it was really too localised to be a muscle. I went for an X-ray and the doctor said:

"It will probably show up in a couple of weeks," because that is what generally happens with a cracked rib.

Saturday 11 February

Manchester City 0 United 3

I got a phone call at 9.30am from Ken Ramsden, our assistant secretary. "The game's in doubt," he said. "Bernie Halford's been on the phone and said torrents of rain are expected."

So I got ready and then went down to Maine Road right away. I arrived at 10.20am and the pitch was alright. Wee Stan Gibson was out there working away, mopping up the wet with a sponge roller. He is a great groundsman and a brilliant bloke. But the rain was coming down so I stayed there until about 11.30 and asked Bernard Halford, the secretary of Manchester City, when the referee was due. He said 12, so I said, "Well you'll let me know if he's going to have to make a decision."

I went away to The Copthorne and had lunch with the players. Then I drove right back to Maine Road and got there about 12.15. The referee came out at about 12.40pm and said there was not a problem. I was delighted the game was on. If it had been off, Keane would have been suspended for the cup tie. And, as long as it didn't turn into a swamp, I felt that that was going to be a good surface for us.

In the first half City went at it hell for leather. I didn't think we gave young Philip Neville the right support defensively but he got through it simply because of his great ability. I knew he was going to tire because he had a lot of work to do defensively. With the pitch being as soft as it was, I said:

"Right, Kiddo, get Scholesy warmed up at half time. We're going to make the change five minutes into the second half."

I think it was actually six or seven minutes when we made the change, and the game opened up for us.

Although we had some real incisiveness in our play in the first half, we always looked as if we could score goals against them, but weren't controlling the game. Once Scholes came on, it just opened the door for us. It gave us that extra man in a forward area and we started to really play well. We got a goal about 15 minutes into the second half and from then on we could have scored a few.

The pleasing things for me were McClair's and Cole's performances. The two centre backs, Irwin and the goalkeeper were outstanding. I said to them after the game:

"If you start playing like that now, we'll have absolutely no problems."

We've got to stop losing goals away from home. Once we do, we'll be back to our best, our real best – even without Eric Cantona. I feel we'll be a real formidable side again.

If you look at our away goals we've lost two at Leeds, three at Ipswich, two at Blackburn, two at Southampton, two at Queens Park Rangers and two at Chelsea. That's not Championship form. I always think if we score two away from home we'll win a game. We should be winning games scoring two. So if we are getting back to that form of defending I think we've got a really good chance now.

Andy Cole has begun to fit in and I think his play shows that he has real intelligence. At Newcastle, Beardsley, Lee and Clark played a lot of tight little passes in the middle, a lot of combinations and zig-zag passing. All Andy needed to do was operate in that central area. People used to say he never worked his channels. But just because of the way Newcastle play I'd have thought that would be very difficult. Because if he had worked the channels they'd have no striker, unless they'd continued their midfield players' running through. But they didn't really do that, although Lee would make runs in there, certainly, and Beardsley would eventually come in. So Cole used to stay in there all the time because he knew what was going to happen.

Now Cole's come to us and he is already playing differently. He has started to operate in the channels. So people are saying,'Oh, he's working really hard.'

But I think what is happening is that he says, 'I'll move out here because if I can get the centre back out here, I can always get a winger to come up and join me and then I'll get off back into the space the defender's left.'

He does that because he knows we've got that pace going up there to join him all the time. So he can set up, get out there and go away all the time. He's a good thinker and that was what produced two of the goals today.

The derby was a really good, determined performance by us. The only disappointment was that the atmosphere was terrible; the City supporters were disgraceful. I've never seen that before. Every time I turned round there were people fighting in the main stand. And when the City supporters started on the Munich songs at the end, it was pretty disgusting.

In 1985 it was Heysel, in 1995 we're now seeing hooligans pervading the grounds again. Away from home we're getting terrible stick and it's reaching a crescendo. It's disgusting what the players are having to put up with at away grounds.

The City fans at the moment are taking their inability to beat us very hard and that is making it very tough for Brian Horton. You can see he is working very hard and I don't think he deserves what is happening to him at the moment. Despite the fans, it was a really terrific performance, we were right on song. But then just when we were feeling happy with the world, we got hit by the news about Cantona. I came out of the press conference and two of the Sunday papers were there. They told me that Eric Cantona had allegedly attacked an ITN reporter in the West Indies, where he has gone to get away from it all.

You have to just listen without reacting. Inwardly I was thinking: "Bloody hell," but at the same time I was wondering what these news guys and photographers were doing, hunting over the West Indies for Eric? It must have cost them a fortune trying to find him, hopping from one island to another.

But where do we go from here? Inevitably, when I got home it was on the news, although there was no film this time – the police confiscated it. The whole thing has grown out of proportion. When the incident happened at Selhurst Park, it was shown 93 times on television over the next two days – that's more repeats than the films of the JFK shooting. They've probably discussed it more as well.

Venue: Maine Road	*Att:* 26,368			
Manchester City	*goals*		**Manchester United**	*goals*
25 Andy Dibble		1	Peter Schmeichel	
16 Nicky Summerbee		3	Denis Irwin	
18 David Brightwell		4	Steve Bruce	
4 Maurizio Gaudino		6	Gary Pallister	
5 Keith Curle		23	Phil Neville	
15 Alan Kernaghan		8	Paul Ince	58
12 Ian Brightwell		5	Lee Sharpe	
8 Paul Walsh		9	Brian McClair	
28 Uwe Rösler		14	Andrei Kanchelskis	74
10 Gary Flitcroft		17	Andy Cole	77
11 Peter Beagrie		11	Ryan Giggs	
Substitutes				
2 Andy Hill		12	David May (82 mins for 14)	
33 John Burridge		24	Paul Scholes (53 mins for 23)	
9 Niall Quinn (63 mins for 11)		13	Gary Walsh	

Sunday 12 February

Eric is all over the front pages of the tabloids and the phone is ringing constantly. And to make for a really happy day, Blackburn had the easiest possible win against Sheffield Wednesday, who looked as if they were feeling sorry for themselves after going out of the Cup to Wolves on penalties. You could see the disappointment in their performance.

I started off watching it and then after about 15 minutes I said: "Sheffield are not going to win this, there's no point in bloody watching it. They're not going to do it." There's no point in getting all frustrated about it, so I went up to Mottram Hall, had a cup of tea and relaxed.

I think there are a lot of clubs whose last throw of the dice is the FA Cup. Sheffield needed an FA Cup run to keep the whole thing going. One of my theories about the game is that they should start the FA Cup later. It would be easier to retain crowds if they started it on 1 February and made it a quick tournament. I know replays come into it, but it just delays it by a month and the crowds generally tend to go down after their team has been knocked out of the FA Cup.

Monday 13 February

The press are having a field day over Eric. But when you get all the news surfacing and the police are wanting to question him, you say to yourself, 'What are we doing in this world?' There are photographs of Eric's wife, who is six months pregnant, all over the papers. It's absolutely disgusting. What man would not be protective if guys came up trying to taking photographs of his pregnant wife in a swimsuit? So I'm not surprised Eric reacted. What kind of country do we live in? It's unbelievable.

The coaching staff protect the younger players, but at our staff meetings they'll say,'You had better have a word with X or Y, ' because he doesn't look as if he's enjoying it or he's maybe going a bit over the top or getting carried away, or his father's proving to be a bit of a problem – it could be 101 different things.

Today we were discussing Ben Thornley again. It's one of those difficult problems. He's probably looked at the situation, has seen me putting Simon Davies wide left in a number of games, and he knows he would have had that chance if it hadn't been for the injury. He has let it get on top of him a wee bit and he's got a bit heavy. The lad is hitting a brick wall at the moment. He's a stocky lad, anyway, but if he gets heavy he's going to have a real battle.

I phoned his father. He's a headmaster, so he's intelligent; he has good awareness of the situation, and he is realistic.

"We're going to have to really push your boy," I said. "We're just going to have to dig in here, but we're going to stick by him all the way."

Then I had Ben in and I said, "Look, you're going to have to keep your head up. You're really going to have to battle. It's all about how you handle that fight."

I'm getting him to see our nutritionist and will try to get a wee bit of optimism back in his life.

He had a bad injury. There's nothing we can really do because he's not breaking down, although it is obvious there is still a restraint in parts of his game. He's playing in a few reserve games and A-team matches, but there is a restriction in his game. The specialist thinks he should play until it breaks down and should then be operated on. So the boy's in a terrible limbo. He knows his career's stopped really and he's now 20 years of age. He's going to have to battle hard to get a good career for himself.

It's sad, because he is a lovely kid, too; brave, a two-feet finisher, a great crosser of the ball – he has a bit of spunk about him. He was a great talent, a certainty to make it. He had a wee bit of cunning about him. He could get a cross in and get fouls for nothing, but he wasn't a diver because he was brave. And he was good in the air for his height. Hopefully we can resurrect him, get him back.

I keep hoping he breaks down so we can get the operation done and get him rehabilitated properly. It would mean he'd be out for a year, but by the time he's 23 he might have a good career. So that's a terrible dilemma for us. His parents have been fabulous.

This is an international week, with fifth-round FA cup ties at the end of it, which is most unusual – and ridiculous, I think. You can't say it because you've got to support Terry Venables in his quest to make things better. It's fair to say the last England performance was abysmal, which doesn't do the game any good. But no matter how you mask it, it's a ridiculous time to play the game. I'm not surprised Leeds have withdrawn Gary Kelly from the Ireland squad. I knew that was going to happen. That's their last chance of getting silverware. It might be my last chance of getting silverware for that matter – I might not win the League. Who knows?

This evening we had a bowling night in aid of HAWC – Helping Adolescents With Cancer. We had a team of five: four of the lads – David May, Andy Cole, and the two Nevilles – and big Norman Davies. I was supposed to be playing but, because of my cracked rib, I became coach for the night.

Early on in the evening, an oldish man approached me and we had a short chat. Later on there was a buffet. My secretary Lyn said:

"Can you come over after the buffet for a bit?"

"Aye, I'll get something before I go."

She said: "Carl Denver, the singer, would love to meet you." It was the oldish man.

"I didn't recognise you," I said.

"Oh, my hair's turned white," he said.

I asked him how he was doing, and he said:

"I'm doing fantastic. My CDs are selling a bomb in Africa, Australia and New Zealand and I'm doing tours everywhere. I'm making more than I ever did. I'll send you a couple of my CDs."

"Aye, that would be great." I said. "Actually, I met pals of yours in Springburn at the New Year."

Springburn, where he comes from, is on the other side of Glasgow from where I came from. I always remember he had a brother who used to sell papers outside the cinema in Townhead. 'Wimoweh', that was his song.

In the morning, driving in to work, I listen to all sorts – Mike Sweeney on Radio Piccadilly. I like Mike, he's into those stupid wee quiz games with songs. You phone in and he gives you clues. And I'm always tempted to phone in because two or three times I've got it. But I don't, because if I'm wrong he'll absolutely slaughter me. He's always going on about the gigs coming up in Manchester, all the old groups.

Tuesday 14 February

The board meeting was at 12. It's a good idea starting early. We used to start the board meetings about 3pm and not get away until 6pm. Now we start at midday and still get away at 6pm. It's an important time for the club, we're increasing the size of the stadium, making decisions about Cantona and Ince and so on. The board meetings are a bit tense at the moment.

Wednesday 15 February

I was on my way to the reserves' game against Tranmere at Bury, where we play some of our reserve matches, and I heard the England game in Dublin on the radio – the England fans rioted and ended the game. I couldn't believe it.

Sparky played a half but felt his knee. It was a bit stiff so we took him off. They played some good football, but the pitch is a bit dodgy at the moment. A lot of pitches seem to have taken a battering this year.

Fortunately our own pitch is in great condition.

The events in Dublin were appalling, but should we be surprised? I think we've been pretending everything is all right when it isn't, and hasn't been for a time now. There are things that have surfaced in the last year that have brought my attention to the crowd problems in our game. We're finding it away from home. West Ham was appalling last season. That's what disappointed me with Billy Bonds after that game. When I criticised the West Ham fans, he said, "Well Alex is entitled to his opinion" and I was angry. He was a man I looked up to, a person who played the game the right way. A good lad. Someone of whom you'd say, "Well he's a man alright." But the worry of upsetting his own supporters evidently swayed him. He was afraid to annoy his own supporters even though he knew it was the right thing to do.

In the Cup Final the Chelsea fans were throwing things at Giggs when he was taking a corner kick after about ten minutes of the game. By the time we went up and were parading the Cup they were throwing all sorts of things and the press ignored it. It's like the pogroms. Nobody believed it, they ignored it until they discovered it for themselves when the war was finished and they entered the camps. You can ignore things too long. The abuse we get is horrendous. But it was a sad night.

Thursday 16 February

A busy day. In the morning I went up to open a school in Prestwich. Our groundsman Keith Kent's kids are at it. I was asked if I'd go and open it because it'd burned down. And it was cold, way up in the hills there on the way up to Bury. And it was fabulous. Sometimes you need to meet modern day youth to get invigorated, because we underestimate them. We underestimate what a good school can be.

I got up there and there were three girls and three lads, all smartly dressed in uniform, waiting to escort me. And these young girls with their skirts on and the boys too, were freezing cold standing in that wind looking out for me.

"Is this my bodyguard?" I asked.

"Yes, we've to look out for you," they said.

Inside the school assembly hall the 600 kids there all had uniform on – ties and shirts and all – and that was not because Alex Ferguson had come but because their discipline is such that it's that way. It was great. I really enjoyed it. It's refreshing. It was bloody freezing.

In the evening I had to go and open Flixton Club. Now I said in my speech, and it's true, that too little publicity is given to events of this kind. There were a few photographers there from the Manchester Evening News and maybe a local Metro and they'll get a wee photograph in and say something about my speech, about me opening the club and that's because I'm there. They probably wouldn't get anything in the papers unless there was a personality present. There are good clubs up and down the country and people up and down the country who genuinely love the game. They work their tails off to produce a new social club, to show a bit of ambition about themselves and try and get a wee bit better than they are and it doesn't get any publicity. All the publicity today was about the hoodlums, the thugs who were over in Dublin. It's an unfair world. They've done a fantastic job up there. It's a smashing soccer social club, and I hope they do well.

Sparky is incredible. He was in and trained perfectly well today. That suggests that him playing for a half yesterday was about right, but his recovery is just astonishing.

Friday 17 February

So it was a busy week for me. And it isn't helped by the continuing trouble which I am having sleeping. I find that hard. So I had a quiet night. A friend came down for a game of snooker, and then we went out for a meal with some people from Scotland.

Saturday 18 February

Scholesy went through for the reserve game on Wednesday with the flu. He and Butt have been on and off with flu and chest complaints for the last few weeks. And Ince has been another problem in that respect. They're not fit enough. Ince is not fit enough. He may think he is, but he's not. He's just not getting to anyone. If you don't train at our level it shows. And they can't carry on with chest infections and flus and think they're going to handle it on a Saturday. It's disappointing, but you've got to do it; leave them out to get their fitness sorted out, so they're ready to perform up to their capabilities. So that comes into consideration when I'm picking the team. So Sharpey will be in midfield with Ince and with McClair up to come in the hole all the time and give them the problem of whether they stick or twist – whether they should go in to him or wait for him to come through.

Leeds are dangerous – mainly from of their set-pieces. Ray Wilkins called it "the land of the giants" when QPR lost there recently, so we have spent some time this week working on defending against their dead ball kicks. But we also worked on a function getting Ryan off the left touch-line a bit, and making runs into the channels.

This afternoon I went to Everton to see their cup game with Norwich. They won 5-0. An interesting afternoon: embarrassingly easy.

Before the game I was standing downstairs. Dennis Signy, the secretary of the Football Writers Association, was there. He told me he was meeting Bill Kenwright, the Everton director and theatre producer, at quarter-to-three. The doorman overheard, and said, "He'll not be here at quarter-to-three, I can assure you of that."

"Why?"

"He's here every day at one-minute-to-three. I'll put my life on it." This was at about half-past-two.

"Well I'm waiting here to see if he comes at quarter-to-three," I said. So I was chatting away to Dennis Signy and then Kenny Dalglish came in, and shook hands with whoever and then he went back out – maybe to get tickets, I don't know why. And then I saw this young boy, Keith Brown, who's been coming down to The Cliff for a couple of years, with his family. "Hello Keith," I said, and he was a bit embarrassed. And his parents were saying hello, and chatting and Kenny came over after a wee bit.

I said to Keith: "Are you down here as a guest of Everton?"

"No we're here with Kenny."

"Oh," I said, "Well he's got plenty of money, he'll look after you."

I don't think Kenny liked that.

Young Keith was a wee bit embarrassed because he's always loved coming down here training at The Cliff. It happens though, it's happened two or three times. You'll go to a ground, and you'll see a young boy you've had down training with you. We were down at Chelsea on Boxing Day and there was one of the young boys and he had a Chelsea track-suit on. 'What the bloody hell's this?' I thought. He was a United fan, but a Londoner and we'd had him up with his parents and they were really interested. The boy didn't say anything. He was probably scared I'd see he'd signed for Chelsea. But these things happen.

There were quite a lot of football people at Goodison Park. It's good to meet some of the managers at games and at half time you have a wee chat. But we came back out and someone told us Scotland had beaten

France in France. Brilliant! Kenny and I were delighted. A lad behind us shouted out: "Hey! There's Fergie talking to Dalglish." That's one thing you get at Everton, at Liverpool. You do get the wags. Another one started chipping at Ken:

"It won't be like this when we play you in April," he said.

"You're bloody right it won't," Dalglish retorted.

The score was four–nil at the time.

Sunday 19 February

United 3 Leeds United 1

We had some great performers today. In the big games you want them all to perform, and today they did. They are looking fresh. It was a good result for us. I was really pleased. And I was pleased also that there wasn't too much hassle. A few seats were ripped out but I think we can accept that. I thought the away fans were alright actually. I've seen them a lot worse than that. But they had the stuffing knocked out of them with two quick goals. We had the game virtually won in the first six minutes, both goals from corners, and the second was one we had spoken about beforehand. We didn't work on it but we talked about McClair leaving the front post and Pally going in, which is different from what we normally do. And it worked. So it was a great start to the game. You can't ask for better than that. That knocked the stuffing out of them. They couldn't really get going until half time, and then they were expecting their manager to sort it out for them.

I thought we did well tactically. McClair was magnificent, he's such a brainy player. Thinking and moving all the time.

The plan with Ryan worked too. In the first half he did give them a lot of problems by coming off the left side. But at half time, I said: "Look, there's no need to go and do that now. Let's keep our shape and make sure they can't get back in, because we'll get plenty of the ball if you stay wide now, Ryan."

If they hadn't lost the two early goals, they would have set us a tactical problem. They were playing Whelan in the inside right channel to come away into the inside left channel and the deep role in behind our midfield. Because they knew Keane runs on and Ince operates from there they had Whelan breaking off into the space that Keane leaves all the time to go forward. And they did cause us a problem in terms of good possession – either Whelan or Gary McAllister were always on the ball in the first half. But we sorted it at half time. We just sat a wee bit deeper.

Whelan also stayed up in the second half.

So you have to be aware of the other team's tactics. And I think that would have given us a problem if we hadn't scored early. We'd have sorted it and I know we'd have done alright, but tactics are an interesting part of the game.

It was obvious they were going to make changes in the second half. I said to the players: "As soon as they come in they're going to make changes. They must bring Yeboah on, they're two–nil down. In fact I think they might make the two. They might bring Worthington on." I thought they'd bring Worthington on, take off Wallace and put Yeboah through with Whelan. Or otherwise take Masinga off and bring on Worthington. But they took Masinga and Wallace off. And I think at 2-0 down you have to do something, and I think that's the kind of reaction you would expect from a good manager. And Howard's a good one.

I still couldn't see them doing anything, but football's a funny game and you get bad vibes at times. You hit the bar at one end and they go back down and score. It was a sloppy goal to lose, but fortunately they kept their composure, didn't get nervous and they handled it well. The players were in good fettle, they were ready. You could see it, you could smell it in the dressing room. There was a good atmosphere. There was tension, but not a tension that was going to affect them adversely.

Venue: Old Trafford	*Att:* 42,744		
Manchester United	*goals*	**Leeds United**	*goals*
1 Peter Schmeichel		1 John Lukic	
16 Roy Keane		2 Gary Kelly	
3 Denis Irwin		3 Tony Dorigo	
4 Steve Bruce	1	19 Noel Whelan	
5 Lee Sharpe		12 John Pemberton	
6 Gary Pallister		6 David Wetherall	
14 Andrei Kanchelskis		14 David White	
8 Paul Ince		8 Rod Wallace	
9 Brian McClair	4	26 Phil Masinga	
10 Mark Hughes	72	10 Gary McAllister	
11 Ryan Giggs		11 Gary Speed	
Substitutes			
19 Nicky Butt		21 Anthony Yeboah (45 mins for 26)	52
13 Gary Walsh		13 Mark Beeney	
24 Paul Scholes		15 Nigel Worthington (45 mins for 8)	

Monday 20 February

I ended up at a meeting with Maurice Watkins' colleague, Kevin Finnigan, regarding the legal side of Ben Thornley's injury. He has been looking into sueing Nicky Marker for the tackle. That's been proving very thorny. There have been a couple of litigations recently – John O'Neill's case against Fashanu, and the Paul Elliott case against Dean Saunders. I was asked to give an opinion on the Fashanu one but I felt that the fact that I'd been involved with Fashanu in the case over the the

Fashanu/Anderson clash in the tunnel at Wimbledon would make me a poor witness.

But after the Saunders and Elliott case there has been a reluctance from managers to get involved in any of these things. I think the general opinion is that they don't want to see things going to court. The legal people spoke to Gordon Taylor and put a suggestion that there should be an arbitration situation where three witnesses for the plaintiff and three for the other side sit in a room in Manchester, look at the video and come up with an opinion. They would then settle the case through a conversation, rather than go to the lengthy and costly procedure of the High Court. That would, to me, be a sensible proposition.

We also had a meeting at Maurice's office over Eric's situation and then went up to the Portland for a wee chat about other things. Eric and his wife came with their barrister, as well as Maurice, one of his partners, and myself and George Scanlon, who interprets for Eric and Andrei. Ned Kelly, who looks after security, came along too because we've been discussing this the whole week. He goes into the police tomorrow and then Friday we're down at the FA. We don't know where yet, they haven't decided where their hearing is to be held. So it's going to be a big week for us, and we'll have to be bang on. I phoned and got the police round to Eric's house yesterday because the press were bothering him. He had them moved because they've become a nuisance now.

We are also looking at the medical situation. There is a possibility of hypo-glycemia, and we're going to get tests done on that, because we're not prepared to accept these incidents as always 'just being Eric'. We have to look at the situation. Why do the incidents always occur in the second half? So we've been going into a lot of things, in the last few weeks, Maurice and I, the club doctor and the physio. We spoke to Eric about the hypo-glycemia and he was interested.

It was a busy day and I didn't get down to see the reserves because the meetings went on too long. And they lost 2-0. In fairness there have been too many changes. We haven't had any consistency in the reserves this year. Too many injuries. Young ones and old ones. There are no really old ones but the older group of the young ones – the youth team of two years ago – were the nucleus of the reserve team. They've been in now without any consistency. But it was disappointing to see that they lost 2-0. I was surprised at that. Anyway, we'll find out the reasons. Jim Ryan's in the dock.

Tuesday 21 February

Eric went to see the police today, and has been charged with common assault, the lowest form of charge.

George Graham was sacked today by Arsenal, after the Premier League's report on the allegations that he took a "bung" to sign players from Scandinavia.

Somebody phoned me at The Cliff and said George Graham had been sacked. I put the teletext on and called the staff in to look at it. It's a lot of money and if the allegations were proved to be true then you fear for George. But I couldn't understand Arsenal doing it. They knew about it last October or thereabouts. By reputation they've always had a high moral stance. If you go back to that time the two clubs were brought up for disrepute after the battle at Old Trafford, they chose to fine their manager a week's wages. So it is a bit surprising when they've known about this since October that they go and carry out the sacking today.

I don't think we've heard the last of it, but it's sad for a great manager to leave in that way.

A thought just struck me this morning, reading Johnny Giles on Wimbledon. It was an incredible piece, praising Wimbledon to the high heavens for giving Vinny Jones a three match ban for biting a guy's nose and hitting people with toast in restaurants. And we suspend Cantona for effectively six months of football, which could cost us at least £6 million, and we still get stick. It's unbelievable. You just can't win.

I know the standard of the club is great and people say 'It wouldn't have happened in Sir Matt's day would it? They would've thrown Cantona out the door.' But Sir Matt had to contend with a few hotheads in his day. I'm sure Sir Matt was faced with the same things I'm faced with. Certainly we are proud of the credibility of the club and we tried to uphold it, and the Cantona thing was something that really hit us badly. We're not disputing that. But when you've got winners, they get in a situation where the game gets too much for them, and they get carried away. Sir Matt had winners like Nobby Stiles and Paddy Crerand. Denis Law was always booked or sent off at Christmas.

I say all the time that you can't leave your character in the dressing room, it goes out onto the field with you. And people forget that Manchester United teams – no matter who was the manager, who were the players – have always had big games. We're facing a big game every week – cup ties and Cup Finals, because teams are desperate to beat us.

So these players, unlike most players in the game, are in flashpoint situations every week. They're expected to perform at the highest level and players like Keane, Ince, Hughes, Cantona and Schmeichel are naturally emotional players.

And they criticise us about those players and indiscipline. So if it was indiscipline with five it would be indiscipline with 11 of them. But you look at Denis Irwin, Lee Sharpe, Brian McClair, Andrei Kanchelskis, Gary Pallister and Ryan Giggs. Gary Pallister has had about four bookings in his time here – and that's six years. Paul Parker's never in trouble. So if they criticise the Keanes and Inces, do they never think of praising the behaviour of the other players? What you're talking about is their personalities. We don't go out there with intent to tarnish our name. They go out to win the matches and they are emotional players involved in cup tie situations. They are real competitors and from time to time it goes over the top. Teams are wound up to play them and they're going to get right stuck in to them and there will be a few tackles flying about. The one thing about Manchester United and all the teams where I've been is that we'll not have any players rolling about playing for fouls and getting players booked. That's the one thing I say to every one of them. They get up and play. They don't moan about it, they get on with it. And that, I think, is a great credit to them all.

The press have been so critical of us since the Cantona thing happened, it's about a month now, it's been unbelievable. So we just have to, as they say, bite the bullet. But the Jones situation has actually been a perfect ending to the month. It's been a great booster for my philosophy about the need to defend your players and the part the press play in influencing people's minds.

Wednesday 22 February

Norwich City 0 United 2

We flew to Norwich this morning. It was the most horrendous flight, the biggest fright I've ever had in my life. The plane hit the runway in a crosswind and as it careered across the pilot tried to pull it back and it tipped right over. The wing tip was inches from hitting the ground. The captain did say that was the nearest you'll ever get without crashing. So that was a good start to the day.

It's very easy to joke afterwards and Mike Edelson said: "Well it could have been the Norwich clock outside Old Trafford."

"I told you never fly in February," someone else said. It's sick. But it was a fright.

Some of them don't like flying, so of course there's this argument about whether we should fly or not. Ince and Pallister don't want to fly, they want to go by coach. Others want to fly and there's a bit of banter about it. I think next time there will be more people who don't want to fly. Incey says he went white!

During the game I kept telling myself that the performance was like Southampton, when we flew down and the first half was murder. I didn't think we played that well in the first half tonight although we were 2-0 up at the interval. I thought we did quite well but I didn't think we were exceptional.

At half time I said: "We'll be better in the second half", because that was the case in Southampton. And I was just wondering whether the flight had anything to do with that. We got there at lunch time, they had their lunch and went to bed. It's something we'll just have to look at.

But maybe scoring the two away goals at Norwich was the reason for the low-key performance – an attitude of 'We've won the game, let's just keep the ball.' In the main they did keep the ball very well, but they were never really threatening with it. It was across and back and across. They just kept tidy possession, which is not a bad thing really, but I always like to get a wee bit of risk attached to the game and we didn't provide enough. I left Denis Irwin out just to give him a rest. It's been a hard season, he's been brilliant. He's had a World Cup. He's one of the few along with Gary Pallister who've not had a rest.

In fairness Norwich worked very hard. I had a wee chat with John Deehan after the match and he was asking me about their game on Saturday against Blackburn. I said playing three at the back may be an option.

"Well there's one of two ways of approaching it," I said. "You can play the two markers against their strong ones. but they don't have Sutton, and Newell has been out for that long it's going to be difficult for him to get into the swing of things right away."

"Well," he said, "we've been doing quite well with the four-four-two. We've been working hard at it in training."

"Well stick by it," I said. "You've got to stick by it."

The one thing I have to pick up on from the Norwich game is the attitude of our supporters. I was disappointed by them at Norwich. They started chanting: "We Hate Leeds United." I don't know how all of a sudden this has come on the agenda for Manchester United supporters.

It's never been heard before. But Leeds United to my mind are not important as an item in our lives. I don't know why they were going on about Leeds United.

I shall mention it in the programme and I hope they listen, because I don't like that. We're always going on about clubs chanting Munich and all that. We've got to be above that sort of thing. It was disappointing, really disappointing.

At least the flight back was all right. The wind had dropped and it was raining, so we had a safe journey back and we were in for 12 o'clock.

Venue: Carrow Road	*Att:* 21,824		
Norwich City	*goals*	**Manchester United**	*goals*
24 Andy Marshall		1 Peter Schmeichel	
16 Carl Bradshaw		16 Roy Keane	
5 Jon Newsome		4 Steve Bruce	
10 John Polston		6 Gary Pallister	
2 Mark Bowen		5 Lee Sharpe	
6 Neil Adams		8 Paul Ince	2
19 Andy Johnson		14 Andrei Kanchelskis	16
8 Mike Milligan		9 Brian McClair	
20 Darren Eadie		17 Andy Cole	
22 Mike Sheron		10 Mark Hughes	
7 Ashley Ward		11 Ryan Giggs	
Substitutes			
3 Rob Newman		3 Denis Irwin	
34 Simon Tracy		13 Gary Walsh	
15 Darryl Sutch		19Nicky Butt	

Friday 24 February

We feel devastated. Eric was banned until 1 October. It's a savage sentence. His last game was 25 January. His next game may be the beginning of November by the time he gets match fit after being out for so long. It's effectively a nine month ban so it's understandable for us to feel a bit let down by it all.

People say that we should not have suspended him and left it to the FA. That would have been an abdication of our responsibility, but we did feel aggrieved that having heeded the FA's message, further punishment was heaped on our suspension.

There were three members of the FA Commission – Ian Stott, Gordon McKeag, and Geoff Thompson. Some people thought we got off lightly and there were rumours afterwards that one of them was not satisfied, and had wanted a ban to the end of the year and a £100,000 fine.

In *The Guardian* there was an article about a player in the non-league who chased across the pitch and jumped into the crowd and assaulted a fan. I think he broke his jaw. And he got a two-week suspension from the FA!

Two things stick out in my mind about the hearing: the three hours I spent in the room observing Eric and how he's handling it; and the press circus after it.

We got there about 11 o'clock. George Scanlan, the interpreter, was present as well as two from France, Jean-Jacques Bertrand, Eric's adviser, and Jean-Jacques Amorfini from the French PFA. Gordon Taylor, Maurice Watkins, Ned Kelly, Eric and I made up the rest of our party. We were there until about half-past-two, or three o'clock. Eric was so placid, and he handled the whole thing really well. I said to him before we heard the verdict, "No matter what the verdict is you say nothing. If anybody says anything it'll be me." I had no intention of saying anything, but I felt that by saying that to him I would be taking on the protective role for him by saying that if anyone was going to lose his temper it was me.

We were called quickly to the meeting. It was half past eleven when we went in, and we were in for about three-quarters of an hour. Maurice kicked off with the first submission, then Jean-Jacques Bertrand said his bit and I said mine, and then Eric just made his apology. The panel asked us a couple of questions.

Whilst admitting the charge, there were considerable mitigating circumstances which were put to the commission. There was a lot of remorse from Eric. He has suffered terribly with the press. Nobody can understand it until you're in it yourself. His wife and kids have been subjected to unbelievable pressures since this happened. His chances of bonuses and of winning Cup Finals have gone. The captaincy of France has gone. We talked about the serious provocation, and Maurice gave the commission written details of what had been said to Eric by the fan. I mentioned in my submission the hatred shown to us away from home and emphasised that it's not just happening to Manchester United.

I also spoke about Eric's professionalism as a footballer. He's the best prepared footballer I've ever had. He's first at the training ground, he does his own warm up and then he does our warm up. He trains brilliantly, and then he practises after training and he's the last to leave the car park, signing autographs. He's happy to do the hospital visits whenever you ask him to do anything. He's a model pro, an absolute dream of a footballer.

And there's that part when you say to yourself: 'What is inside that man?' There's a volcano there. And you never know what makes it erupt, because he is so placid and quiet. We mentioned all sorts of solutions; that we were looking into the medical and physical side of Eric, because all the sendings off have occurred in the second half of games.

Ian Stott asked Eric a beauty of a question through Maurice.

"Is it a fact that you are a kung fu expert?"

And Eric looked bemused at this and said, "Qu'est-ce que sais? What are you talking about?"

Ian Stott repeated it: "Is it a fact that you are actually a qualified expert in the martial arts?"

And Eric replied, "No."

It was a cracker. The question surprised everyone present. I looked across at one of the FA boys, who was taking minutes of the meeting and I could see that he was thinking 'What do I write down here? What a question. Should I enter this into this official inquiry?' I couldn't believe it.

After the verdict was read out, Graham Kelly, David Davies, Maurice and I went into a room to discuss the FA's statement. We were horrified with what was proposed. Maurice was seething, really seething at the statement. It was so prejudicial.

"You give that out and you'll be in the High Court by Monday, I can assure you," he said.

So they went through the statement and changed it all round, because it was really horrendous stuff. In fairness, Graham Kelly and David Davies handled it very well once we had made our point.

So after getting the verdict and digesting it and having discussions with Graham Kelly, David Davies and Maurice, I was drained. We also had to prepare our own press statement before the press conference.

Before we went in, we discussed it. We decided that Eric wasn't going to say anything, but I said, "Fine, but you've got to face the music. You've got to go in there and be there." Which he did.

Maurice asked me, "Well do you think you should answer questions?"

"If I start answering questions it'll go on and on and on and on. You know, it'll extend to who's going to replace Cantona – is it going to be Cole, or Hughes, or McClair? Who are you going to sign? So it's going to extend right on. And I don't think we want that. I think that you should answer the questions."

I think we did alright. Questions were all directed to Maurice but prefaced with "Does Alex think this?" or "Does Eric think that?" This was a way of trying to embarrass us into responding because we'd gone down that road and this was a way of getting around our policy of silence which I found quite amusing. I thought it was interesting, I quite enjoyed that part. But I was just wanting to get away.

Then one guy at the very end said, "Alex, you must answer this – How do you think it will affect young boys and all that?" Obviously he was a news man he didn't know what anything was.

I said, "Look, I'm happy to talk to sports journalists at any time but this is not a sports journalist. Maurice will answer your questions." I just left it there. I wasn't in the mood to answer questions and I didn't think I was going to benefit anyone.

I don't think the Dublin situation helped, and the Vinny Jones thing didn't help. Giles did that article applauding Wimbledon for giving him a three match ban. We gave our player a 21-match ban and were criticised. We felt we were being crucified to appease the press after all the criticism of the FA for being weak, and after all the hysteria of the past couple of weeks with the Dublin riots and the 'bung' scandals, and the match-fixing allegations and the behaviour of Vinny Jones in Ireland.

Some of the press coverage has been outrageous. I know a lot of the journalists and I've seen their behaviour abroad. How they can pontificate and moralise when you see how they behave themselves is beyond me. I've seen some of them in fights and arguments and all that type of thing. Of course you can blame drink for that, but equally you can blame the emotions of any footballer in that situation where a guy's provoking him. You never know. Nobody knows how people react. You lose your temper, I've done it myself. As long as human beings are human beings it's going to be that way. Not everyone can be like Bobby Charlton. Winners are winners and there are very few angels like Gary Lineker.

It was a hard, hard day. Eric and his wife went off to Paris. They were probably doing the right thing – getting out of the road. They went over on the Chunnel. I came home absolutely exhausted. I went to bed about nine, I think. I had nothing to eat. I got a cup of tea and went to bed.

Saturday 25 February

Everton 1 United 0

This was one of the tougher away games. Physically tougher. They're setting out their stall very well to get results, and they are very difficult to beat. And with the game starting late, because roadworks on the M62 delayed the fans, we knew that Norwich had drawn at Blackburn. So we went gung ho in the last five minutes and put Pally up. And it never came off. You can't really deny them the result. They've worked hard at it. We didn't have any really bad players and we worked really hard. Our lads worked their socks off, so I'd nothing to say to them after the game. You deserve better but if you get chances like we did, you really do need to take one or two of them. So I wasn't too disappointed. I suppose with Norwich drawing it alleviates the pain a wee bit, and the concern and the fears.

Norwich got a good result at Blackburn – 0-0. It looks a real surprise, but perhaps it isn't, because Blackburn's pitch is starting to go a little and it is hard on bad pitches. But we are getting to that stage in the season where you get these surprises. You can never be sure of a game of football. That's why Andy Gray was being a bit optimistic last night on Sky, saying both teams were going to end up with 93 points. There will be surprising results.

I thought they'd play three in the middle of the park, trying to stop the service to Sparky. So I thought, 'I'm going to play three in there and make sure they have to work to get that protection' – so I left out Andrei. It doesn't give you the right balance, it has to be said. It was one of these questionable team selections you take a chance on. You say to yourself during the game, 'Well we'd have been better just leaving it,' because you can fine tune too much some times. And at half time I said to Andrei, "Keep warmed up because you're going to be coming on." Just when I was thinking of doing it, they scored.

Everton play a bit gung ho, the cup tie sort of thing, but we should have scored five goals. We opened them up a bit. With the Hughes and Cole partnership openings are bound to happen anyway. But if your strikers have got five clear chances between them away from home, you should win.

I thought Sparky should have scored with Incey's ball to his feet for the first one. With the next one I think he expected the defender to have a touch on it and it caught him off guard. He had a great chance there. Then Cole had three chances. He hit his first one well, but he pulled it wide. And the second one he should have scored was a one-on-one with Southall.

If either one of them had scored we would have won one–nil. If we'd established a lead we would never have lost it. If you get five chances away from home and you're not taking them then you're always going to be suffering. I thought we played quite well; we dominated it, really. They had their usual start to the game where everything's wellied into your box, and we handled it alright. Then we started to get hold of the ball, and in the last 20 minutes of the first half we played well. From the moment they scored in the second half we were all over them.

But it was a week in which it was very difficult to get angry about a game of football.

Venue: Goodison Park	*Att.* 40,011		
Everton	*goals*	**Manchester United**	*goals*
1 Neville Southall		1 Peter Schmeichel	
4 Earl Barrett		3 Denis Irwin	
5 Dave Watson		4 Steve Bruce	
26 David Unsworth		6 Gary Pallister	
3 Andy Hinchcliffe		5 Lee Sharpe	
13 John Ebrell		8 Paul Ince	
17 Joe Parkinson		16 Roy Keane	
10 Barry Horne		9 Brian McClair	
18 Stuart Barlow		17 Andy Cole	
16 Anders Limpar		10 Mark Hughes	
9 Duncan Ferguson	58	11 Ryan Giggs	
Substitutes			
31 Stephen Reeves		14 Andrei Kanchelskis	
7 Vinny Samways		13 Gary Walsh	
10 Daniel Amokachi		19 Nicky Butt	

10
On Our Way to Wembley

Sunday 26 February

Darren came up to see us last night. We watched the Benn-McClellan fight, in which McClellan collapsed. I was really worried about him. I knew there was something wrong when he kept wanting his gum shield to come out. It's not what a boxer normally does. I could see the helplessness in his face.

I'm having a hard time with Darren at the moment. He's such a good boy, and dedicated. He thinks of nothing but football. Darren has been working hard and he is a bit down because he's been having a tough time at Wolves. I hope he gets a move because he has to get away. He'll get a football club and he'll be a good player. The manager told him he's been their best midfield player this season and he's then left him out.

That symbolises the horrible part about English football; why England will never win World Cups – we just don't have enough people who believe in playing football. You've got a really good footballer like Darren, and he can't get in the Wolverhampton Wanderers team because the manager believes in a different way of playing. He has had success at Watford and Villa with his approach and I don't think he is going to change. That brings you to one of the reasons why England will never win the World Cup. We have so many different styles of play, whereas in Germany and Italy the players all play the same way. That makes continuity of selection and pattern difficult and that is essential. Something really dramatic is going to have to happen to our game. Terry Venables is the one man who's got a vision, he's got an imagination about the game at least.

Monday 27 February

The *News of the World* came up with the headline yesterday, "Fraud Cops to Quiz Fergie." What? All it says is that the Norwegian police investigating the "bung" allegations want to talk to all the managers who know Rune Hauge. When you read the story it does not suggest that I have done anything illegal or contravened the rules regarding transfers. So why such a large headline suggesting I was involved in some wrongdoing? I spoke to Maurice Watkins and we are sending that along to the barristers for an opinion. Reading the papers for libel is almost turning into a full time job for Maurice.

Preston have asked for David Beckham to go on loan for a month. We've agreed, because we have everyone fit. It's something we find good for some of the young players. We sent Keith Gillespie to Wigan at one stage, and Neil Whitworth went on loan a couple of times. It does them good. It just toughens them up a little and gives them a better insight into the luxuries we give them. They go down there and they have to fight for their training kit and that type of thing. I'm not saying it's always like that but it's a different world and they appreciate it when they come back.

David's one of the later developers in our club, and it'll give him good experience. He's coming on well, he'll be a really good player, but we felt a month there would maybe help put him in the running when we bring him back at the end of it. A wee bit of experience of playing in that division, where it's quite tough and you've got to battle, will help him.

Tuesday 28 February

Andrei asked for a transfer today. I was really angry.

We had a practice game in the morning and I explained to the team:

"Look, this selection thing is a headache and I've just got to start again, make sure I get the team with the right balance. This is what the team's going to be on Saturday."

I had to leave Sharpey out. I explained what I was going to do. It's my job to make sure I pick the team I think is right. It's not easy for me. We had a practice game and I thought he'd understand.

After training I was to go home and take Cathy to the airport because she was going to Glasgow and I was going to Belfast. But George Scanlan came at lunchtime and he and Andrei wanted to see me which was when he asked for a transfer. I was absolutely furious.

I went to Belfast to do an evening for the Shankhill Community Project, for PHAB, the Physically Handicapped Able Bodied. I was on a panel with Ally McCoist for Rangers, Bertie Peacock who used to play for Celtic, and Malcolm Brodie, a smashing journalist.

I'd agreed to go a couple of months ago. I thought it was a worthwhile thing to get involved in, particularly with the Peace Process going on. Everybody was relaxed and determined to get it through. And in that hall, although it's the Shankhill Community and it's a Protestant area, they were a completely mixed bunch. It was really refreshing to see that.

We went to City Hall first. What a gorgeous building. The mayor's deputy was there and he said: "We're going to see this through. I'm speaking for every Irish citizen. We're going to see this through and we're going to get it through."

Then there were a thousand kids in a leisure centre and a lot of parents. But oh my God, the bedlam! You couldn't hear yourself. I couldn't hear what Ally McCoist was saying or what Bertie Peacock was saying or Jackie Fullerton, who hosted it. But it was a lovely night. I stayed with Terry Smith, who used to work for Granada and now works for the BBC in Belfast.

I enjoyed the meal after the show. Terry took me to his local hotel out in the country and we had steak at the bar. The people were just sitting at the bar chatting away and it was really relaxed. It was the first time I've eaten steak for about six months. I just find eating red meat fills me up too much and I feel heavy after it.

I felt it was worthwhile going, but by doing that I couldn't go and see the Youth Team play at Villa Park. It took ages to get the result. Kiddo said he would keep his mobile on, but every time I phoned it I heard the words: "The mobile phone you are calling is not available."

Then I phoned Darren.

"No, I don't know the result," he said.

"Phone them and I'll phone you back."

"They won't answer the phone," he said.

"Bugger you," I said, and I forgot that one.

Then I tried Ken Ramsden. He didn't know the result, but he said he would try and get it and phone me back. I then phoned Kiddo's wife.

"Well it was 3-2 at half time. To us."

"Was it? That's good."

"Aye, he phoned me and told me 3-2. He phoned me at 8.20pm."

I should have worked it out. With a 7pm kick-off for a youth match, that was way into the second half. Eventually I got the result. It was fabulous.

Wednesday 1 March

I was up early in the morning to come to Glasgow. I was the Scottish Television analyst for the Barcelona and Paris St Germain European Cup quarter final.

I like going into Glasgow, it's an exciting city. I get people saying to me, "I was up in Glasgow last week and I didn't realise what a lovely city it was." It's amazing how a stigma can last forever. No Mean City must have been written 40 years ago, but how that image about the Gorbals and razor gangs has stuck in people's minds. It's always been a tough city, there's no doubt about that. Where I came from was tough but I think it's like anything else: if you want trouble you'll get it.

If I go to Glasgow I never get away from wee Jim Rodger. He just seems to know exactly where I'm going. He's incredible. I'd just walked into the Marriott and I was greeted with: "Oh, wee Jim Rodger is looking for you."

"But the plane only landed ten minutes ago," I said.

"Oh, he's in the phone booth." So I went through.

"Where have you been?" he said. "I've been looking for you."

"I've just bloody arrived. Christ!"

He uses that Marriott as his office. I'll phone up the Marriott and say:

"Jim Rodger, please." They don't ask, "Is he resident?" They just say, "He's over there, just hold on a moment."

In a way Jim's been a bit of a mentor to me, he's been an influence in my life since I was 15 years of age. I've a sort of a chequered career with the press. I'm not on the middle of the road. There's a lot I don't like, not because of what they write, but because I just don't like them. Their personalities don't impress me. Their demeanour doesn't impress me. But some do and it's black and white to me. But wee Jim's been a tremendous source of encouragement and support throughout my life. You can't escape him. And of course, people underestimate him so much it's unbelievable.

The game was engrossing. I was in the studio analysing the game with Walter Smith. It was the first time I'd done it for a while. It was a really good game, too. In the first half Barcelona played it without strikers. They played two wide with no central striker. And they had Bakero and Beguiristain making the runs in the hole. They did quite well. The first half of a lot of European games apart, perhaps, from when we play in them, is all cat and mouse. Nobody really does anything. But with Barcelona it's always keep the ball, pass it, pass it, pass it, hoping that your concentration goes and then they'll get someone in. But they missed Romario. You can see that they're going to miss him.

In the second half, Paris St Germain were brilliant: aggressive, good defenders, quick to the ball. The boy Georges Weah up front gave Barcelona's defenders a nightmare.

Thursday 2 March

Paul Scholes has torn ligaments on the ankle so he'll be out for a month. It happened in a training game, too. He went up for a high ball and came down on it badly. We put it in plaster and immoblised him.

Friday 3 March

Andrei's request for a transfer is all over the papers. I was furious because the reporters didn't ring me to check the story or get the club's position.

I went to a charity snooker evening with a friend of mine, Gordon Broome, at the house of another friend, Peter Hember. It was in aid of HAWC. Dennis Taylor and Joe Swail were the snooker players. There were about 70 people watching. I played Dennis Taylor. I was being sponsored per point. I practise quite a lot, and I'm not bad. I broke off but the cue-ball hit the jaws of the pocket. He got 81 – he would have got the maximum but he got a bad break with one of his reds. I think I got about two shots in all – I got maybe 15 or 16 points, so the charity did get something out of it.

But then I played Joe Swail and I got 39 points. He still beat me, but only on the brown. Then I played a member of the public and I won that well.

It was a great night. A beautiful house and beautiful snooker table, and I think they raised about £10,000. It is great that in that sport the professionals can go out on a Friday night and do that sort of thing. All I can do is go and talk about football – we can't go out on a Friday night and put on a demonstration game and banter with the punters like Dennis and Joe did. Dennis Taylor was great company. He is a very funny man – and a great Blackburn fan, so there was a wee bit of banter going on. "You'll be glad I let you win this frame," I said to him. "As long as we win the League!"

Saturday 4 March

United 9 Ipswich Town 0

It was a marvellous performance, you could have set it to music. The harmony was perfect, everybody was buzzing about the place. Their movement, their passing, their passion, was the sort which happens just once in a lifetime.

We could have scored three in the first two minutes, actually: Andy Cole had a good chance; Incey had a header wide of the post at the corner kick he should have scored; then we didn't follow the next corner in and it went right by everybody, and that was only the first two minutes. But once we got the first goal it was all systems go.

It was 3-0 at the interval. I knew Blackburn were only winning 1-0. I didn't mention Blackburn Rovers, but I said to them at half time: "Look, make sure we get the goals today. The one thing we take out of today is the goal difference. It's an opportunity you cannot miss. I've never won here by more than five goals, you know. Never. And that's a condemnation of you lot sitting there. Absolute condemnation of the lot of you." A few of them laughed at that. But they started the second half with two goals in eight minutes. They were five up with 35 or 40 minutes to go. It's once in a life, because in the context of a 9 -0 win or a big score you miss open goals. You miss sitters. We didn't miss any real sitters. The goalie made three good saves. We hit the bar twice, but we never missed any real sitters.

Once it went to nine I didn't want any more. I looked at George Burley and thought: 'Hell, it's a sore one for him.' I felt sorry for him. Jim Ryan was sitting near me and he said: "You looked really unhappy towards the end of the game. Why?"

"Unhappy?" I asked.

"Yes," he said, "you seemed to be thinking about something."

"I didn't want them to score ten."

"Why?"

"Because of their manager."

"Why? Why is it worse to score ten?"

But it is. It's unthinkable for a manager, to lose 10-0. At the end of the game George was really emotional. He was going to go away but he stopped. I went across to him and said, "Look, I'm sorry about that, but you've got to do it." He just walked away. He never came in for a drink and I can understand that.

I had three 8-0s at Aberdeen. I'll always remember beating Airdrie 8-0 in the Cup because Bobby Watson was the manager at Airdrie at the time. We played with each other at Rangers. Bobby and I were really good friends. We still are, we're always in touch. But I wasn't the same at Aberdeen, I was more volatile. I used to say to Bobby when we were talking on the phone that maybe he'd lost a game, and he'd phone me and I'd say: "Well sod it, it's heading for the harbour time." When you lose a game, head for the harbour and jump in.

During this game we went to 8-0 at Aberdeen. Stevie Archibald scored four that day. Bobby leant over into the dug-out and asked, "What way is that bloody harbour?"

We beat Motherwell 8-0 in a League game and we beat Meadowbank 8-0 in a League Cup game. But I couldn't tell you anything other than that Archibald scored those four. I remember that because Tottenham were there and that's when they made their move for Archibald. And other than that I can't remember who scored the goals. I remember at the Motherwell game John McMaster scored with a side-footer from 25 yards. But he had that wonderful football brain and touch. He saw the goalkeeper going one way and he bent it. Side-footed it along the ground. Other than that I couldn't tell you, but I'll remember this because Cole scored five.

When I arrived at the ground there were a lot of supporters having something to say about Andrei: "Don't let Kanchelskis go!" – that type of thing and: "It's your job to pick the team." They're saying he's just got to learn to accept it. Amazing. Although he's a favourite, our supporters don't like players asking away, as Paul McGrath and Norman Whiteside found out.

An incident before the game amused me. While I was giving my team-talk it was interrupted by Andy Cole's mobile phone. That's a a first. He was completely unconcerned and answered it.

Venue: Old Trafford *Att:* 43,804

Manchester United	*goals*	**Ipswich Town**	*goals*
1 Peter Schmeichel		1 Craig Forrest	
16 Roy Keane	15	19 Frank Yallop	
4 Steve Bruce		5 John Wark	
6 Gary Pallister		6 David Linighan	
3 Denis Irwin		3 Neil Thompson	
14 Andrei Kanchelskis		18 Steve Palmer	
8 Paul Ince	72	7 Geraint Williams	
9 Brian McClair		14 Steve Sedgely	
11 Ryan Giggs		21 Stuart Slater	
17 Andy Cole	19/37/53/65/87	33 Alex Mathie	
10 Mark Hughes	55/59	11 Lee Chapman	
Substitutes			
5 Lee Sharpe (45 mins for 16)		10 Ian Marshall (63 mins for 7)	
13 Gary Walsh		4 Paul Morgan	
19 Nicky Butt (79 mins for 4)		23 Philip Morgan	

Sunday 5 March

I went to the East Anglian Supporters branch "do" last night at Old Trafford. There were a lot there, and it was a nice atmosphere. I was only there for half an hour because I'd friends down staying the weekend and had to go and meet them. To have their trip for such a game was incredible, as I said to them: "You know we're always looking to be successful as a club and the club's in a good position, but you'll never get many 9-0s. It's once in a lifetime, so savour your night."

One of them said: "Who do you think your star was today, Alex?" My star? Cole scored five but they all played marvellously. It's not a day for picking out stars, it's a day for remembering, because maybe it'll never happen again. It's difficult to see it ever happening again. They could change the rules of the game, they could make goals another two yards wider if the Americans have their way. But at the end of the day, I can't see it happening.

I had the players in for massages with Andy Pinkerton. We only had one or two injuries. Keaney had a problem with a hamstring and Brucey got a bit of a knee knock. Other than that everybody was all right.

Darren was at the Villa versus Blackburn game and he thought that Blackburn was boring and just defended for the whole of the second half, but it's still a result. You get a few in the press who are, perhaps, starting to swing against them a wee bit in the sense that they're going to have to represent England in Europe. I just don't think they could possibly do well in Europe. But they could get there, because they're likely to churn out results like they did yesterday, just scoring early and just hanging on. I really thought Villa would get something yesterday.

Monday 6 March

I phoned George Burley this morning and I had a good chat with him:

"Maybe it's the best thing to happen, you never know, if the players react to it in the right way. You know what you've got to do. If you need advice, any time you need anything, please phone me. Don't be afraid."

I made a point about his team and the real problem he has.

"I know," he said. "But I can't do anything about it."

They just lack pace. That's what suited us, because we've got so many quick players on our team and they've got seven players on the team who can't run. They've no legs, no pace. You can carry one or two centre mid-field players, but in key positions you've got to make sure that they've got a bit of pace or at least can read the game. John Wark has no legs left, but he reads the game. He needs others round about him to run. On his own, John's own game would be right if all the other bits around about him were OK. But when they are lacking in pace in some of their positions it's a bit bloody harder. But it was a fabulous performance.

I went down to London to do an LWT show, *Sport in Question*. They had problems with one of their panel so Bob Patience phoned me. Bob's been a good friend of mine since he used to write in the Daily Record thirty years ago. So I agreed. It was all right but it's just that continual quick controversy about Eric that comes up.

Tuesday 7 March

Wimbledon 0 United 1

The weather was appalling. I'd stayed in London overnight, but Manchester airport was closed for a time this morning, so there was a delay on the team's flight. It wasn't so bad down here, although it has been pouring with rain.

Things have changed a lot since we let David Beckham go to Preston. As it happens, it's a lesson, but I think we just got off with it. I would have involved David in tonight's game, as it turned out, if he had been with us. Scholes has got the ankle injury, Kanchelskis is away with Russia, Keane is out with a hamstring, Butt is suspended and David May is injured, so we are almost down to the bare bones.

I was doing a piece with Hugh McIlvanney. He came to the hotel in Croydon at lunchtime. We spent about two hours together, then I went to get some sleep before we had a Managers' Association committee telephone conference. We started at 3.15pm and finished about 4pm. I'd only got about ten minutes sleep before we started, so I was just ready to get another half hour when the door went. It was Ken Merrett. He said there was a ground inspection at 4.20pm.

"When did you hear this?"

"Five minutes ago. I thought you'd better know."

"Let's get down there right away. There's no way we're not going to be there."

So we dived in, and there was a local referee, so I just reminded of the rules regarding cancelling games.

"It's not a danger to players and you can see the lines, remember that, Mr Mitchell."

"You don't need to tell me," he said, "I know."

"I know you know," I said, "but I know too."

So I managed to get the decision delayed until 6.15pm. I didn't want any decision made there and then. We wanted the game on, to get it out of the road. I don't know what Joe Kinnear wanted, but I just got the feeling that he would have been happy for it to be postponed. The problem is that Palace are the landlords, and they have their League Cup semi-final tomorrow night against Liverpool, so they wouldn't want us to play and the ground to cut up badly.

I reminded everyone, police and all, I said: "Look, they've entered into this arrangement with Wimbledon, they have to live with that. You can't put a game off because there's a game on the next day. That's not a reason for cancelling."

Wednesday evening

As the game progressed I was sorry I opened my mouth. Bloody hopeless we were. But I knew what they would do. I knew exactly what they would do. They'd either play one in front of the back four to stop the supply, or one behind to mop up the supply. I knew they'd do that. And one up the pitch. We're the only team Wimbledon change their style for. They did it last year to beat us 1-0 and they did it again. It's hard to play against them. They don't let it flow, they foul, they compete for everything and they continually knock you back towards your own half. You are continually picking up all the loose balls, you are continually starting up the game and there is no flow. And the pitch was terrible. It was a bad performance, too. There was no life about us.

Finally, we nicked it in a controversial ending. They had a boy sent off for a second bookable offence – encroaching at corners. There was a lot of fuss afterwards about it being harsh, and complaints about him only being a yard inside, but he was much closer than that. Maybe it was a soft one, but you couldn't have that much sympathy. Joe got a bit carried away, and it all got silly.

We pushed Steve Bruce up and the skipper nicked it. It was the sort of result which makes you think we'll be all right, that we will do it, because it was a terrible pitch, a bad night, and we weren't playing well, but we dug in and got the result. Lucky! but that's it.

Venue: Selhurst Park	*Att:* 18,224		
Wimbledon	*goals*	**Manchester United**	*goals*
1 Hans Segers		1 Peter Schmeichel	
2 Warren Barton		27 Gary Neville	
4 Vinnie Jones		3 Denis Irwin	
10 Dean Holdsworth		4 Steve Bruce	84
12 Gary Elkins		5 Lee Sharpe	
15 Alan Reeves		6 Gary Pallister	
16 Alan Kimble		8 Paul Ince	
20 Marcus Gayle		9 Brian McClair	
21 Chris Perry		17 Andy Cole	
36 John Goodman		10 Mark Hughes	
37 Kenny Cunningham		11 Ryan Giggs	
Substitutes			
25 Mick Harford		18 Simon Davies	
23 Neil Sullivan		13 Gary Walsh	
26 Neil Ardley (85 mins for 20)		26 Chris Casper	

Wednesday 8 March

I watched Palace and Liverpool's Coca-Cola Cup semi-final at Selhurst Park on television and the ground was the same as for our game. You couldn't see any real penetration because the pitch was dead. One pass to Fowler was the only time the game was opened up.

Thursday 9 March

Roy Keane was injured in the first half on Saturday. I said to him: "You'll need to work hard at that. Make sure you come in early in the morning and do your remedial part." He has been doing it religiously, so I hope to have him for Monday.

Blackburn scored after two minutes last night again. Against Arsenal, with all the experience they've got! It makes me wonder sometimes if there is any tactical preparation in our game. I don't know, but how teams prepare to play against Blackburn Rovers amazes me. When John Deehan asked me about it, I said: "What you must do is start right, because Blackburn always start well." If you get over the first 25 minutes you've always got a great chance against them. They win games by scoring early goals. That's the way they work it: getting an early start to the game and then just stifling the game and playing off of people, living off it.

Friday 10 March

There was a dinner for Ray Wood – a lovely night. Bobby and I were the speakers. There was a full house, about 400, with a lot of the old players there, so hopefully we raised a few bob for him because he's been struggling after his bypass operation. He had three caps for England but the great thing he said in his speech was: "But the more important thing: I played for Manchester United." It was nice that he was really warm about the club.

When most people come here it's the pinnacle. It's the biggest thing for them, I mean whether you're a manager or a player. Even if they don't do well, even if it's not turned out right for them, that experience of being here is always something. Whether they've got that great affinity to the club that a lot of players have had then it's probably a debatable point. But most of them have cherished their days here and always have an affection towards the club.

Our older players, the ones in the '48 team, are so affectionate towards the club. One or two from the late-Sixties team have just a wee bit of bite about them. Not bitter, but more of an edge. Maybe it's a generation thing. The people who came after the war, the players and others, are far more disciplined people. Or more subservient, possibly, and were happy with what they got; happy with the job, happy just to get a few pennies.

I think there are a lot of people who can never accept what the modern player earns.

Some people are trying to retire me. A couple of days ago, Bill Thornton, who is a very nice man, phoned up and wanted to do an interview. He works for the Daily Star. I don't particularly like the Star, I must admit. I did the interview yesterday and then he phoned me up and told me his editor had changed it. The interview is on the inside, but on the back page there's me saying "I will retire in two years." Unbelievable.

So then, of course, Bob Cass is on the phone. He'd been on earlier in the week, and had asked if I was retiring. I'd said no. But now he had seen the Star. "What the bloody Hell's this I'm reading in the paper. You're retiring in two years time? I've bloody done my story for Sunday saying you're not retiring."

"You carry on with that," I said.

"Will you be there in 1999?"

"Of course I'll be here," I said. "I hope I'm here in 1999."

"Good, I want the exclusive in 1999."

"Bloody hell, that's four years away."

Cathy's going up and down to Glasgow all the time at the moment between her mother who's not so good and her sister Bridget, who is waiting to have a pacemaker fitted. So I had to cook for myself.

Saturday 11 March

We trained in the morning. Then Kiddo went to watch Robbo and Middlesbrough at Bolton, and I went to Liverpool – Tottenham with Les Kershaw – a fabulous game. First half was a fantastic game. End to end. It was really good exciting stuff.

What you notice about the present Tottenham side is the fitness. They ran Liverpool off their feet in the second half. It was the physical thing that beat Liverpool, because Tottenham were just running round them.

They should have been two or three up at half time, but Liverpool are one of those teams who are always in with a chance. Tottenham left Liverpool's left-hand side of the pitch empty. They left Babb or Walters on the ball, they didn't bother about that. And they tried to just squeeze all the space in centre midfield so that Barmby could run on to support the strikers. He was running between Babb and Ruddock all the time. Sheringham pulled off of Scales and left Klinsmann to just go through the middle. So they gave them a lot of problems both tactically and physically.

I arrived at Liverpool at 2.20pm and they wouldn't let me through to the car park. They said I was too late. So I was sitting there and all these Liverpool supporters were going round the car giving us stick. The attendent said: "I'll need to radio in." He then said: "What's you're name?"

"Alex Ferguson."

So he said into his transistor: "Alex Ferguson."

Then he turned back to me and said: "No, you can't. Park your car there. In the side street there. Just park it there and come back and move it at five past three after the game has started." I parked it there, anyway, and all the Liverpool supporters are giving me absolute pelters. There's nothing worse than a Liverpool supporter when they are doing well. They're bad enough at the best of times. Well, the banter. In fairness, nothing really nasty. One or two were a wee bit sort of stupid but nothing really terrible or anything like that. They were giving me a bit of stick, though. We're playing there next week – was I not supposed to go and watch them? So I got into the ground and I gave my key to the steward.

I said: "Look, this is the problem."

He said: "I'll move it, no problem."

So at half time, I went down to get my keys and he said: "Oh, they put a ticket on it." Can you believe that?

When I was coming back I met Ian Ridley, a journalist.

"Good result for you at Coventry," he said, "1-0 Coventry."

"Oh Good," I said.

So I got upstairs and Les Kershaw was standing talking to Terry Darracott, who used to be at Everton. "1-0 Coventry," I said.

"Oh great!" but then he proceeded to tell everybody.

"Les, don't tell anybody or you'll just put a jinx on us."

"I'm not superstitious," he said.

"I am!" I replied.

With about six minutes to go I said: "I'll go and get the car, bring it up to the door." I knew it'd be time up at Coventry because the Liverpool game had been delayed for ten minutes because of some traffic problems. And when I got into the car, Blackburn had equalised in the closing minutes.

I went home and it was one of those great nights you get in the house. My older son, Mark, and his wife were up and eight of his pals from Scotland had come down for our game against Queens Park Rangers. My niece Lisa from Aberdeen was also staying. She's come down for some job interviews. She's South African but she's been over here for five years now. Cathy's still in Glasgow, so Tessa made this magnificent pasta sauce.

And she's there cooking away and all this tribe are sitting chatting. I looked at the waste disposal in the kitchen. There were two carrier bags of empty bottles and cans. "Who's thrown all that away."

"This is a warm-up – it's just a warm-up," they said.

"Bloody Hell!" They'd only got in at five o'clock. they must have drunk six or eight bottles and cans of lager each before their dinner.

So I said: "Would anyone like some wine?"

Every hand went up. I collect wines and I've this full case of '85 Margaux and as it's a full case I could afford to take some. So I opened four bottles and went out of the room. So I was gone and they were thinking, 'Och, it's still warm-up time!' the mistake I made was opening it before the meal was put on the table. I had to go and get two more bottles for the meal. But it was terrific listening to their banter. I knew them all when they were wee kids. Some of them are 6 foot 3, massive boys, now. All 26-27, all at school together. It was good, I enjoyed it. So eventually the six bottles of wine were done and I said: "What time are you going out at?"

"Oh, about quarter to nine."

I said, "Right, I'll book your taxis now." I just wanted to get rid of them to try and clear up the debris. So the taxis came about twenty minutes to nine and they all went off into town. Never came back until three in the morning. I said, "Thank God" – you should see the debris. There must have been at least eight dozen cans and bottles. Unbelievable!

Sunday 12 March

United 2 Queens Park Rangers 0

I've been wary of QPR ever since they beat us 4-1. We've never taken them for granted again. I thought it would be a toughish game and it proved that way.

We had a fitness test on Roy in the morning. He felt OK but wasn't dead sure so the risk was too great. We put him on the bench and with Giggsy feeling his calf at half time I had to put him on. If we'd have been 2-0 up I'd have put Neville on, but it was too big a risk.

I said to him: "Just sit in the middle of the park, sit in front of the back four. Just stop the supply up to Ferdinand and you'll do the job."

First minute of the second half he made one of those 40-yard runs of his. He went right through, squared it, and the goalkeeper saved it. I said: "Bloody hell, they just don't listen to you." Roy has got that great enthusiasm to play. He's a marvellous player, physically and mentally tough.

We won reasonably comfortably without too much excitement. I felt that if we'd really needed it we could have found another gear. But credit to Queens Park Rangers, they battled. The two centre midfield players, Holloway and Barker, are little terriers. They can give you a hard time. And of course you're always wary of Ferdinand's threat: his pace and his ability in the air. He had one chance early on when he ran past Steve Bruce, because he's got that change of pace. It was on his right foot, too. Fortunately he just ended up going a wee bit too wide.

It was a 1pm start and we were waiting for the semi-final draw, so I watched the Everton-Newcastle game. I fancied Everton to win 1-0, which they did. I just said: "In the draw, let's get Crystal Palace or

Wolves." So I was happy with that draw.

You know when you say something that you wish you'd never said? The thing I said was in Cassy's piece this morning about my retirement. "Eventually somebody'll take over," I was quoted as saying. It didn't mean anything, but seeing it in cold print, I said to myself: "That's a terrible thing to say when you've got Brian Kidd, here." So at the press conference after the game I said that Brian Kidd is instrumental to the future of the club and that if he wants to be the manager he has every right to expect it.

It was my anniversary this weekend and Cathy is away. Crafty so-and-so – she never said a word.

Venue: Old Trafford *Att:* 42,830

Manchester United		*goals*	**Queens Park Rangers**		*goals*
1	Peter Schmeichel		1	Tony Roberts	
27	Gary Neville		16	Danny Maddix	
3	Denis Irwin	53	3	Clive Wilson	
4	Steve Bruce		14	Simon Barker	
5	Lee Sharpe	22	2	David Bardsley	
6	Gary Pallister		15	Ruus Brevett	
14	Andrei Kanchelskis		20	Kevin Gallen	
8	Paul Ince		6	Alan McDonald	
9	Brian McClair		7	Andrew Impey	
10	Mark Hughes		8	Ian Holloway	
11	Ryan Giggs		9	Les Ferdinand	
Substitutes					
16	Roy Keane (45 mins for 11)		12	Gary Penrice (62 mins for 15)	
13	Gary Walsh		13	Sieb Dykstra	
27	Philip Neville		5	Karl Ready	

Monday 13 March

We had a medical meeting. We have one every so often. Les Olive and Mike Edelson from the board, my two physios Robert Swires and Dave Fevre, Kiddo and myself all attend. We just go through the whole thing about the treatment of players, the surgical part. We discussed Paul Parker's operation, for instance. David May is having a hernia op.

I had a chat with Kiddo about Cassy's story, in case he was a wee bit upset. And I'm sure he was. "You know I wouldn't ever dismiss you," I said. "I know that," he replied. "It's just the way they come out, these things."

He said: "But you shouldn't be retiring, anyway."

"I know," I said. "I feel all right."

In the evening I had a HAWC charity dinner. I've been speaking at quite a few dinners, but you don't always know exactly how to pitch it. At the Ray Wood dinner I spoke about the season, about the Champions' Cup and I spoke about the Cantona incident, how we handled it and why we handled it and how I felt the FA let us down. At the HAWC dinner I was uncertain, but the organiser said: "They love to hear you talk about how you progress as manager." So I did a bit of both. Before I started, I had a chat with Peter Reid who was there with Mike Walsh and Jim Smith.

I made a point, which is true, that in tracing my career it's all about your relationship with your chairman. The bad spell I had was when I had a bad chairman at St Mirren. You become vulnerable. But I had a good chairman at East Stirling, Willie Muirhead. He still writes to me. He's an absolute character. always giving me stick for something I've done or said. And of course I had a wonderful chairman at Aberdeen in Dick Donald.

Tuesday March 14

We had a board meeting. It was straightforward for a change; nothing at all really to discuss. The Cantona issue is behind us now.

Afterwards I had a meeting with Alan Austen. He's got one of the most difficult jobs at Old Trafford – he's in development. The advent of the National Lottery is killing the development a bit. They're having to think of new ideas to keep in the stream of activity. So I was going over some ideas with Alan, trying to help him, thinking of the best way to use the players in this situation.

Wednesday 15 March

United 0 Tottenham Hotspur 0

In the first half some of the football was brilliant. We had about seven clear-cut chances. If we'd have scored, we'd have won. In the second half we had to go a bit gung ho and Sharpey got himself stranded up the pitch, and they got in behind him. Klinsmann began to cause us problems and Brucey and Pally were a bit hesitant, a bit nervous. But that'll be the hardest home game we'll play. The hardest away game will be at Anfield on Sunday. But it was a game we should have won and I was a bit disappointed that we didn't.

I know our club, and I half expected us to draw. You expect us to take it to the last gasp. That's the way we are. I don't think it's ever going to change. I don't think we'll ever win a Championship easily. It'll always be the third, fourth, last game of the season. But that's the way it's going to be and you just have to accept it. It was a great opportunity to go a point behind Blackburn and really they would've been worried then. But now it comes down to only one defeat. They can't afford a defeat and we certainly can't. It's a critical time for us. No doubt about that.

Klinsmann is a good player. Good movement, good mobility about him, elasticity in his body, he's terrific. He's surprised everyone. He is a bit of a diver, but he's trying hard to rid himself of that in Britain because he'll not get away with it. I think he has comported himself well, in his interviews, too. They are clear and concise and there is always something to them.

Spurs were impressive once again. Their running stood out, as it did at Anfield. There is that definite influence of Gerry Francis – this physical thing. I just wonder whether they're going to be like that in the last weeks of the season.

If we get to the Cup Final and meet them there, I just wonder what they'll be like on Wembley day – whether they will have that same running power.

There are all sorts of theories about how you prepare players. British teams who have done well with the physical input on the field have managed to be successful in many ways. Tottenham have got talented players to go with that running power, which makes them a difficult team to play at the moment. But how do you gauge and how do you spread out the work load so that they are still going strong when it comes to the vital part of the season, when you need a result? Do you have that knowledge? It'll be interesting to see what Tottenham are like come that part of the season. Will Gerry reduce the amount of training or maintain it? I must find that out as the season goes on.

Venue: Old Trafford *Att:* 43,802

Manchester United		*goals*	**Tottenham Hotspur**		*goals*
1	Peter Schmeichel		13	Ian Walker	
3	Denis Irwin		2	Dean Austin	
4	Steve Bruce		5	Colin Calderwood	
6	Gary Pallister		6	Gary Mabbutt	
5	Lee Sharpe		3	Justin Edinburgh	
14	Andrei Kanchelskis		11	Ronnie Rosentahl	
8	Paul Ince		9	Darren Anderton	
9	Brian McClair		15	David Howells	
17	Andy Cole		7	Nicky Barmby	
10	Mark Hughes		18	Jürgen Klinsmann	
11	Ryan Giggs		10	Teddy Sheringham	
Substitutes					
19	Nicky Butt (76 mins for 9)		14	Stuart Nethercott	
13	Gary Walsh		1	Erik Thorsvedt	
27	Gary Neville		20	Darren Caskey	

Thursday 16 March

I watched the video of the Spurs match again. We had seven really good chances – scoring positions and shooting positions. I don't know how Andy and Sparky missed theirs. When Andy hit the bar and Sparky had the one that went under his feet. The chances we missed were incredible.

With the Liverpool game coming up, we had the players in for a massage this afternoon. It's always going to be a big one, Liverpool.

Friday 17 March

We didn't do anything at all because Andy Cole was getting treatment on a thigh injury. I spent my time thinking about the best way to play Liverpool. They play this peculiar system of three centre backs with two full backs pushed on, but not actually playing a sweeper. Babb tries to take the extra forward, whoever it may be, on the right-hand side. And if someone runs beyond Bjornebye, he takes that too. It's an odd system, but they've won the League Cup with it. You wonder whether it would work at the highest level.

Plans for the new stand have been finalised, which is good news, but next season the stadium's going down to 32,000 while we're building a completely new North Stand. We need a bigger stadium. For the moment we are going to go to 55,000, but I've got ambitions to go up to 65,000. All you need is organisation. There's already a mail-order system. What you do is make sure it's season tickets for 55,000 and the other 10,000 are floating. That allows for FA Cups, for away fans, for the floating fans that come on the day or visitors from Ireland, or New Zealand and Australia... or Timbuktu!

Paul Parker has had another set back. It's unbelievable. I thought we'd have him for the next couple of weeks. I was looking forward to that, because we've a problem at the minute with the full back positions. Irwin is fine, but Sharpe's not happy playing there, and if I could get Keane fully fit and into centre midfield, I know I wouldn't want to leave him at full back. He's the one who will spark off our charge – if I can get him properly fit.

Saturday 18 March

Willie Miller, my old captain at Aberdeen who got sacked as their manager a few weeks ago, has come down to see the game tomorrow. He came with us to City versus Sheffield Wednesday in the afternoon.

Freddie Pye got us an extra couple of boxes. He's been a good friend to me since I came down here. Before the game he was full of the joys and I said: "I've put you on my coupon today."

"Oh Christ," he said, "that's us beat." And after 20 minutes they were beaten. I couldn't believe it. Just like the last time I went – against Tottenham – they could have been five down at half time. Instead, they got one back just before the interval. When a team scores on half time, going in at the interval with that goal behind them changes the game even if they are still behind. It's often decisive. City scored right after half time and won 3-2 and Sheffield just kept missing chances.

I didn't enjoy the game simply because you look at the managers. I'd one eye on the game and one eye on how they were handling it.

I spoke to Trevor before the match and I could see he was worried. You can see in some people's eyes that it's not happening for them and he's under pressure. Brian Horton is in the same situation. It is very easy to forget the days that you were under pressure. And it's a great reminder to see other managers in the situation that you were in. We were never in that situation of being relegation material, but that situation where you're not getting what you expect out of people, not reaching the targets you've set yourself. And for Trevor, who's at a good club at Sheffield Wednesday, and Brian Horton who's at City – two big clubs – you know that their expectations have not been reached. It must be really frustrating and hard for them. And of course, the press don't help. There's always somebody who's supposed to be taking Brian's job. It must be really hard for Trevor and Brian.

You wonder if maybe it'd be better if Franny Lee said: "Here's a five-year contract, it's your job, run with it." But there's always the speculation, there's always that imponderable question: what's going to happen.

After the game I met the team and we came over to Chester for the night – a nice relaxing hotel. I've settled the tactics and I really fancy us. I can't see them having the legs in midfield to handle us.

Sunday 19 March

Liverpool 2 United 0

It was a really disappointing performance at this stage of the season. When you're looking for United players to put their medals on the table, Anfield is the place to do it and show why they won them. It certainly never materialised and it brought home to me the possibility that it's been forgotten how our success over the past few years was achieved. Although Liverpool didn't play that well they were the better team, particularly in the first half. The second half we had a lot of possession but never looked really like scoring except for the two chances that Giggs and Hughes had.

When I watched them against Tottenham, my thinking was that we'd win the match in midfield. Instead, we swamped our own play; we had too many people around the ball, no spread in our game. What I decided to do was leave Andy on the bench and play Sparky on his own which, in the past, he's done very well against Liverpool. He probably had his worst ever game against Liverpool. He wasn't alone. You expect Paul Ince to rise to the occasion in that sort of game, but he didn't. There were a lot of disappointing performances.

One of the things in big games is that players really need to listen to what we're trying to achieve tactically. And we decided that Paul Ince should play more on the left-hand side than centre midfield, so that when McManaman was looking to have a free role, he would come up against Paul. Paul Ince is the best in the business at winning in these types of situations. The idea was for Ince to cover that area, and let McClair and Keane look after the rest. But Paul kept drifting to the right in the first half. Their first goal actually began with Paul making a run down the right. He beat a man, passed it to someone who crossed it, Wright headed it out, and McManaman was free, right up the park. Although we got back at it and made a few mistakes, if Ince had stayed on the left-hand side and disciplined himself, we wouldn't have had any problem at all from McManaman.

Should I have risked Andy Cole? It wouldn't have been any worse, put it that way. And the performance of Andrei Kanchelskis, you wonder what's going on in the boy's head.

You expect Liverpool to be revved up, you expect their players to be climbing mountains. The only thing you have to question, which I'm sure Roy Evans will be doing, is why can they not do that against Tottenham in the Cup? Why can they not do it in a League game against Coventry?

It is almost a reversal of the situation in the Manchester United-Liverpool games when I first came to the club. When United played Liverpool they'd have climbed mountains – always did well against them. Liverpool were scared to play United in those days. Although they were having great success, they were always fearsome about playing United and never really played to their potential because United never allowed them to settle.

And now the reversal is there for everyone to see. We've been a great success in the last few years, Liverpool have had hard times. And that's their Cup Final for this season. So it's a great tribute to us maybe, but our response was not acceptable. I said to the players at half time and after the game: "Some of you will not be here if we don't win the League this season. Some of you won't be here after the end of the season." And I think it may be time for changing two or three of them. Hunger is the most vital organ in our club. It's always going to make us, because we've always had players with good ability here. We've never achieved anything in the past because they've lacked something. That is not going to recur.

It's disappointing and I felt, having drawn with Tottenham in a game we should have won and played well in, fate was conspiring against us. I feel that people want Blackburn to win the title, and there was no better demonstration of that than when Sherwood had a four-pointer reduced to two points to save him from a four-match ban. I felt that was crucial to them.

You see that kind of thing and the complaints they've made about referees all the time this season. The press doesn't really pick up on that. If United complains we'd be moaners, whingers. So you just get the feeling that everybody wants them to win the League, and all the fates are pointed that way.

Willie Miller came across for lunch to the hotel. It was good to see him and he was looking cheery. As if he was relieved to be out of the whole thing. We had a chat about Aberdeen, and it was interesting listening to Willie reflecting on the situation. I said:

"You know, we had that great team, it was all players with desire, plenty of players who wanted it." And he said:

"You look at the Aberdeen team now, none of them could have got near the reserve team at that time." That's the dramatic change. Sad to see it.

Venue: Anfield	*Att:* 38,906		
Liverpool	*goals*	**Manchester United**	*goals*
1 David James		1 Peter Schmeichel	
5 Mark Wright		3 Denis Irwin	
6 Phil Babb		4 Steve Bruce	
12 John Scales		5 Lee Sharpe	
15 Jamie Redknapp		6 Gary Pallister	
17 Steve McManaman		8 Paul Ince	
10 John Barnes	61	9 Brian McClair	
20 Stig Bjornebye		14 Andrei Kanchelskis	
23 Robbie Fowler		16 Roy Keane	
9 Ian Rush		10 Mark Hughes	
25 Neil Ruddock	88	11 Ryan Giggs	
Substitutes			
16 Michael Thomas (61 mins for 10)		17 Andy Cole (46 mins for 5)	
30 Tony Warner		25 Kevin Pilkington	
11 Mark Walters (88 mins for 25)		19 Nicky Butt (83 mins for 16)	

Monday 20 March

Moss Bros came to have me try my kilt on for the investiture. Two or three of the players saw me and had a good laugh. They were really impressed. I said: "It's class, this is class, son. You won't see this every day in your life." There was a bit of banter. Brian said: "Jesus Christ,

Boss, you're not going to wear those socks with Umbro on them, are you?"

"Bugger off, you," I said.

Everybody wanted their photograph taken with me: the stewards and the staff and the groundsmen.

I was meant to go to a dinner in Dublin as speaker, but it was cancelled at the last minute because some guy couldn't go. A night in was what I needed, anyway.

Tuesday 21 March

I was concerned that people had bought tickets in Dublin, expecting me to be there. So I phoned a friend of mine in Dublin just to make sure there was no press reaction. He said: "I haven't seen anything. I didn't even know there was a dinner on." But you've got to be careful if people expect you to be at a dinner and you don't turn up. I was angry about it.

Wednesday 22 March

United 3 Arsenal 0

I heard shocking news at lunchtime: Davie Cooper, who played in the Scotland team when I was manager, had collapsed and was in critical condition.

When I heard what happened, I phoned Walter Smith, who said to me: "I don't think there's much chance."

Davie was a player in the Scotland team, whom I've always admired. He's a lovely lad. He said in his book that I was the best manager he'd ever worked under – a lovely compliment.

He told a story about me and five-a-sides in Mexico - about how I celebrated a goal at my age. I think he said: "He obviously didn't score many goals as a player." I wrote a letter saying: "I'm going to have to consult my lawyers about this. It's libellous as far as I'm concerned. You want to look at my record at Rangers," because he was with Rangers at the time.

So he wrote back: "I went through the archives. I cannot find any note of you scoring a goal." We had a wee bit of correspondence going for a bit . That was in about 1988 or 1989.

Wednesday evening

I said in the programme that I had questioned whether we still had the desire to win. The players responded well. We needed the first goal because Arsenal played it tight. They set up a system of man-marking. And they were really going right through with their tackles. Almost from the start I could see what was going on, and I said: "Oh, the referee's going to have his work cut out here." Fortunately he booked Keown, and he booked Bould right away for going through from the back.

But once we'd scored the goal we did well and in the second half we could've run up a big score. You can understand why they're disappointed in their League form. Having a lot of players is sometimes a problem. They've got about seven strikers. They've bought Kiwomya and Hartson plus they've got Smith, Campbell, Merson and Wright. Sometimes you don't know what the best team is. They've got heaps of midfield players – they've got Hillier, the boy Selley, Morrow, Jensen, Schwartz.

They'd made a couple of changes, went man-to-man in the middle of the park, with Keown and Morrow, but once they were down, I didn't think they were going to win. I felt for Stewart Houston a bit, because it's a difficult time and it's a difficult position for him. George Graham is a marvellous manager and you look at the situation and wonder if Arsenal have been wise.

Sharpey played very well. His record against Arsenal is brilliant. He had a bad time against Tottenham because he wasn't happy playing left back after he had scored against QPR. He doesn't enjoy playing left back and it's probably brought up against him, in the sense that he's going to have to make his way – either him or Giggs – over to centre midfield. But he's done quite well in centre midfield.

The referee also booked Wright just before the interval. Then Wright had a wee skirmish with Steve Bruce in the tunnel. He is a lucky lad, because we're prepared to let it drop, and Bruce is prepared not to take it any further. It wasn't serious. It could have developed into something but the players were good and got Brucey away from him. I said to the big guy: "What the hell's going on now?" He apologised. Wright is quite a lucky player because he treads a thin line at times. He's an excitable lad – even off the pitch. People of that nature never change. Good striker, though.

Maybe if he'd gone to a club where they do a lot of linking and he was forced to go and link and develop his technique he could have been a better player, but Arsenal have used him in the way they think is best. He's been a great buy for them.

After the game, I drove down to London with Ned Kelly and a friend of mine for my investiture in the morning.

Venue: Old Trafford	*Att:* 43,623		
Manchester United	*goals*	**Arsenal**	*goals*
1 Peter Schmeichel		13 Vince Bartram	
16 Roy Keane		2 Lee Dixon	

4	Steve Bruce		6	Tony Adams
6	Gary Pallister		12	Steve Bould
3	Denis Irwin		3	Nigel Winterburn
14	Andrei Kanchelskis	80	23	Ray Parlour
8	Paul Ince		14	Martin Keown
5	Lee Sharpe	31	21	Steve Morrow
10	Mark Hughes	26	10	Paul Merson
17	Andy Cole		31	Chris Kiwomya
11	Ryan Giggs		8	Ian Wright
Substitutes				
9	Brian McClair		32	Glenn Helder (57 mins for 23)
25	Kevin Pilkington		26	Lee Harper
19	Nicky Butt		11	Eddie McGoldrick

Thursday 23 March

We stayed at Selfridges. Sir Richard Greenbury sent his car to pick me up and take me to the Palace. It was a long day, because there are a lot of people there and I was one of the early ones – the CBEs go first. The Prince of Wales said to me: "I'm glad to see someone who's properly dressed."

I felt I looked smart and after the investiture a lot of Scots people came up and said: "We're so ashamed we didn't wear a kilt." They said: "We thought we'd come to London and, you know..."

I said: "This is the place you should wear it. In fact, the only thing I've not got that I should have is my Claymore!" It was terrific Highland dress. The thing that made my mind up about it was a photograph in a magazine of Sean Connery in his kilt. Blackwatch tartan. He looked magnificent. And I said: "That's it. I'm definitely wearing it."

It was the first time I'd been to Buckingham Palace. What a beautiful building. You get to see the parts of it that no one else sees. The investiture is done in the ballroom.

It was wonderful. Afterwards photographs were taken. There were a couple of journalists there. A guy said:

"Can I do an interview afterwards?"

"Fine," I said.

And a girl said: "Can I do one too?"

"Oh yeah, fine."

I was thinking it was about the investiture but the first guy said: "We're going to talk about Davie Cooper."

"Why?"

"He died this morning."

"Oh Christ." I said. "I can't talk about that."

And the girl said: "Can we talk about Eric Cantona's sentence? He's got two weeks."

"Bloody hell, you're joking."

"No, it was on the radio."

I phoned the chairman on the way back to the hotel.

"I can't believe it," he said.

With everything that's going on," I said,"that's absolutely disgraceful."

We went back to the hotel where we had a private room – all my family were there and we had the film people videoing and taking photographs because I hadn't waited for the photograph in front of the Palace. Leaving aside the Cantona decision, which was stunning to say the least, we had a great lunch. They all stayed on but I was tired and went up to bed. We were going out in the evening with Sir Richard Greenbury and his wife Gabrielle. I phoned Eric, who was out on appeal at that stage.

"I'm really disappointed for you," I said, because Isabelle was really taking it badly. "You get home to her right away. Make sure she's all right." Eric's having a horrendous time. He's got feelings like everyone else, but possibly doesn't show them.

In the evening we went for a lovely Italian meal in Picadilly and had a great surprise – Paul McCartney came in with all his family. I hardly noticed him, it was my wife who noticed.

"That's Paul McCartney's wife," Cath said.

"Where's Paul McCartney?"

"There he is." He was sitting right beside me.

I said to myself: 'Well, there's an ordinary guy. His wife's straightforward. His friends are just straightforward, ordinary people.' One of them started chatting to me: "Great result last night. I really hope you do it."

Paul and I said hello. It was his daughter's birthday. No matter how much money he's got, no matter what success that he's had, he's handled it the right way. No pretensions, no big-time Charlie stuff.

We went back to Richard's flat and opened a 40-year-old bottle of red wine. He said: "It's a special day for you, I'm going to open this." He reminds me a lot of myself – that type of determination. You can see why Marks and Spencer is so successful.

Friday 24 March

The Ian Wright-Steve Bruce skirmish got some coverage this morning. There's always somebody going to talk. Steve got a black eye, so it was difficult to hide, but we haven't said anything. It was best that we just left it.

Inevitably, the main topic was Eric's sentence and, horrifyingly, some of the papers supported the magistrate.

The players are away on international duty, so for once I've been able to have a bit of a break. I've bought a flat in London and I went across there at lunchtime. It's really because my two sons are in London now and my grandson's down there. It will be handy to have, knowing I'm not always going to be having to use hotels. One of my sons, Mark, is a merchant banker and he says it is a good time to buy before they all start coming in from Hong Kong in a few years' time. It's a nice flat, but even as an investment we could sell it on.

Saturday 25 March

We had to stay down in London to go to Sopwell House in St Albans today to sort out the menus and the room lists for my son's wedding in June. I couldn't go to the Youth Team game because it's one of those things – if I don't get it done I'm dead. Cath said: "If you think you're going to that Youth Team game, I'll not be here when you come back."

We tried to sample all the different menus. It's obscene. You are eating all the time, and end up feeling terrible. It was fortunate that I had my mobile and Ken Ramsden kept phoning up with the score every ten minutes in the hotel, while I was taking my lunch. By the end of lunch it was half time.

We are flying up North tomorrow for a christening.

Sunday 26 March

We went to the christening, then I went on to a dinner. A dinner! My weight was right down after all that training I'd been doing, but it all comes back. Well, maybe not all of it, but you feel sort of bloated.

Monday 27 March

Davie Cooper's funeral was today. Last night I was about to fly up to Glasgow and phoned Walter Smith and he said: "Righto, I'll get you picked up at the airport."

While I was waiting in the airport lounge Denis Law came in. I love Denis. He's one of my favourites, a fabulous bloke. We get on the plane together, and who should come in but Graeme Souness. He was in a different row, back a bit. We were talking about the Cantona thing and people were saying: "It never would've happened with Matt."

So I asked him: "What would Matt've done? "

He said: "He used to shake his head and say to me, 'What am I going to do with you Denis?' Every Christmas I was back in Scotland, celebrating Christmas, he just shook his head. It's just the players you've got.

Paddy was always banging into people in games."

Denis is funny, so we had a good time. He was going to Russia with Scotland for the BBC and he said: "I've got my cheese, my ham and my crisps in my bag."

"Christ, it's not that bad," I said.

"We're staying at an hotel called the Eurostar, that tells you everything," he said. The Eurostar, that's the one. So we had a good laugh.

Then Graeme Souness and I met up and got driven into Ibrox because we were going on the Rangers coach to the funeral. I like Graeme, he's a good guy. On the way back we had a chance to have a talk for quite a while.

"You know the mistake you made at Liverpool? You were too impetuous," I said.

"Aye, I know, but it had to be done," he said. "We had a dying team, an old team."

"Everbody knew that." It was an old team all right and a lot of the things he did were right. I told him he'd done it too quickly.

"I know that now," he said.

I think he's got an impetuous nature, but he gave a lot of young players a chance. He showed he had the balls, the courage to do that at a difficult time for the club. Kenny obviously saw that himself. Maybe that's what got to Kenny. They were an old team and what do you do with an old team? I felt that myself when I came to this club. I had to admire Graeme that day, because when we came out of the funeral, a Rangers supporter came up to him and said: "It's your effing fault." Can you believe that? The mentality of a person who could do that. I was stunned. I would have jumped the guy. But Graeme was controlled, he was fabulous.

He said: "I'm here to pay my respects to Davie and that's what I'm going to do."

And the Rangers supporter started: "You signed Maurice Johnston!" The real root of it was religion, because he had signed a Catholic. I felt sorry for Graeme, but he held his nerve well. He's a man of real substance.

It was a nice service and Walter Smith spoke very well. It was very emotional and difficult for him. Ally McCoist spoke and was very funny. Only Ally could get away with it. It's always difficult to know what to say but I think it's nice to reflect on the personality of the deceased. Ally told a funny story about the team doing its pre-season warm ups, with Gary Stevens always a good 50 yards in front of everybody. Davie was not a great pre-season trainer and he said to Ally:

"For Christ's sake, can't you get him to slow down?"

"He won't listen," McCoist said. "There's no way you're going to get him to slow down."

"Well, throw him a ball," Davie said.

Walter was telling us that when he became assistant manager under Souness, Davie Cooper went up to him on his first day and said: "How the hell are you going to coach me? I played against you at Dumbarton and you were hopeless. You'd nae left foot, you couldnae run, you couldnae cross the ball. How are you gonnae coach me?" And he was dead serious and walked away. Walter said, "Christ. What a start to the day that is." On your first day your star player comes up and questions your ability to coach.

It never occurred to me, but when you think about it, guys like myself who weren't big stars like Charlton and Muhren but became managers of really good players could be asked: "Well what have you done as a player?" It's true, that. But the ordinary player can become a good coach and manager because he has to think differently. I think managers who've been great players expect all their players to be as good as them. They expect them to be able to do anything they tell them because they could do it as players.

My job, however, is to try and realise my dreams. I would've loved to have been Denis Law. He was my hero. I would have loved to have been Denis, even as a player, even though Denis was only about a year older than me. Sometimes I would hold on to my cuffs in the way Denis did. I always made sure that the ball went in if it rebounded off the goalkeeper. There were little things that you picked up off your heroes – and everybody's got heroes.

Before we went to the funeral, I was up in Walter's office, and he said: "Have you seen this morning's *Daily Record*?"

"No."

"Your man wants to join us: Kanchelskis."

"Cathy told me not to trust you," I said.

"We're not interested," he said. "What does he think? I've enough Russians." (They've got two up there.)

I came home and watched Norwich and Ipswich and quite enjoyed it.

Tuesday 28 March

When I came out of the funeral yesterday I saw Andy Goram in front. When I said hello he was very sheepish. Today, I found out why. Apparently he had attacked me in the papers that day. He said that you wouldn't treat a dog the way Manchester United has treated Jim Leighton. I'm not letting him off with that. How does he know how Manchester United treated Jim Leighton? Jim Leighton got treated the same as everybody else at this club. No different. We've had no complaints about how everybody's treating him. Being dropped for the Cup Final is not easy – I got dropped in 1965, so I know exactly what it's like. I was told at two o'clock that I was dropped, and I was the top goalscorer. Jim Leighton got dropped because he deserved to be dropped – he wasn't playing well enough. He's harboured this grudge, and says he'll never speak to me again. I don't see what he's going on about. If you play well you pick yourself, if you play badly, you drop yourself.

Anyway, so much for Andy Goram. I gave him his debut for Scotland too. But it's all that old goalkeepers' union.

I'd agreed to speak at a dinner for Neil Fairbrother's testimonial. It was a good night. I took an Eric Cantona shirt which raised some money for him, so he was quite pleased. I only do certain dinners for good causes. The comedian was Mike King who is really funny. Neil Midgely was a brilliant MC.

Wednesday 29 March

Steve Bruce's appearance before the FA disciplinary commission is tomorrow, and I have to be at the Dover Football Club tomorrow evening, so I decided I might as well go down to Bruce's Commission. I watched England play Uruguay.

Uruguay just booted the ball up the park all the time. England found it very difficult. What a frustrating night for Terry Venables. He obviously wants to try and see this system through, but I think in the home matches he'll find it difficult. I said that from the start.

Anderton's a breath of fresh air for them and I thought he did well. I thought that defensively they were all right. Adams and Pally had no problem.

Thursday 30 March

Evidently I missed a good fight by going to Wembley. I was meant to be going to Stockport's dinner before I decided to come down to London. Apparently the dinner ended in fisticuffs between Danny Bergara and the chairman.

We went to the commission armed with a video. I said, "Do you think

Steve Bruce is a dirty player?" They listened to us. When they said, "two matches", I thought the two-match ban was extra, and I was a bit unhappy and I just hopped it. I think maybe they were saying, "What on Earth was he unhappy about."

When I got outside, Ken explained that it was two matches only. The commission were very fair and I must let them know that, although Brucey will miss the semi-final. When people miss the semi-final when they're given bookings in League Cup ties, it's a bit hard. They should change it.

I went for a cup of tea at the Royal Lancaster with Brucey and Ken. I asked the owner if I could get an hour's sleep and he gave me a room to bed down in. Then I got the train down to Dover in the afternoon. It was one of the old trains with those old-fashioned compartments. It was the first time ever I'd been through that part of the world. It's a great relaxing ride, going by train.

I had to drive back to Gatwick that night because I'd got a 7.25am flight, so I said: "If you could do your auctions at the end of the night it would help me, because I can get away at 11 o'clock after the speakers." Jackie Blanchflower was speaking next, so I did my bit and they started the auctions and raffles. At 11.10 they were still doing auctions and raffles so I had to make my apologies and leave. I didn't like doing that, especially as Jackie Blanchflower is a fabulous speaker.

Friday 31 March

My intention was to do a function this morning with a view to Sunday's game. But Kanchelskis rang and said he wasn't fit, Ince is having bother with his back and Sparky has a neck injury, so I have had to put the function back until tomorrow.

At last, some better news. Eric's appeal was successful. He has been sentenced to community service instead, not prison, which seems much more appropriate.

I can't think of any subject that's ever caught more press attention than Cantona. Since 25 January I have felt as if I've been on a roundabout which you can't get off because it won't stop. It's pressure we don't need, no doubt about that.

There was a survey in *The Independent* when the original case came up – of the last 10,000 cases for common assault, there have been only 562 convictions. And of the 562, four hundred and twenty odd had previous convictions. Of 124 who had gone to prison for common assault the first time, I think 80 odd had a weapon. So you're talking about maybe 30 people out of 10,000 in Eric's situation. I'd like to know what those 30 did.

The reason for jailing him was the fact that he was a hero. He's been a hero to many young people. In a legal sense that's balderdash. In a moral sense I think we're all responsible for that in sport, particularly a club like Manchester United. I think morally we have a responsibility and duty to what we represent and how we represent it. I think Eric is well aware of that now, but not in a legal sense – in a court of law. The day after he was sentenced, Lord Denning crucified the magistrate. At that moment I think we knew that it was going to be all right when he appealed.

There was a terrific article in one of the Sundays. The writer made the point that Eric was sent to jail because, in the words of the magistrate, he's a hero to these millions of young kids. He's a great player and he's a good-looking guy. So what about that ugly left back who plays with a third division team who's been kicking wingers up and down the pitch for years. What do we do with him? Give him two weeks' holiday in the Caribbean and £5,000 to sort his warts?

Then there was the article from the boy Richard Kurt in The Independent last Tuesday, pleading with Eric to stay. He said: "you're idolised, you'll never get that anywhere else. You've got to make your mind up about that now. You'll never get what you're getting at United – anywhere in the world – nobody'll idolise you the way we do. Yours has replaced the Pope's photograph in my house. I used to pray every night to the Pope, I now pray to you." Fabulous. It was a great article, which ended by saying, "You once said playing for Manchester United was the perfect marriage.' If that was so, have we given you grounds for divorce?"

I had Richard Greenbury staying with me at home. We went for an Italian but I was feeling rough. I think I've got food poisoning. I had an oyster down in London, that's what did it.

Saturday 1 April

I was up all night. I went to training, but was feeling terrible, so I went back to my bed and stayed there all day. I got up in the evening and went for a lovely meal with Richard, his two sons and his daughter-in-law.

There was still doubt about Andrei's fitness. He has come back from Russia feeling this, feeling that. Then he told me he was given eight injections in order to play for Russia. Two in each arm, two in each buttock. I find it amazing that anyone would allow himself to be given those injections.

Sunday 2 April

United 0 Leeds United 0

A game of complete frustration. Leeds just came and killed the game. They didn't go forward, they didn't make threats to us. Two years in a row and I don't think they've had one strike at goal. They don't normally do that against other teams, but they do it with us. I think it's more pressure on Howard playing us than any other team. Their support were more happy with a draw than winning, just because it stopped us. That support, they are the worst. I can understand them wanting a result, but they're chasing a UEFA Cup place and they need wins.

I couldn't fault the players. I think it was one of those days when it just wasn't going to go in for us. Some of the things that happened in that second half were unbelievable. And the referee, dearie me. To stop you twice when you're through against their back four. Once we had a player injured and once they had a player injured. So either way it was wrong. So disappointing; frustrating – an experienced referee like that, too.

But the nature of the game is that you've got to win, and they've definitely put us under tremendous pressure in the League. That's why I had to come out after the game and say: "Blackburn can only throw it away," and hope that will put a bit of pressure on them.

Gary Neville was outstanding today. I'd been a bit unsure about him in the pressure matches, which was why I played the more experienced Lee Sharpe at full back against Liverpool. I think Gary can be a bit impetuous and in the atmosphere at Liverpool you need people who are cool. But he's improving. This has been his best performance. He'll play in the semi-final.

Venue: Old Trafford *Att:* 43,712

Manchester United	*goals*	**Leeds United**	*goals*
1 Peter Schmeichel		1 John Lukic	
2 Gary Neville		2 Gary Kelly	
16 Roy Keane		6 David Wetherall	
6 Gary Pallister		4 Carlton Palmer	
3 Denis Irwin		12 John Pemberton	
8 Paul Ince		10 Gary McAllister	
14 David Beckham		3 Tony Dorigo	
9 Brian McClair		23 Andrew Couzens	
17 Andy Cole		21 Anthony Yeboah	
10 Mark Hughes		9 Brian Deane	
11 Ryan Giggs		8 Rod Wallace	
Substitutes			
24 Paul Scholes		15 Nigel Worthington (88 mins for 8)	
13 Gary Walsh		13 Mark Beeney	
19 Nicky Butt		19 Noel Whelan (82 mins for 9)	

Tuesday 4 April

Robin Barwell from BBC Television wanted to bring a crew down to do a bit of filming of the Youth Team and perhaps interview one or two of them with regard to a report on drugs in sport which has just been published. Why do they always want to come to us?

I've had a call from the FA about reports on referees. They think I did them more objectively than any other manager in the League, and they think it's disappointing that I've stopped. I stopped doing them weeks ago – after the Cantona thing. Two bad tackles on Cantona, one on Cole in the first half – I just hope that David Ellery is right on his toes on Sunday.

I went down to Palace to have a look at them against Aston Villa. It was a dreadful game. And Villa scored a perfectly good goal. A good header hit the underside of the bar and came down a foot-and-a-half over the line. I don't think the linesman was in a great position – I don't think the floodlights are that great there anyway. But it was so clearly a goal. The referee was maybe 30 yards behind it, so it was difficult for him, but the linesman was six yards from the by-line. That could get you relegated. But it was a dour game. From the first minute it was a nil-niller.

At half time somebody came up and said: "Blackburn are drawing 0-0; Queens Park Rangers are murdering them."

"I don't like hearing that," I said. "I heard that on Saturday. I've been hearing that for the past few weeks." And just like at Everton on Saturday they sneaked it 1-0. It's not so much disappointing and frustrating as depressing. You say to yourself, 'Is that the way to win at football?' But at the end of the day you can understand their determination. You can understand that trench mentality to try and win it. It's a big prize. But it's amazing. I wonder what Kenny's philosophy is, when you think of how he brought Barnes and Beardsley to Liverpool and the way Liverpool played. Interesting, very interesting.

The press have plugged Blackburn all the way, but I think even the press are starting to realise that Blackburn are winning games and coming out and saying: "We're not interested in entertaining." It's so frustrating. You see that they're just going out there to destroy games and they could win the League. I find it hard to fathom. Kenny Dalglish was one of the best players ever. He embraced every concept of one's imagination as a footballer. I think much of it must be down to Ray Harford.

I was supposed to be at the Chester and Wales branch dinner but because of the Palace game I had to withdraw.

Wednesday 5 April

Crystal Palace is a long trip, whichever way you go. Les Kershaw came with me last night.

We went round the M25 and came back through the centre of London.

We did a good session. We are now gearing up towards the semi-final.

Thursday 6 April

Ryan did a shooting session.

I had to go and make the lottery draw at Old Trafford for the Development Association. It's an important thing for them because, as I said, they're up against it with the National Lottery now.

Friday 7 April

We closed the doors and had a practice game. I'd picked my team. I wasn't going to wait for Kanchelskis. We played at Old Trafford to get a bit of peace and quiet and tried to get the young boys to play the way that Crystal Palace play. It's funny because it's not in their mentality to whack balls into the corners all day, but I said to them: "Do it!" It was quite funny seeing them whacking the ball over their shoulders. "Take two touches in the middle of the park," I said, "Then whack it in the corners."

Tonight, I went to the old boys' dinner; the former United players' dinner. They made a nice presentation to David Meek for his services to Manchester United, because he's covered the club for 37 years. He said in his speech: "It's very nice to be remembered by you all, but maybe I should forget what you're like."

I said: "It's amazing people's lack of memories, David." He's a smashing lad, David, and he's done his job well. You can trust him, and that's almost unique in this profession nowadays.

Saturday 8 April

We did all the set pieces again in training. I was at a loss what to do, really. So I went home, had a look at my reports on Palace again and tried to get into my bed for half an hour, but I couldn't sleep. So I watched the Grand National and backed the second horse – Party Politics. I had backed Master Oates as my main bet but I had a saver on Party Politics.

I was concerned about the Youth team's semi-final. I'd arranged for the coach driver, Hugh Jones, to phone at half time with the result.

"2-0," he said.

"Brilliant!"

"It should be ten," he said. "They're playing magnificently."

So I relaxed, I wasn't worried about them anymore. I got the final result 3-0, and was happy with that. I never expected them to do so well. They're getting better all the time and they've got a genuine chance of winning it. We've got two outstanding players – Cooke and Neville, and hopefully two or three others have got a good chance of making it.

We travelled down to the New Hall at Sutton Coldfield. A beautiful hotel, I don't know why we've never gone there before. It's full of history. It opened in 1200 – fascinating.

Sunday 8 April

United 2 Crystal Palace 2

I knew right away when they started hitting the corners in and Peter dropped a couple. We were faffing about, giving ourselves a hard job. And we didn't keep the ball well in the first half. So at half time I said: "Bloody well get penetration in our game! Get people running through!" So it was on my mind right away to put Butt on. He did a quick warm up, we put him on and he started to tear them apart – making great runs through. So we'll see. He's definitely put himself in the frame.

On Tuesday, Young went off with an injury and I thought it was his knee. 'There's no chance he's playing Sunday,' I thought. The same went for Coleman because he limped the whole game. But some London clubs are doing this oxygen tent treatment and both players made it. Remarkable! I was amazed.

I felt a wee bit for the manager when you read all the stuff that's been in the papers. Ron Noades has obviously made the money by having a bit of business acumen. He can't be thick. He must be intelligent. And Alan Smith was a teacher at one time, so you say to yourself, 'How could they get themselves into a public slanging match like that?' But maybe Alan is too honest for his own good because he'll never win that and I think he's already said as much.

I saw Alan Smith after the game. I said: "That result could keep you in the Premier Division. You don't need to go to Blackburn on Tuesday now, the last thing you need is another defeat." I think Blackburn may be sick a bit too. They'd be thinking, 'Oh Christ, extra time, we'll murder them on Tuesday.' So in a way it's a good result for us and for them. I want Blackburn to go straight to Leeds, because that's going to be tough. My feelings are that if they lose a game they may not win another one. I think they could go completely. What they're doing is hanging on, it's like an old ceiling starting to sag with water. You know it's going to go, but you don't know when. It may last until the plumber gets there, but if it doesn't, it's all going to come down.

Darren came out to see me before the game and picked up his tickets. I had a good chat with him. He went on as a sub yesterday and, he said, got a great ovation from the fans. I think the fans have been wondering what the hell's going on. He says he did all right. They played him outside left, which is not his position, but he says he got in the box a few times. So hopefully he's going to play on Wednesday night. It's been a frustrating time.

I've been in games this season and while you're playing or maybe you're travelling to a game, you say to yourself, "I wonder how he's getting on? I hope he's doing well." It's amazing how it can grip you. I just feel that he's never going to be a Graham Taylor player. I've had to get him an agent because I find it difficult to be involved personally. I got Paul Stretford to look after him.

Fathers are always biased, but I think I can judge objectively, and I don't think Darren deserves what's happening to him. I look at the game and try to analyse where he's going wrong. I look for any flaws, faults. I keep telling him that he needs to get a goal, which he's been poor at. Or he needs to get his head in a wee bit better in the air. Other than that his style is terrific. He's up and down the pitch and he passes the ball. He's always wanting the ball. He's got great vision. I've been down to see him about five times now and he won the man of the match twice from ITV-Central Television.

An unhappy end to the day. There was a brawl in a pub at Walsall between the two sets of supporters and a Crystal Palace fan was killed.

Venue: Villa Park *Att:* 38,256

	Manchester United	*goals*		**Crystal Palace**	*goals*
1	Peter Schmeichel		1	Nigel Martyn	
27	Gary Neville		22	Darren Patterson	
16	Roy Keane		5	Eric Young	
6	Gary Pallister	96	14	Richard Shaw	
3	Denis Irwin	69	12	Chris Coleman	
28	David Beckham		20	Ray Houghton	
8	Paul Ince		4	Gareth Southgate	
9	Brian McClair		16	Darren Pitcher	
5	Lee Sharpe		11	John Salako	
10	Mark Hughes		9	Chris Armstrong	91

11	Ryan Giggs	8	Ian Dowie	33
Substitutes				
19	Nicky Butt (49 mins for 28)	3	Dean Gordon (45 mins for 12)	
13	Gary Walsh	19	Rhys Wilmot	
24	Paul Scholes	21	Ian Cox	

Monday 10 April

There were some suggestions that the game should be postponed because of the death of the Palace fan, so I had to have one or two discussions about that.

I came in at my usual time and I watched the video twice because I wanted to be certain about a few things in it. I had big Peter Schmeichel in to discuss his part. After a long discussion I said: "Take the video and check it yourself."

I brought the youth team all in and congratulated them: "The only thing you've got to worry about with Tottenham, the one thing they've got in their favour, is that they think they can play." Bill Shankly called them the "Drury Lane Dancers". They think they can play the big-time Charlie down that one, but I said, "I don't expect boys from the North to be bothered by that."

A friend of mine's got a bakery in Bury and he's won an award for his gateaux, which I went to present.

I had to come in to discuss Eric's future with Jean-Jacques Bertrand, the chairman and Maurice Watkins. Afterwards I went to parents' night at Old Trafford where young players who are joining us next year come with their parents to be introduced to Manchester United. The PFA representative was there, the education girl from the college came along, and we went through the whole thing and had a bite to eat. Finally I went to the reserves match so it was a long day, but a worthwhile one.

I had a long chat to George Graham on the phone and he was telling me Ray Harford's in for the Arsenal job. He was quite bright and breezy. I was amazed by some of the things that were going on at Arsenal.

Tuesday 11 April

We're sending Andrei to another specialist tomorrow. hopefully, we can find what the problem is this time. He's been talking about going to a specialist in Germany, but we are reluctant to do that because we think that the best people are available in Manchester. We've tried everything and had everything checked; his prostate, his back. It's really disappointing because we need him in our team. Its a time when we need everybody to pull together with the Cantona situation which was such a nightmare for us – and now we've got Andrei's problem too.

Peter Schmeichel wasn't very happy when I criticised him for his problems with the corners. He got his agent, Rune Hauge, to phone me. I had Peter in and said: "Look, just go and look at the video." He looked at the video and Rune has just phoned to say Peter agrees with me. Well done Peter!

It's unbelievable the way video has changed things. When I started as manager you had to wait for television highlights, if your game was televised, to confirm what you were trying to convince players of. I remember a situation we played at St Mirren and I said to our goalie: "What were you doing there?" He denied that he had got in the wrong position. It was on television that night but I couldn't record it because nobody had videos then.

So I got him in on Monday.

"Did you watch it?"

"No," he said.

"I bet you watched it, and I was right!"

Now every game is videoed. But in the heat of the moment players don't think they make mistakes.

The goalkeepers' union never likes admitting to mistakes. I remember Bobby Clark at Aberdeen. Bobby used to gather all the goalies around about him after the game and analyse the whole match. They would never criticise each other – ever.

We went back down to New Hall and I watched Hibs on Sky. They lost 3-1.

Wednesday 12 April

United 2 Crystal Palace 0

You never know what is going to happen. This morning everything was relaxed and peaceful, we felt at peace with the world. It was a lovely sunny day, there was good banter, we went for a walk in New Hall's beautiful grounds, we had a quiz, it was all good fun, and we had an FA Cup semi-final to look forward to. But you just don't know what is ahead. Ten minutes into the second half, Roy Keane was sent off for stamping on Southgate, and once again all hell broke loose and we were being pilloried.

In the team talk I said about the need to behave; the fact that we would be under scrutiny because of the death, and the need for calm at this match. I warned that Palace were an aggressive team.

I was confident. I felt we had made our mistakes in the first match, we had Steve Bruce back who brings enthusiasm and defensive knowledge, and I thought his presence would help us cope better with their aggression.

In the first half we were in complete control. But by the interval we had problems with Keane, who had a badly bruised, cut ankle from a nasty tackle, and Giggs, who had pulled a hamstring. So it was a question of who was going to come off.

Both were getting treatment at half time. Roy went into the treatment room, Ryan stayed in our dressing room. Palace were in the home dressing room, which is right next to the medical room. The walls are thin and you could hear through them. I was flitting from one to the other, but in the medical room you could hear what they were saying, and there was some very aggressive stuff. I don't know whether that had a bearing on what was to come.

In the end I had to keep Giggsy off. Roy said: "Give me five minutes." And just when I was going to take him off, he said: "Give me another five," and in that time the incident occurred. It was a bad tackle by Southgate, on his bad foot, and he reacted. He knew immediately that what he had done was wrong. He knew he shouldn't have done it. I said to him, "What were you thinking of?"

Once again United are in the dock. We got through the rest of the game, and went back to the deadest dressing room I can remember. Doug Ellis sent in a bottle of champagne, which was nice of him, but there were no celebrations. We are in the final of the FA Cup for the second successive year and no one was celebrating. Everyone sat there thinking: 'What have we done now?' It was a nightmare come true.

Venue: Villa Park *Att:* 17,987

Manchester United	*goals*	**Crystal Palace**	*goals*
1 Peter Schmeichel		19 Rhys Wilmot	
27 Gary Neville		22 Simon Grayson	
4 Steve Bruce	30	14 Richard Shaw	
6 Gary Pallister	41	5 Eric Young	
3 Denis Irwin		3 Dean Gordon	
19 Nicky Butt		20 Ray Houghton	
8 Paul Ince		16 Darren Pitcher	
16 Roy Keane		4 Gareth Southgate	
5 Lee Sharpe		11 John Salako	
10 Mark Hughes		9 Chris Armstrong	
11 Ryan Giggs		8 Ian Dowie	
Substitutes			
9 Brian McClair (58 mins for 11)		21 Ian Cox (81 mins for 16)	
13 Gary Walsh		25 Jimmy Glass	
24 Paul Scholes		23 Ricky Newman (81 mins for 8)	

11
Double Disappointment

Thursday 13 April

We should have woken up to headlines celebrating our return to Wembley. Instead – predictably – we were slaughtered once again. I won't defend Roy's action, but once again people's reaction to it is out of proportion. He is young – 23 – and it was his first sending off. He knows he shouldn't have done it, it was an impulsive reaction to being badly fouled.

Yesterday's match was sensitive, but if it is a sensitive match, isn't some of the responsibility also on the Crystal Palace captain? He should be the one to set a standard. He wasn't even booked for the bad tackle, but he deserved to be sent off as much as Roy Keane did for his response to it. During the game, Dowie blatantly elbowed Gary Neville off the ball. The press has always blamed us, but this morning their response was just over the top.

The FA did take action: Roy has been charged with bringing the game into disrepute. There is the suggestion that they will impose a further ban on top of the automatic three-game ban. If that happens, Roy will miss the Cup Final – which is what more than one paper was demanding this morning. If the FA does take action, we will not stand idly by. The chairman came to see me this evening and in the nine years I have known him, I have never seen him so angry.

Inevitably, I didn't sleep. Again I just tossed and twisted and turned things over.

Friday 14 April

We seem to be living in an endless nightmare at the moment. Trying to prepare for tomorrow's game at Leicester seems unreal in view of everything going on.

I phoned the chairman this morning. It is getting to him too. He said: "I haven't slept a wink."

We had a press conference as usual on the day before a game, but with a difference: Roy Keane came along to make a public apology. It gave the journalists an opportunity to see the damage to his ankle.

I am finding it impossible to sleep. I got about two hours' last night. I need sleep, but I don't know how.

Saturday 15 April

Leicester City 0 United 4

I said: "Now, for goodness sake, behave! Go and enjoy the game." And they did. The young players did very well. Some of the movement off the ball was tremendous, and we had really good moves for two of the goals. Leeds scored a last second equaliser against Blackburn, so we have cut the gap a little.

Venue: Filbert Street *Att:* 21,281

	Leicester City	*goals*		**Manchester United**	*goals*
33	Kevin Poole		1	Peter Schmeichel	
2	Simon Grayson		3	Denis Irwin	
3	Michael Whitlow		4	Steve Bruce	
4	Jim Willis		5	Lee Sharpe	33
19	Colin Hill		6	Gary Pallister	
10	Mark Draper		8	Paul Ince	90
18	Gary Parker		9	Brian McClair	
22	Jamie Lawrence		10	Mark Hughes	
9	Iwan Roberts		17	Andy Cole	45/52
6	Mark Robins		19	Nicky Butt	
25	David Lowe		27	Gary Neville	
Substitutes					
15	Brian Carey (55 mins for 2)		24	Paul Scholes (55 mins for 10)	
1	Gavin Waro		13	Gary Walsh	
8	Mark Blake (74 mins for 25)		28	David Beckham (46 mins for 5)	

Sunday 16 April

I kept thinking about Blackburn's game yesterday. They managed to get an early goal again, but this time they failed to hang on to it. Is that the turning point? I just have this feeling it might be.

There was more bitter criticism in today's papers. They ripped me to pieces. It's as if the critics want me to break up the team and sell off every player who gets sent off.

Do they expect me to come out and criticise Roy publicly? Provide headlines for the player's mother to read and make enemies of not just the player but his entire family and circle of friends? The one principle I have always had in management is that we do not do our disciplining publicly. When Jesus Christ came off the cross, there were three people waiting for him, and the players know that when they come off the cross I will be there for them. The worst scenario in management is losing the support of your players. This last year has been a nightmare in terms of discipline, but because I have never had a year like it, I can't fairly be accused of being responsible for undisciplined sides.

Monday 17 April

United 0 Chelsea 0

My optimism didn't last. We have now gone scoreless for three home games. Without Giggs, Kanchelskis and Sharpe we were up against a brick wall. Chelsea just sat back and defended, and we hadn't the pace out wide to turn them. Yet we should have had a penalty when a defender handled. Even Glenn Hoddle admitted it afterwards, although he claimed that the defender was pushed. But there wasn't anyone there to push him! For us to get a penalty at Old Trafford I think a player would have to be shot. Anyway, I think that's it. That result is just the boost Blackburn need.

Venue: Old Trafford	*Att:* 43,728		
Manchester United	*goals*	**Chelsea**	*goals*
1 Peter Schmeichel		13 Kevin Hitchcock	
27 Gary Neville		2 Steve Clarke	
4 Steve Bruce		27 Gareth Hall	
6 Gary Pallister		5 Erland Johnsen	
3 Denis Irwin		6 Frank Sinclair	
28 David Beckham		21 David Rocastle	
8 Paul Ince		25 David Lee	
9 Brian McClair		17 Nigel Spackman	
17 Andy Cole		10 Gavin Peacock	
10 Mark Hughes		9 Mark Stein	
19 Nicky Butt		8 Paul Furlong	
Substitutes			
18 Simon Davies		12 Craig Burley	
13 Gary Walsh		23 Nick Colgan	
24 Paul Scholes		7 John Spencer	

Tuesday 18 April

I had a friend down from Aberdeen. He made a bookcase for me on Sunday and last night I went home, made dinner and we spent the evening filling the case with books. I was so depressed because we'd only drawn that I had one glass of wine too many. Blackburn were playing City and I didn't even bother watching it, but then someone phoned and said: "City won 3-2," so that draw with Chelsea means we have closed the gap by a point. It was still a missed opportunity, though.

I do now think that Blackburn have gone. Three years ago we drew at Luton when they were already relegated. That same day Leeds drew at home; but within four days we had lost the League, because we were on the slide. It just all goes, and there is nothing you can do about it. And, at that stage, I didn't have anyone to bring in to reverse it. The following year Robbo came back at the right time, and even last year, when things were a bit sticky around the semi-final, he came in. But Blackburn don't have a Robbo. They might scramble a result or two, but when you get into that slide it preys on your mind.

Simon Davies asked for a transfer today. I had put him on on Monday to try and solve our lack of width, but he hadn't obeyed instructions and it nearly cost us as goal, so I took him off again. I've told him he can go at the end of the season.

Eric begins his community service today, so the media circus is back at The Cliff – cameras everywhere.

Thursday 20 April

Went to Dublin for the Irish Player of the Year awards. A smashing night, and plenty of Irish hospitality.

Friday 21 April

The players – apart from the injured and Paul Ince – are away on international duty. Roy Keane has not joined the Ireland squad, but Jack Charlton wants him to go over anyway.

Saturday 22 April

I said to Roy: "Jack Charlton wants you to go to Ireland and join the squad." He said: "I'm struggling, Boss." I told Roy to phone Jack and tell him.

I went to watch the B team play Oldham at Little Lever, then went to see Middlesbrough at Barnsley. I went over Woodhead, and it snowed! I stopped at a pub for a sandwich and a glass of beer, sat in front of a great log fire reading the paper, and thought: "It's great having a day off."

It was a great game. Kenny was there – he apparently got into an argument with some people in the stand. Maybe the pressure is getting to him!

Sunday 23 April

I phoned Pop and said:

"You've no problem now, you are so strong." Middlesbrough have definitely made it now, so we will look forward to seeing him in the Premiership next season. But I said to him: "Don't bother playing against us, because you won't get a kick!"

Monday 24 April

We spent the whole day negotiating with Eric – a really good day for United because it looks as if he's going to stay.

Eric came in at 11am with Jean-Jacques Bertrand. The initial meeting went on for 80 minutes, but then Eric had to go to go off for today's community-service stint. Jean-Jacques, Maurice Watkins, the chairman and I carried on talking until about 3pm. Then the chairman took Jean-Jacques to his office to discuss alternatives, and I did some paper work. But I said to the chairman:

"One thing is obvious: he really wants to stay. So we've got to find a way of doing it, because if we sell him, what with building a new stand, how do we find a replacement? That would cost £6.5 million."

Contrary to what was being said in the papers, Milan were not offering a large fee. "We might get them up, but if you are going for Le Tissier or Collymore, you are talking £6.5 million, which represents a big deficit. So financially, it's common sense to try and get the deal done."

We discussed the other problems, such as security. We may have to consider taking our own security with us to away matches. There are problems at away grounds, even getting off the bus, but the FA has never come up with any constructive solution.

There is also the situation on the field to be considered. Eric knows he has got a temper, other players know he has got a temper and they will try to provoke him – players will do anything to get a result and Eric will have to contend with that.

Eric came back around 5.15pm and we agreed a deal at 8.40pm. The most important thing was that he wanted to stay. He turned down a lot of money from Inter Milan to do so. We agreed we would take a couple of days to decide that this is definitely what we want, and Jean-Jacques will return on Thursday so that we can announce it to the press on Friday. The contract reflects the situation, the need for Eric to play and, in fairness, Eric suggested that the pay should be tied to him playing. Now I'm quite enthusiastic about it all.

Wednesday 26 April

Kiddo said: "The way Eric is talking to the players, it sounds as if he is going to stay."

Neil Ramsey, Paul Parker's agent, came in. Paul is concerned about his future. He won't play again this season, so he has only played one League game all season, and his contract is up next summer.

I went to see Darren play for Wolves' reserves at Everton. He had a good wee battle with John Ebbrell. I sat with Joe Royle and his father. Joe said: "How comes Darren isn't getting a game?"

Thursday 27 April

Jean-Jacques phoned and told the chairman he wasn't going to come over, which seems to be a good sign.

Friday 28 April

It was a good day for United fans. Eric signed a new three-year contract. There had been some more bad press because the story had leaked in the papers this morning, and what with the papers rehashing all the old stuff, some were saying it was a disgrace that Eric was getting a pay rise. But he's been offered a £4.2 million contract by Inter Milan. Are we to give him a pay cut to show his loyalty? We decided to attack the situation in the press conference this morning.

We had a staff meeting at Old Trafford. I'm going to so many meetings, I'll need to stop being there so much in the afternoons. I'm virtually having to divide myself in two – half at Old Trafford, half at The Cliff. It's very difficult – I do feel that if I'm not at The Cliff, my presence is missed.

I had my moment of glory: I played for Maurice Watkins's lawyers' team against a team from Leeds in the gym. I have to say I was brilliant – scored two and made six. That's my story.

Saturday 29 April

I am wracked with pain in the legs and back. Playing on the hard surface in the gym takes its toll.

Went to watch Everton play Wimbledon. A dour affair.

Sunday 30 April

Blackburn lost at West Ham. Watching it I said: "What a pity we've made a mess of it," because we've had too many chances. If we had won 1-0 against Chelsea, we would do it. Blackburn haven't played well for six weeks. Once you go at this stage of the season, there's nothing you can do – you're helpless, you're struggling through games. There will be no *crème de la crème* from Blackburn now. It'll be sheer battle. Game after game they've been hanging on, kicking the ball into the stand and you have to admire their guts. They might get through just by battling, but I feel it is going to be very difficult for them now. The one thing they can't contend with was what they found today: a team fighting as hard as them, a team fighting for its life. They didn't have an answer.

Monday 1 May

Coventry City 2 United 3

Our performance was excellent. Butt, May and Scholes – the young ones – all did terrifically. We had the usual United cliff-hanger – ahead twice and twice level through losing bad goals. Nail-biting stuff.

Gary Neville got booked after about five minutes, so he now is in danger of missing the Cup Final.

Venue: Highfield Road — *Att:* 21,885

Coventry City	*goals*	Manchester United	*goals*
13 Jonathan Gould		1 Peter Schmeichel	
25 Marcus Hall		27 Gary Neville	
5 David Rennie		6 Gary Pallister	
6 Stephen Pressley	72	12 David May	
2 Brian Borrows		3 Denis Irwin	
28 Kevin Richardson		9 Brian McClair	
31 Gordon Strachan		19 Nicky Butt	
8 Roy Wegerle		24 Paul Scholes	32
15 Paul Cook		17 Andy Cole	55/79
9 Peter Ndlovu	39	10 Mark Hughes	
19 Dion Dublin		5 Lee Sharpe	
Substitutes			
17 Alan Pickering		28 David Beckham (76 mins for 24)	
27 Mike Marsh		13 Gary Walsh	
30 John Filan		29 Pat McGibbon	

Tuesday 2 May

A meeting with Keith Gillespie's solicitors. The *Daily Mirror* said I had got rid of him because he was a bad boy off the pitch, so he is suing them. I will certainly be a witness. He is a fantastic boy and I never had a moment's bother with him.

Wednesday 3 May

I had a long meeting with Andrei and his translator George Scanlan. The vibes I get from George are that Andrei just wants us to put an arm round his shoulder and reassure him that we want him. It was a disturbing meeting.

Thursday 4 May

Another meeting – this time at 7.50am with Ben Thornley and his father about his progress. Coming in at that time shows how concerned his father is, which is brilliant. He is getting closer. Hopefully he will take the next step in pre-season.

In the evening I spoke at a dinner for Neil Fairbrother's testimonial. The other speaker was David Lloyd, the Lancashire coach and former England batsman. He was the best speaker I've heard in ages – composure, timing, funny.

Friday 5 May

Training this morning was absolutely fantastic. It was a joy to watch – the quality of the work was superb. Kiddo has done fantastically well to maintain such a level. And there is a buzz about the place, the mood is terrific, you can sense we now believe we can do it.

Yet another meeting – this time with Gordon Taylor of the PFA about Jovan's work permit, about Ben's case against Nicky Marker, and to clarify a dispute with Arsenal regarding Matthew Wickes, a youth player whom we have allegedly poached. This is all nonsense.

Saturday 6 May

We had the usual Friday session: boxes and so on. Then Ryan's hamstring went again. I am worried about him playing in the final now. I thought he would be an important player for us, especially without Eric, Andrei and Andy.

Scholes did so well at Coventry I want to play him tomorrow. I've been worried about Incey's form. His energy in games has not been great. You wonder if the court case is affecting him. I'm tempted to leave him out, to play the same team, but that would mean more controversy.

I went to Everton versus Southampton. When I got there Sir Philip Carter, the former chairman, said: "Have you got a season ticket here?" There were lots of people with "Ferguson" on their Everton shirts and I said to the doorman: "I didn't realise how much I was appreciated here!"

Sunday 7 May

United 1 Sheffield Wednesday 0

David May got an early goal, then he was injured. Gary Neville went into centre half and was brilliant. If he was an inch taller he'd play for England as a centre half. He's a marvellous centre half. He might even get away with his lack of height like Martin Buchan did, because he is a good reader of the game, he's decisive and strong.

I said afterwards that I'd picked the wrong team. Paul Scholes found it hard to play as an all-round midfield player. Having got an early goal there is always the danger of just protecting what you've got, and although we didn't play badly, there was no getting a second goal, which always keeps your supporters on edge. But once Nicky Butt went on, I wasn't worried that we would lose it. Now we will see how Blackburn respond against Newcastle tomorrow.

I said to Choccy beforehand: "I was going to leave you out until I saw your record against Wednesday."

"You'd better not," he said.

"Well," I said, "that's to pay you back for the rubbish you write about me in that column of yours."

His diary in the United magazine is brilliant. I told him we should give him a five-year contract for the magazine.

Venue: Old Trafford *Att:* 21,885

Manchester United		*goals*	Sheffield Wednesday		*goals*
1	Peter Schmeichel		1	Chris Woods	
3	Denis Irwin		2	Peter Atherton	
5	Lee Sharpe		3	Ian Nolan	
6	Gary Pallister		10	Mark Bright	
8	Paul Ince		11	John Sheridan	
9	Brian McClair		12	Andy Pearce	
10	Mark Hughes		14	Chris Bart-Williams	
12	David May	5	16	Graham Hyde	
17	Andy Cole		17	Des Walker	
24	Paul Scholes		19	Guy Whittingham	
27	Gary Neville		25	Michael Williams	
Substitutes					
19	Nicky Butt (52 mins for 24)		7	Adem Doric (82 mins for 19)	
13	Gary Walsh		13	Kevin Pressman	
23	Phil Neville (24 mins for 12)		8	Chris Waddle	

Monday 8 May

Blackburn won 1-0. Afterwards, Tim Flowers had a go about people questioning their bottle. I was questioning their ability to perform under pressure. They were very lucky against Newcastle – they've been lucky for weeks, so there is nothing wrong with us saying these things. It's just part and parcel of modern sports psychology. They did the same thing last year: there was a headline on an Alan Shearer interview on the morning they beat us that read: "Let's see your bottle now." Well, we showed it, we won the League. Now it's up to them.

Tuesday 9 May

I'm a bit more hopeful about getting Ryan fit for the Final, although we are having to work on it.

Wednesday 10 May

United 2 Southampton 1

At last, a penalty when we needed it! It was 1-1 with just over five minutes to go when Andy Cole was pulled back, and the referee gave it. Denis Irwin scored.

You get your money's worth watching us. Mark Hughes missed a great chance after two minutes; after six we were a goal down. Bad defensive work letting Magilton run between the two centre backs from midfield, although to be fair, Magilton has good vision. But we missed that early chance and when Pally hit the post with a header, I thought it might be one of those days. But we plugged away and got the equaliser, Andy taking it very well. The second half was a siege. We had to work hard, though, because Alan Ball has done a great job at Southampton.

So now it is down to the last games – us at West Ham, Blackburn at Liverpool. I felt it was important to dismiss all the talk about Liverpool not trying. I can't believe that after the job he has done, Roy Evans could be betrayed by his players in any way.

Venue: Old Trafford *Att:* 43,479

	Manchester United	*goals*		**Southampton**	*goals*
1	Peter Schmeichel		13	Dave Beasant	
3	Denis Irwin	80	3	Francis Benali	
4	Steve Bruce		4	Jim Magilton	
5	Lee Sharpe		5	Richard Hall	
6	Gary Pallister		6	Ken Monkou	
8	Paul Ince		7	Matthew Le Tissier	
9	Brian McClair		9	Neil Shipperley	
10	Mark Hughes		10	Neil Maddison	
17	Andy Cole	21	14	Simon Charlton	5
19	Nicky Butt		15	Jason Dodd	
27	Gary Neville		16	Gordon Watson	
Substitutes					
24	Paul Scholes (76 mins for 10)		12	Neil Heaney (57 mins for 3)	
13	Gary Walsh		1	Bruce Grobbelaar	
28	David Beckham		21	Tommy Widdrington (76 mins for 7)	

Thursday 11 May

Had a meeting with Andrei and Grigori Esaylenko, his agent. I told him we recognised our faults and that there had been a breakdown in communication, but that we could only act on what our medical people tell us. I hope things are sorted out now because we don't want him to leave.

Gary Neville was up before the FA for reaching 40 points, but as we had a board meeting I couldn't go. Ken Merrett went with him – we felt there was no way he was going to be banned anyway. He was fined £1,000.

After the board meeting, Kiddo and I drove to London for the first leg of the FA Youth Cup Final against Spurs. And Gary Neville was in the dressing room pleading poverty. He said: "When I got a lot of those points it was in the reserves, before I got my new contract. I was playing for reserve-team wages."

"That's a terribly sad story, Gary," I said, "just wait while I get my handkerchief out. I'm heartbroken for you. You'll need your Cup Final win bonus now."

"Boss, I can't afford £1,000."

It was a disappointing game. We lost 2-1, but neither team played near their full potential.

Friday 12 May

We had an open day for the press to show how relaxed we are. The players have enjoyed their football this week, we've taken it down to the wire. Brian McClair presented me with the Scottish PFA's merit award, which was nice.

Saturday 13 May

We did a light session, then travelled down to London in the afternoon. Paul Ince had received a death threat, so the hotel was swamped with CID. You couldn't move for security. The Red Arrows airforce team were staying there too, so there were a lot of uniforms about, which was quite comforting. Paul just stayed in his room.

Sunday 14 May

West Ham 1 United 1

So near and yet... If you had seen the game with 15 minutes to go, you would have said we were certain to win. We were battering them, but it just wouldn't go in for the winning goal.

I left out Mark because I decided to play five in midfield, to try to draw their sting and control the ball to start with. I thought we wanted to be patient, not get carried away and get desperate like we did in Gothenberg. It was not easy leaving out Mark – he's a legend at the club, he's scored so many vital goals – but he has not been at his best and I hope this will give him a jolt and he will win the Cup for us.

But it was going well until we gave away this soft goal. I can't believe that this five-foot five-inch winger could cut in across our defence and sidefoot the ball home. Right against the run of play, just when we were starting to get a real grip on the game.

So I put on Mark. We got the equaliser before the hour, so there was plenty of time. But the goalkeeper made three fabulous saves and it just wasn't to be. But I loved it. At the end I said, "Well, that's Manchester United." Nobody ever gives in at this club. Everyone was running their socks off, it was great to watch, even if it brought disappointment.

And I fancied Liverpool to beat Blackburn. I thought if they wanted to win it, they could win it. Blackburn have been "gone" for weeks now. They've no engine left. They have run themselves into the ground for the whole season.

Venue: Upton Park *Att:* 24,783

West Ham United	*goals*	Manchester United	*goals*
1 Ludek Miklosko		1 Peter Schmeichel	
2 Tim Breacker		27 Gary Neville	
8 Mark Rieper		4 Steve Bruce	
4 Steven Potts		6 Gary Pallister	
12 Keith Rowland		3 Denis Irwin	
17 Michael Hughes	31	19 Nicky Butt	
26 Don Hutchison		16 Roy Keane	
7 Ian Bishop		8 Paul Ince	
10 John Moncur		5 Lee Sharpe	
11 Matt Holmes		9 Brian McClair	52
9 Trevor Morley		17 Andy Cole	

Substitutes

30	Les Sealey	13	Gary Walsh
18	Simon Webster (88 mins for 17)	10	Mark Hughes (45 mins for 19)
6	Martin Allen (85 mins for 26)	24	Paul Scholes (79 mins for 16)

Monday 15 May

How do you come to terms with losing the League? Usually I watch the video of a game the following day, but I just can't come to terms with the failure and I haven't been able to face the video. It's almost as if I'm scared to watch it. I keep thinking about those last 15 minutes. I just don't know how we didn't get the ball into the net.

The players have the day off to recover. Saturday is now so important to the club.

It was a big day for United because we had the second leg of the Youth Cup Final. We invite all our scouts, the schoolboy signings and their parents, the youth players and their parents, and the Tottenham players to dinner at Old Trafford before the game. It's an opportunity to let people know how pleased we are with their assistance, and how important youth football is to the club. I spent a pleasant two hours chatting. The game was exciting, and went to a penalty shoot-out. Paul Gibson made a marvellous save to win us the Cup. A great credit to the team, and to Eric Harrison. It was his fifth Youth Cup final in 12 years – and his second success.

There was a touching moment at the start of the game. As I went to my seat, everyone in the ground stood up and applauded us into our seats. I was proud of that, and said on the tannoy at half time how much I appreciated it.

Tuesday 16 May

Now we can forget West Ham and concentrate on Wembley. The players and staff were all fitted for our Wembley suits at Garçon. I hope we are as smart on the field as off it.

Then we went to Mottram Hall for a swim, sauna and massage.

Wednesday 17 May

We trained at Old Trafford. There was a press day today for the players' pool.

Ryan Giggs is making good progress.

Thursday 18 May

Today was the vital day in our preparations. I decided to do the functions today, and pick the team. I spoke to Ryan, watched him train, and then decided to make an early decision so we would get the thinking right. I decided to leave him out. He was a bit disappointed, but he knew he was not 100 per cent fit. He said: "I'd love to be sub, but I don't want to let you down."

"You've never let me down," I said.

We had our second press day and I had our pre-game press conference today so that tomorrow is clear. The players had lunch at Old Trafford, then we travelled down to our hotel in Windsor.

Even now we can't be allowed to go about our business quietly. First there was a story that City want Kiddo as their manager, which I think was simply mischievous. He is an integral part in United's success and will be even more so in the future.

Then there was a story that Andrei still wants to leave, supposedly because he doesn't get on with me. I'm not going to get involved in that one. We will wait and see what happens when he comes back for pre-season.

Friday 19 May

We trained at Bisham Abbey. Ryan's hamstring felt a bit tight, but I said to him: "It'll be OK, it won't break down."

Saturday 20 May

United 0 Everton 1

A disappointing day. I didn't think we deserved to lose. We were in total control in the second half, but Choccy was unlucky with a header which hit the bar and Neville Southall played the way he hasn't played for years – the second time in a week we ran into a keeper having an inspired day.

We lost a bad goal. Ince lost the ball and we had just about everyone in front of it. Brucey had just pulled up with a hamstring so wasn't very mobile, but we were over exposed and they caught us on the break.

I was sure Ferguson and Stuart would play, but I made the point in the team meeting that if Ferguson didn't make it, they would then play Stuart through the middle with Limpar wide. That was what happened, and for an hour Limpar had a really good game. When Ferguson came on they lost their shape.

Giggsy needed reassuring in the morning that he would be all right, and when he came on in the second half he did really well.

I was pleased for Joe Royle. After 12 years' service with Oldham he deserved a big club and a trophy. But he was never stretched fully at Oldham. Now he will be.

Venue: Wembley *Att:* 79,592

Everton	goals	Manchester United	goals
1 Neville Southall		1 Peter Schmeichel	
2 Matt Jackson		27 Gary Neville	
3 Andy Hinchcliffe		4 Steve Bruce	
5 Dave Watson		6 Gary Pallister	
26 David Unsworth		3 Denis Irwin	
6 Gary Ablett		19 Nicky Butt	
16 Anders Limpar		16 Roy Keane	
23 Barry Horne		8 Paul Ince	
17 Joe Parkinson		5 Lee Sharpe	
8 Graham Stuart		9 Brian McClair	
14 Paul Rideout	30	10 Mark Hughes	
Substitutes			
10 Daniel Amokachi (69 mins for 16)		11 Ryan Giggs (45 mins for 4)	
12 Jason Kearton		13 Gary Walsh	
9 Duncan Ferguson (50 min for 14)		24 Paul Scholes (72 mins for 5)	

Sunday 21 May

Nobody likes losing championships and cups, particularly to see it all go in seven days. But it was still a successful season in a very testing year. I cannot think of a year in which a club has had so much stick and handled it so well. That reflects our club, a club full of determination, perseverance and great heart.

Looking back over the season, there is no team which has tried to win in the way we have. We have played football, always entertained, we never shut up shop or wasted time. Anyone who has watched us this season has had their money's worth, and I'm proud to say that.

There were crisis points and watersheds. The European Champions' League was a major disappointment. A little less naiveté and a more negative approach would have got us into the next phase, but is it a crime to be positive? I think we should be more careful defending away from home, but not negative.

The Cantona incident was the major crisis. Only a fool would say it didn't cost us the League. I felt we were capable of winning the League anyway, but Eric would have guaranteed it. The decision by the Board to suspend Eric until the end of the season was surely enough, but the FA's disciplinary committee thought otherwise. I think we can thank the press for that.

Injuries wrought havoc. The side that won the Cup 12 months ago did not play together once. We had three hernia operations in the last two weeks of the season – Andrei, Brucey and Keane. Paul Parker had both knee and ankle operations.

But there were the positive sides. The signing of Andy Cole took everyone by surprise it was so quick. Hopefully he will be a marvellous signing for United. I can't wait for Andy and Eric to get together next year. Andy will definitely get us 30 goals next season. With Eric getting his regular one goal in two games, we should get another 50 from the rest of the team, and 80 goals is the championship.

Defensively, we've had a fantastic year. Pallister, Bruce, Irwin, Neville – they've all had fantastic seasons. Peter Schmeichel is close to reaching his peak. In the next five or six years he is going to be phenomenal. If Pally looks after himself, he could spend the next five years playing for United.

But perhaps most satisfying of all is the emergence of the kids. Gary Neville has come on brilliantly. Yesterday he again switched to centre half and was immaculate. Paul Scholes also came on and made an impact, and Nicky Butt has now made himself a first-team player. Next season I shall be looking for others to follow their example.

Wednesday 24 May

A happy note to end on: Paul Ince was cleared today.